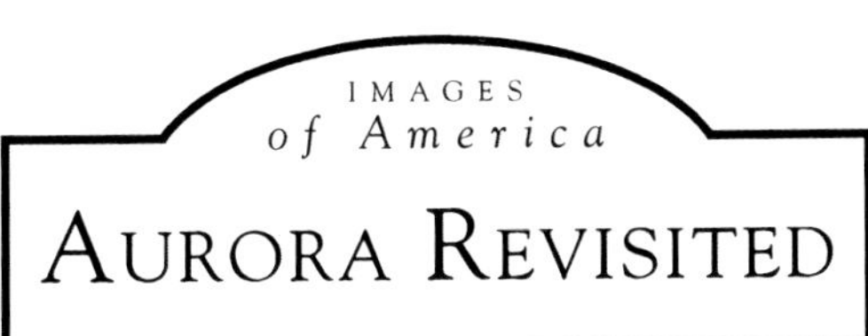
IMAGES
of America
AURORA REVISITED

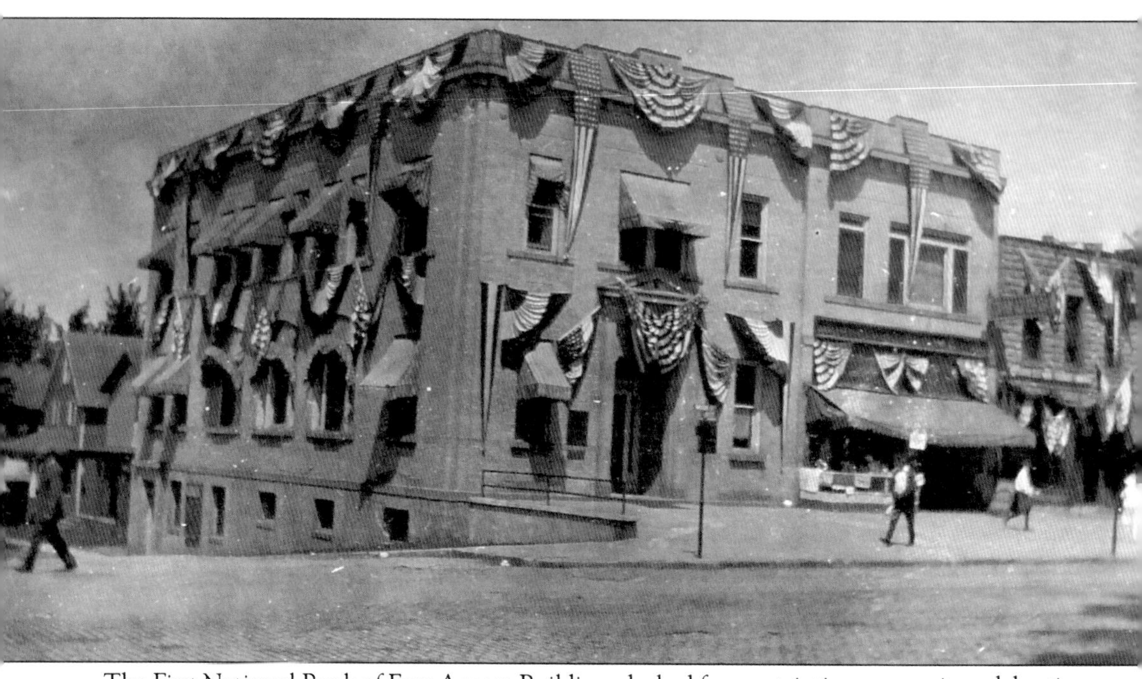

The First National Bank of East Aurora Building, decked for a patriotic community celebration, was constructed on the northeast corner of Main and Church Streets in 1912. Though not the community's first bank, the First National Bank of East Aurora was unique in that it was chartered by the federal government and issued US bank notes under the provisions of the National Banking Act. The building has been home to a number of other financial institutions in the years since. Edward M. Cummings's Rexall Drugstore occupied the eastern portion of the building when it first opened. (Courtesy of the Aurora Town Historian's Office.)

On the Cover: For decades, local families flocked to Emery Park for picnics, especially after church on Sundays. This image of children enjoying the playground was taken shortly after Erie County purchased 175 acres at the southeastern part of the town in 1925 and converted the property into one of the first county parks in the nation. The park has since grown to more than 480 acres. (Courtesy of the Aurora Town Historian's Office.)

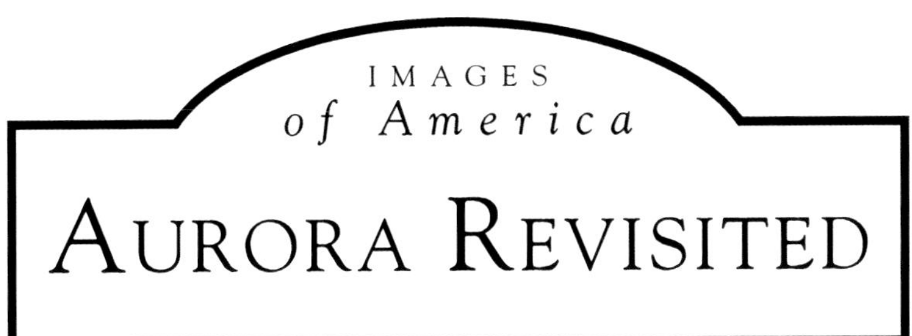

Robert Lowell Goller

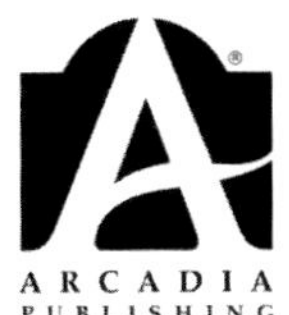

ISBN 978-0-7385-7598-8

Published by Arcadia Publishing
Charleston, South Carolina

Printed in the United States of America

Library of Congress Control Number: 2011923100

For all general information, please contact Arcadia Publishing:
Telephone 843-853-2070
Fax 843-853-0044
E-mail sales@arcadiapublishing.com
For customer service and orders:
Toll-Free 1-888-313-2665

Visit us on the Internet at www.arcadiapublishing.com

To the citizens of the town of Aurora:
past, present, and those yet to come

Contents

Acknowledgments 6
Introduction 7
1. Aurora is Born: 1804–1860 9
2. The Town Grows: 1861–1879 25
3. Horse-Racing Capital: 1880–1889 35
4. Lights, Water, and Roycroft: 1890–1915 49
5. A Town in Transition: 1916–1929 81
6. Aurora and the Great Depression: 1930–1940 101
7. A More Modern Aurora: 1941–1970 111

Acknowledgments

Aurora Revisited would not have been possible without the assistance and guidance of many, especially the Aurora Historical Society, whose support and resources made this project a pleasure; Grant M. Hamilton and the team at the *East Aurora Advertiser*; the previous Aurora town historians and volunteers, whose tireless efforts to preserve the community's history are reflected in this book; the editors at Arcadia Publishing; and Jason A. Gonser for his guidance, patience, and unfailing support of all my endeavors. Regrettably, mistakes in available historical records are inevitable, but thank you to those I have called upon to answer questions and review information for *Aurora Revisited* in an effort to avoid factual errors as much as possible. Finally, I am eternally grateful to the elected officials and citizens of the town of Aurora and village of East Aurora who have entrusted the town historian's office to me since 2007. It continues to be an honor and privilege.

Unless otherwise noted, all images are from the collection of the Aurora Town Historian's Office.

—Robert Lowell Goller

Introduction

The town of Aurora and its principal village, East Aurora, have been likened many times to Andy Griffith's Mayberry and Bedford Falls of the Christmas classic *It's a Wonderful Life*.

It is no surprise. There are many striking similarities. Main Street retains a hometown charm of small shops, familiar faces, and a vintage theater that was inaugurated during the silent movie era of the 1920s. Tree-lined streets serve as gateways to stately homes, many built more than a century ago.

Aurora takes pride in its unique history. It is one of few communities of its size that can boast two National Historic Landmarks. It has been home to a US president; an Iowa governor; acclaimed artists, writers, and craftsmen; and championship racehorses.

However, fame alone does not build a community. Ordinary citizens courageously took chances and made sacrifices to build Aurora. Those who enjoy Aurora's charm today owe a debt of gratitude to the vision of the earliest settlers, who saw great potential in this tract of land along Cazenovia Creek in Western New York. Aurorans since then have built upon that vision.

The images in *Aurora Revisited* offer a photographic time line of the community's progress, from a small farm town to a growing modern community that has strived to retain its unique heritage. While it is impossible to delve into every person, place, and organization that has had a hand in shaping Aurora, this book aims to provide representative snapshots of the town's progress—and the men and women who have contributed to that progress—over the past two centuries. Unlike previously published histories of the community, this book tells the story of Aurora in a chronological format, providing a unique glimpse into the evolution of the town.

The branches of Cazenovia Creek, named for Holland Land Company agent Theophilus Cazenove, connect the village to the unique rural hamlets throughout the town, including West Falls, Griffins Mills, Jewettville, and South Wales. The creek and its tributaries, known for their beauty today, served a vital role in the early days of Aurora, providing power for the lumber, grain, and woolen mills that electrified the community's economy.

Aurora's beauty was appreciated long before the first settlers came to the area in 1804. Native American villages are known to have been in place here as late as the 1500s and 1600s. Evidence shows that Sinking Ponds, now a wildlife sanctuary on the northern edge of the village, served as a Native American community. Remnants of Native American villages, including stone tools, have been found throughout the town and preserved among the collection of the Aurora Historical Society.

An agent of the Holland Land Company surveyed the Middle Road, today's Main Street, and opened the area to settlement in 1803. The following year, Jabez Warren purchased a large tract in what is today the town of Aurora. After clearing a small portion of the land and building a log cabin, he brought his family to Aurora. Soon, a handful of other families—including Warren's son William Warren—joined him, planting the roots for what flowered into a vibrant community. Within a few years, these families established their own churches, taverns, schools, and businesses. Some of those families have never left. Descendents of some of the earliest settlers still call Aurora home.

Following the War of 1812, hundreds more settled in Aurora to take advantage of the relatively inexpensive land, rich soil, and quality of life.

One of those families was named Fillmore. A young Millard Fillmore walked from the middle of New York state to join his parents and siblings, who had settled here earlier. He established his law practice on Main Street, across the dirt road from the honeymoon cottage that he built for his new bride, Abigail Powers. Millard Fillmore went on to a successful political career, ascending to the US presidency in 1850. His home, moved to its present location on Shearer Avenue in 1930, is now a National Historic Landmark museum operated by the Aurora Historical Society. His parents and siblings continued to live in Aurora and are buried in the Pioneer Cemetery.

The arrival of the railroad in December 1867 further opened Aurora to Buffalo and points beyond. Previously connected to the city by only a plank road, Aurora's economy boomed with cheese factories, lumberyards, and other industries made more lucrative by the trains passing through town.

Aurora became the horse trotting capital of the world in the 1870s and 1880s when Cicero Hamlin built his Village Farm. People came from around the world to catch a glimpse of the champion horses, including the handsome Mambrino King, bred at Hamlin's farm. Soon after, the Jewett family members entered the arena, constructing their own horse farm and becoming famous for building the world's only mile-long, covered racetrack off Grover and Quaker Roads.

Elbert G. Hubbard put Aurora on the map again when he constructed Roycroft, his Arts and Crafts Movement community on South Grove Street. Though at odds with town and village officials on many occasions, the eccentric Hubbard brought many well-known visitors to the community, including Henry Ford.

Though Roycroft fell on hard times during the Great Depression, several successful ventures were launched during the 1930s. Vidler's 5&10, an old-fashioned store that still graces Main Street with its red-and-white awning, and Fisher-Price Toys were both founded in East Aurora in the same year.

After World War II, a population spike in the 1950s and 1960s, as well as the expansion of the highway system, led to the introduction of suburbia, including a modern shopping plaza, a new high school, and the construction of the Aurora Expressway from South Wales to the thruway just outside of Buffalo.

Of course, the community's growth has not come without debate over the past two centuries. Some feared the town was growing too fast. Others feared the town was falling behind.

Despite the many transitions, Aurora has fought hard throughout it all to maintain its historic heritage and character. As a result, the community is still, as Elbert Hubbard once said, not a locality but a condition of mind.

One

Aurora is Born
1804–1860

The dawn of the 19th century also signaled the dawn of Aurora. Except for a few tracts set aside for Native American reservations under the provisions of the Big Tree Treaty of 1797, the Holland Land Company had been given control of the territory west of the Genesee River. Having helped Joseph Ellicott survey the 43-mile Middle Road in 1803, including East Aurora's Main Street, Vermont native Jabez Warren came back the following year to make the first settlement.

Education was important to the early settlers. The first school opened in William Warren's log house at the corner of what is today Main and Pine Streets in 1806 or 1807. The school doubled as the town's first tavern. A frame schoolhouse was opened on the west side of Olean Street just two years later.

William Warren was among the 16 Aurorans who served in the War of 1812. When the British burned the city of Buffalo on December 30, 1813, many residents fled through Aurora, staying at the Eagle Tavern at what is today the circle.

The community experienced rapid growth following the war. With the growing population, new businesses and mills along Cazenovia Creek flourished. By 1845, the population of the town of Aurora had grown to more than 3,000. New residents established homes in a handful of hamlets, including West Falls and Griffins Mills. Aurora's commercial position in the region grew with the construction of a plank road, from Main and Pine Streets to the Buffalo city line.

Aurora also entered the political arena. Residents of Griffins Mills formed one of the earliest antislavery societies in the mid-1830s and assisted runaway slaves on the Underground Railroad. Millard Fillmore, who established his law office on Aurora's Main Street in 1823, ascended to the US presidency in 1850 upon the death of Zachary Taylor. Fillmore no doubt disappointed Aurora's antislavery activists when he signed the Compromise of 1850, which included the Fugitive Slave Law. Many historians argue, however, that the compromise postponed the Civil War, enabling the Union to build up its resources enough to successfully win the conflict more than a decade later.

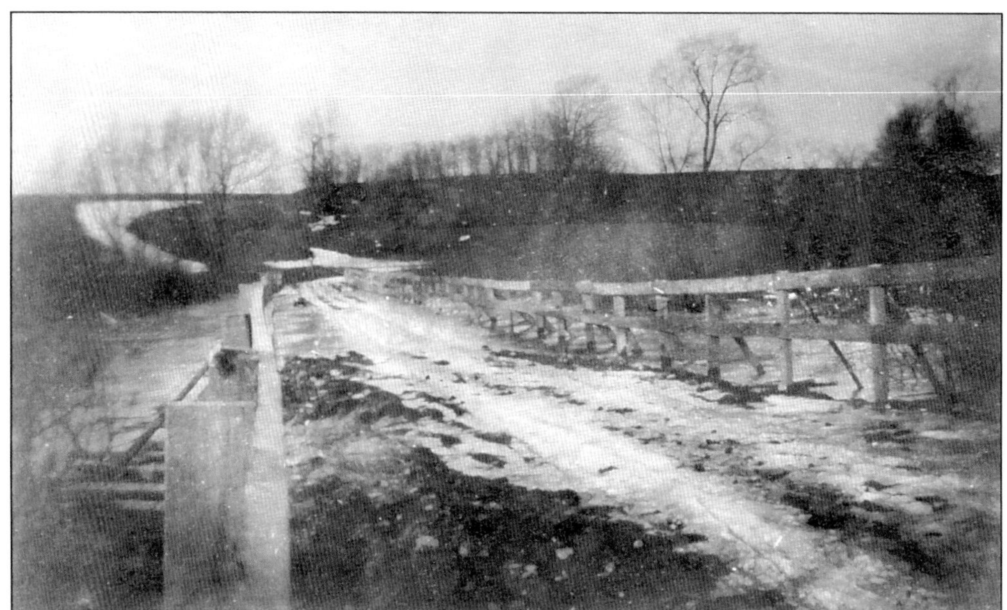

Sinking Ponds, which got its name from the 26 bridges that fell victim to it between 1849 and 1913, was formed by glaciers. A geological survey in 1965 revealed that it was the site of the Hopewellian Native American settlements more than 3,000 years ago. The Kahquah lived in the area around 1645, when the Senecas invaded. Pictured above is the last of the bridges in February 1915, two years after the idea of a bridge was finally abandoned in favor of using Girdle Road around the pond. Shown below are Alfred Davison, left, and Edward Godfrey removing remnants of the 26th bridge on October 14, 1964. Sinking Ponds now serves as a village-owned wildlife sanctuary where visitors can get a glimpse of what the area might have looked like before the first settlers arrived in 1804.

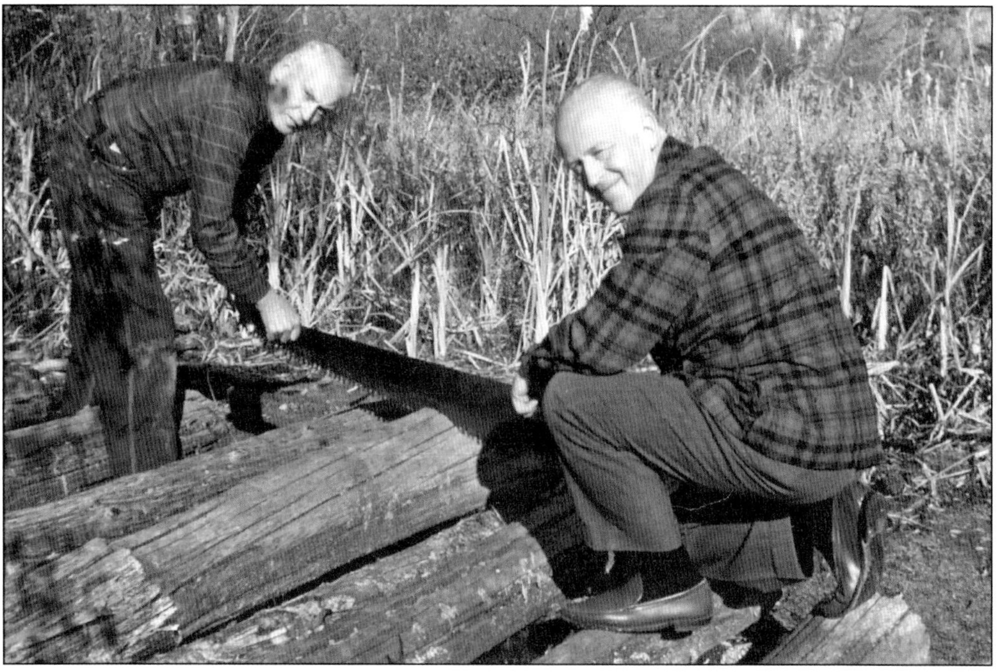

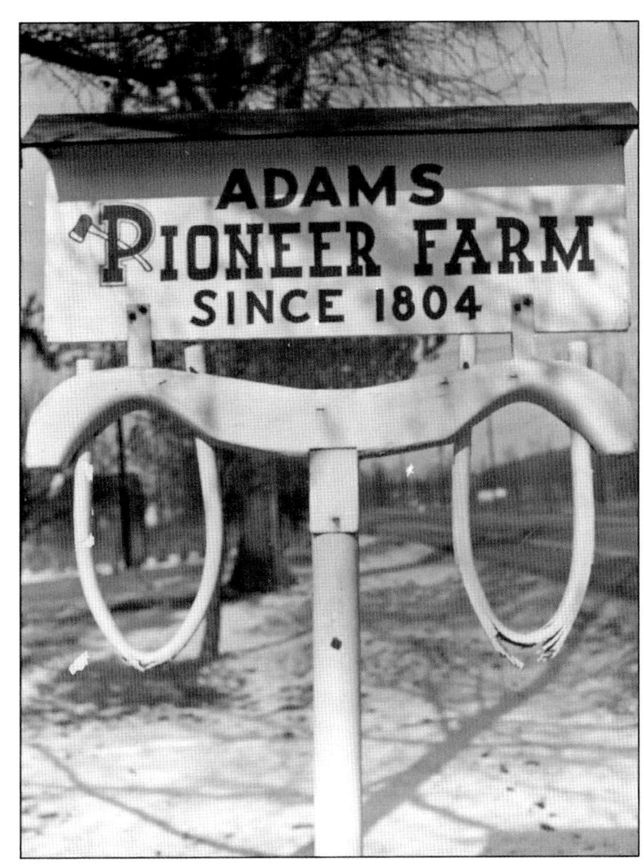

A sign on Olean Road touts the longevity of the Adams farm. Shortly after Jabez Warren arrived, Joel Adams built his house on the old Indian trail that is now Olean Road. After it was complete, he went back to Massachusetts and brought his family by ox team over nearly impassable roads in late 1804. They were the first family to spend the winter in Aurora. Descendents continue to live on the homestead.

A man drives a tractor on the Adams farm on Olean Road in November 1918. Perhaps the American flag is being flown in celebration of armistice that ended World War I, which occurred that month. Members of the Adams family farmed the land for generations after Joel Adams first arrived in 1804. He died on December 9, 1821, at the age of 70. He and his wife, Lydia, are buried in Pioneer Cemetery.

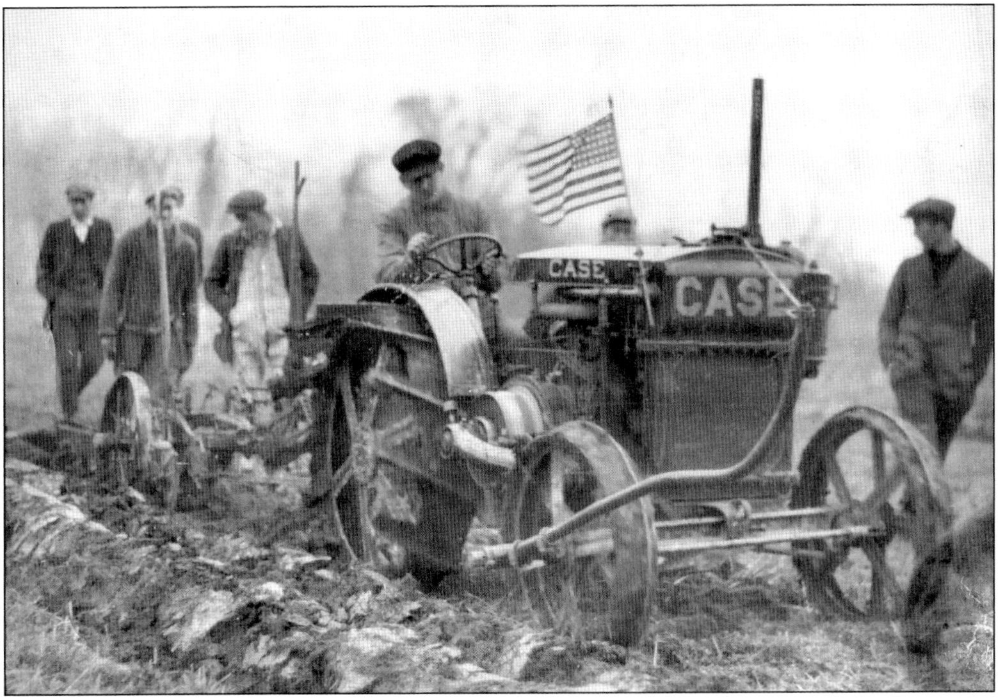

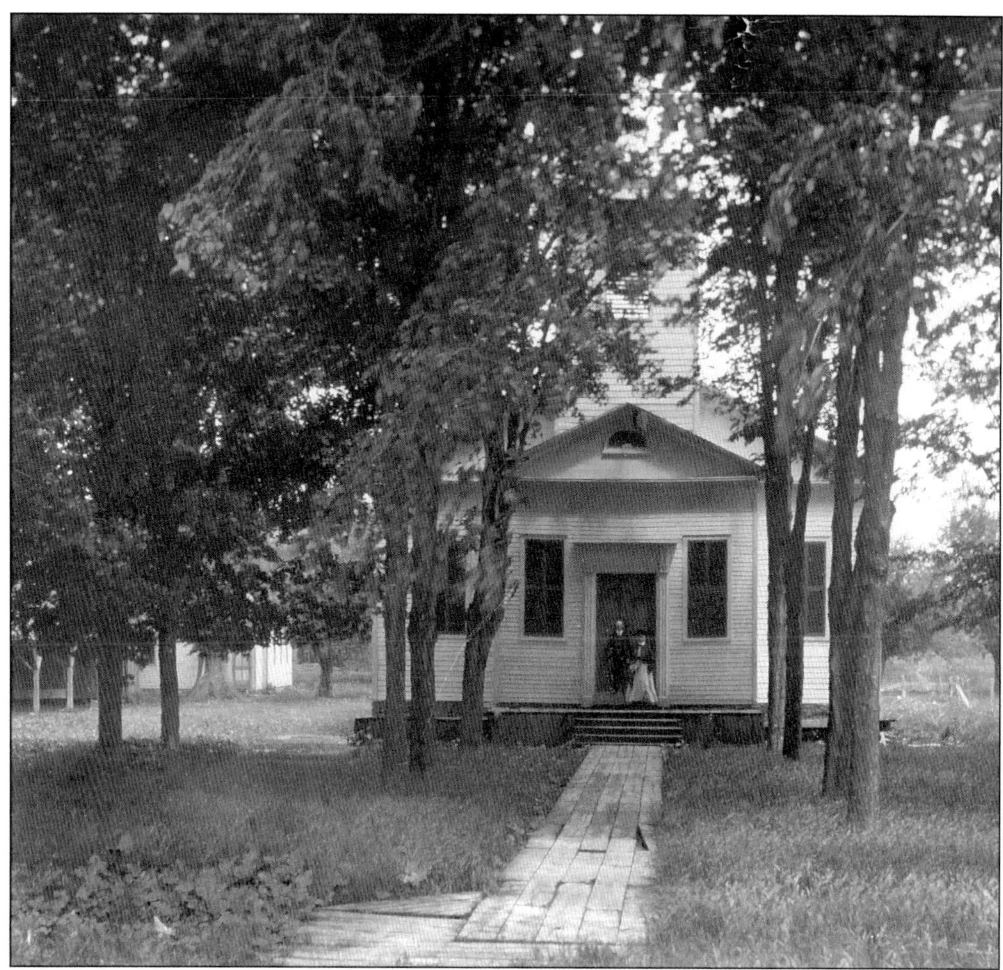

An unidentified couple, possibly the pastor and his wife, stands at the entrance to the Griffins Mills Presbyterian Church, the first church founded in the town of Aurora. It was organized at this Mill Road location on August 18, 1810, as the West Aurora Congregational Church, to reflect the name of the community at the time. The building, which is still used today, was erected in 1831. A belfry was constructed to accommodate a 48-inch bronze bell that was purchased in 1844. Before the Civil War, the church served as a meeting hall for the West Aurora Anti-Slavery Society. The congregation took an official stand against slavery, and it is believed the church building served as a stop on the Underground Railroad, sheltering runaway slaves before they continued their journey to Canada along the nearby Cazenovia Creek.

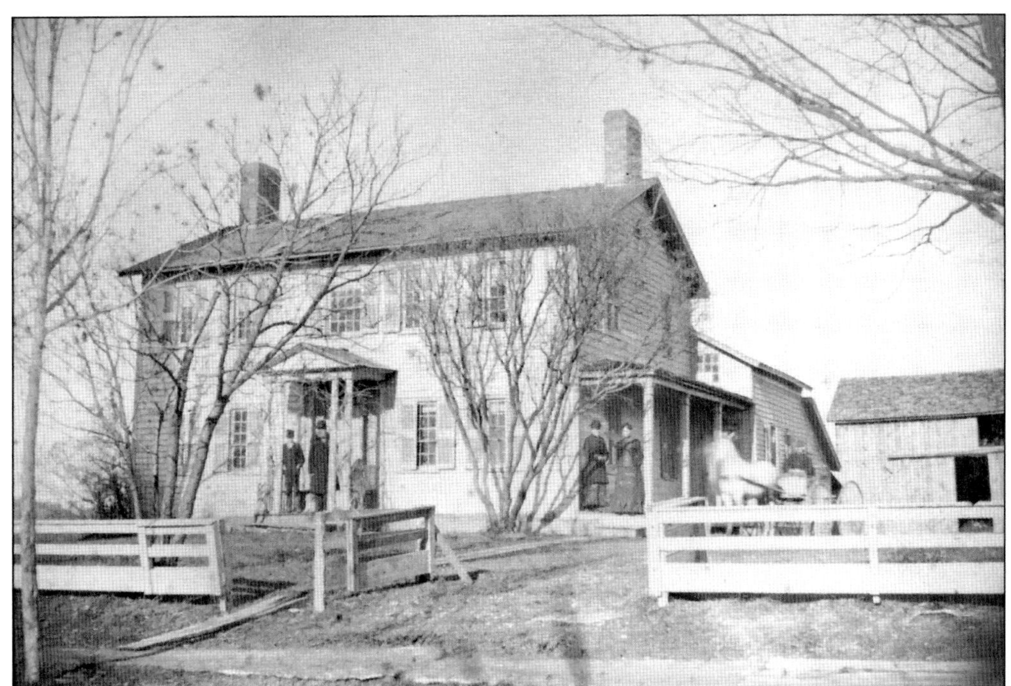

The Federal-style home on the northeast corner of Main Street and Shearer Avenue is one of the oldest in the town. Built by Daniel D. Stiles in 1828, it became known as the Shearer house when Noah and Betsy Shearer bought it in 1838 or 1839. Their son Joseph H. Shearer lived there until he died in 1915 at the age of 91.

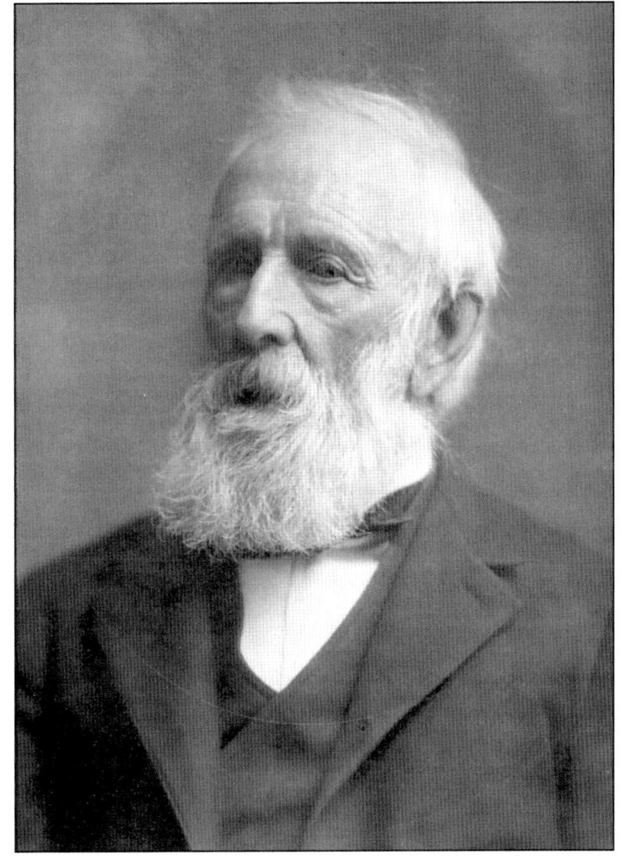

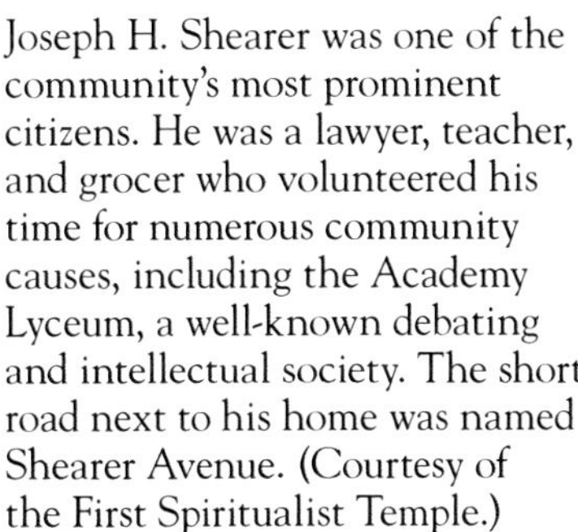

Joseph H. Shearer was one of the community's most prominent citizens. He was a lawyer, teacher, and grocer who volunteered his time for numerous community causes, including the Academy Lyceum, a well-known debating and intellectual society. The short road next to his home was named Shearer Avenue. (Courtesy of the First Spiritualist Temple.)

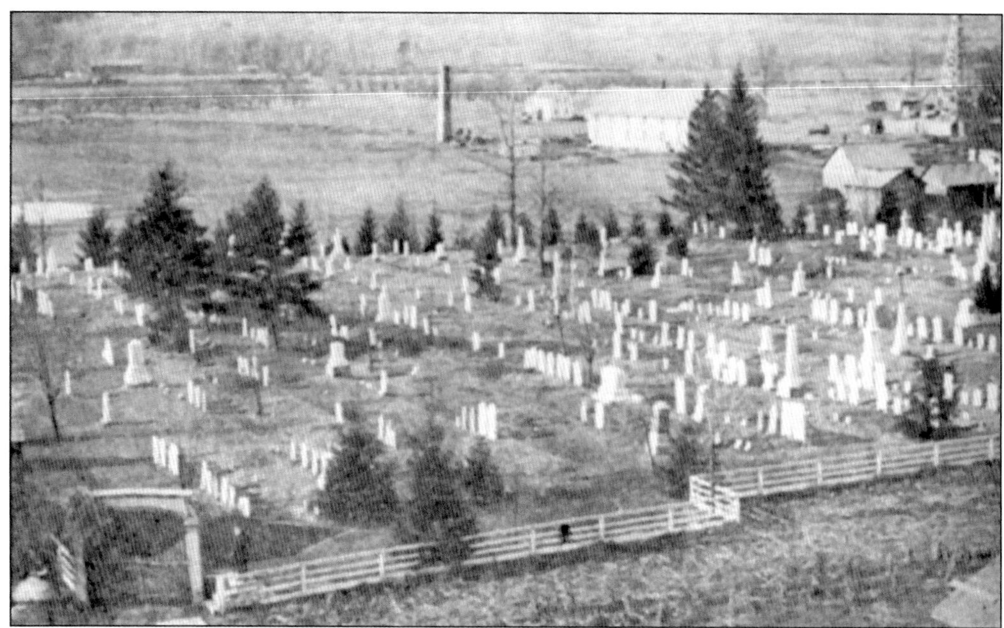

The East Aurora Cemetery, shown in this early view on a card from a local undertaker, was established in 1827 to provide a proper burial ground for the community's earliest settlers. Before the cemetery was established, settlers were simply buried in their backyards. Some caskets were moved to the new cemetery when it opened. One of the more notable plots is that of Pres. Millard Fillmore's family.

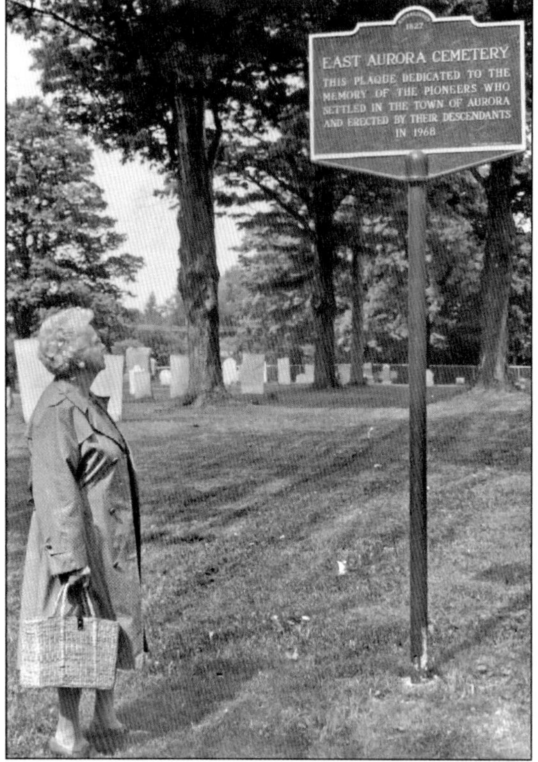

Amy Adams Forden, who was Aurora town historian from 1960 to 1974, admires the historic marker placed at the Temple Place entrance of the East Aurora Cemetery, later known as Pioneer Cemetery. Forden, a great-great granddaughter of early Aurora settler Joel Adams, was instrumental in garnering the approvals and funds needed for the town to take over and restore the cemetery in the mid-1960s.

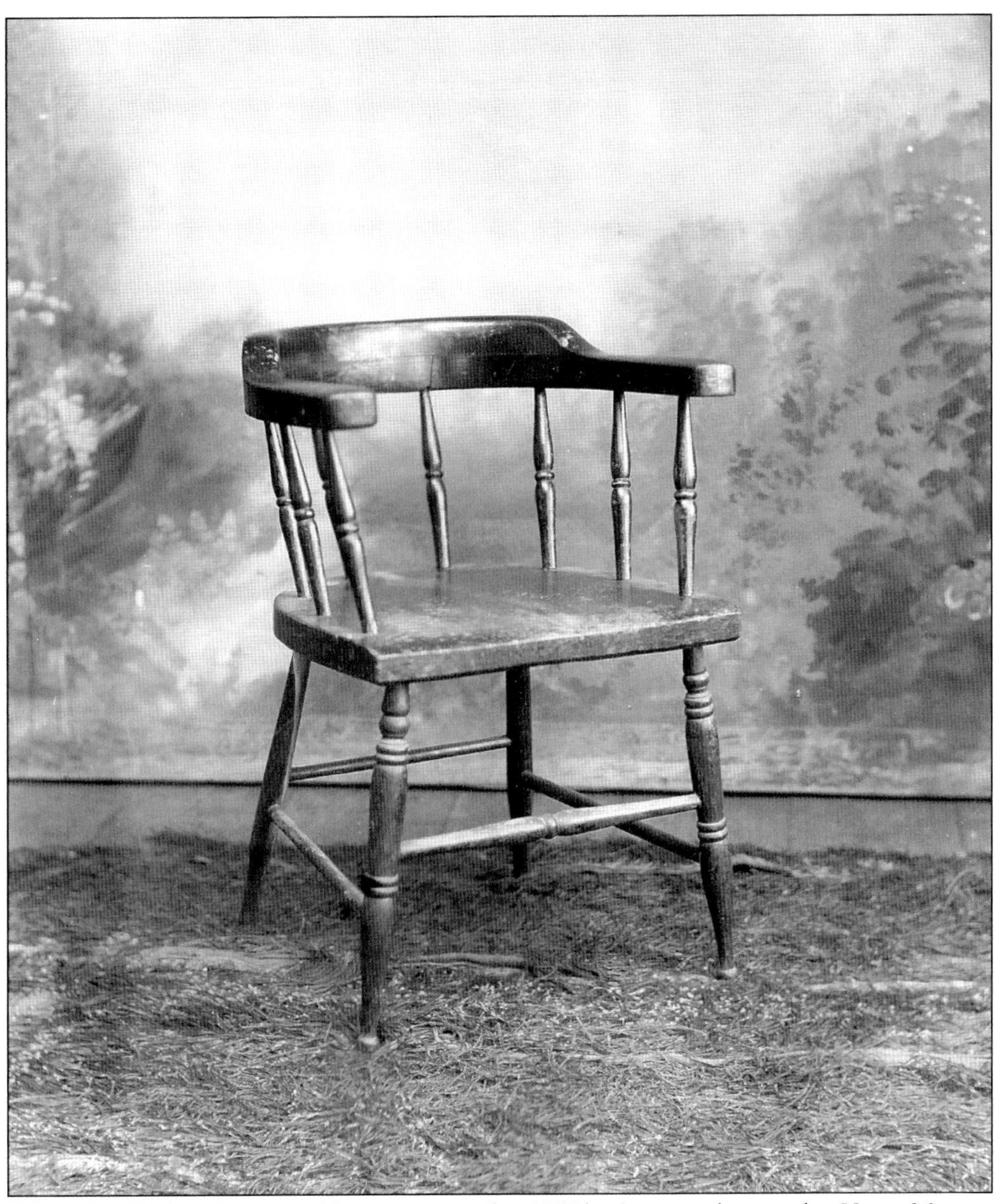

This captain's chair was one of four constructed in 1852 by Aurora cabinetmaker Henry Morrow to furnish the new, shared quarters of the Independent Order of Odd Fellows and Temperence Society in the Regulator Block, which was located on Main Street between Riley and Church Streets. Following a dispute between the two organizations, the Odd Fellows left, and the furniture was divided. The Sons of Temperence continued to occupy the hall until the group disbanded in 1856. The Lodge of Good Templers, a fraternal organization, received the two remaining chairs, but when the lodge disbanded in 1876, the chairs were given to the reorganized Sons of Temperence. When that group dissolved again in 1896, attorney Joseph H. Shearer kept one of the chairs. On August 26, 1902, he gave the remaining chair to the First Spiritualist Society, which was meeting in the Regulator Block. The chair, pictured here at the 1902 dedication, moved with the congregation to the new church on Temple Place in 1911. It is still used during worship services. The fate of the other three chairs is unknown. (Courtesy of the First Spiritualist Temple.)

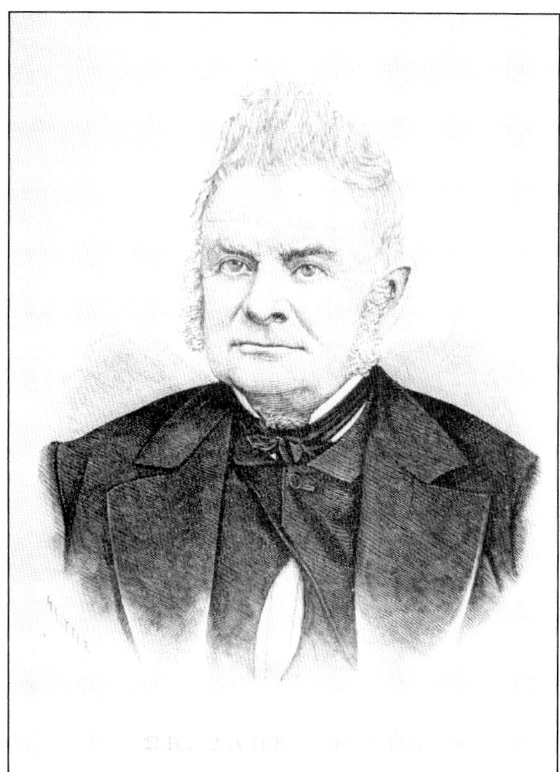

Dr. Jabez Allen was the town's first physician. After arriving in Aurora from Vermont in the mid-1830s, he opened the first drugstore next to his home near Main and Pine Streets. In fact, it is said Dr. Allen made his first house call on the day he arrived. Allen's practice continued for more than 45 years.

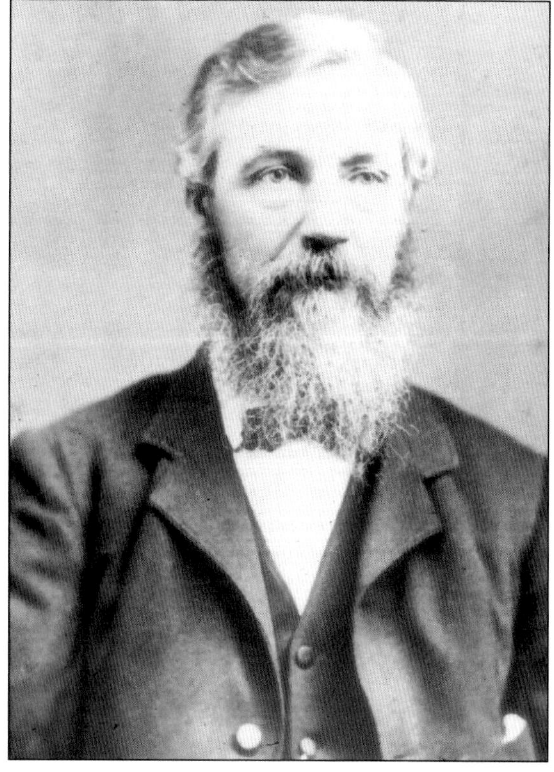

Maj. Gen. William Warren followed his parents, the first settlers, to the town of Aurora in 1805. He served in the War of 1812 in Buffalo, and his log house, located near the corner of present-day Main and Pine Streets, served as the town's first tavern and schoolhouse beginning in 1806 or 1807. He also served as clerk of the Baptist church. He died in June 1879, two weeks before his 95th birthday.

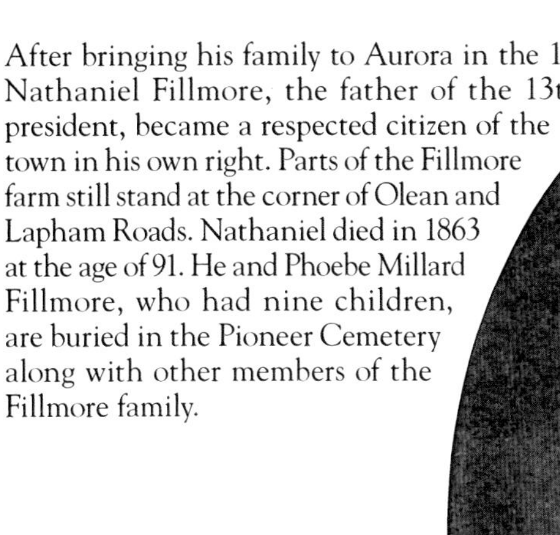

After bringing his family to Aurora in the 1820s, Nathaniel Fillmore, the father of the 13th president, became a respected citizen of the town in his own right. Parts of the Fillmore farm still stand at the corner of Olean and Lapham Roads. Nathaniel died in 1863 at the age of 91. He and Phoebe Millard Fillmore, who had nine children, are buried in the Pioneer Cemetery along with other members of the Fillmore family.

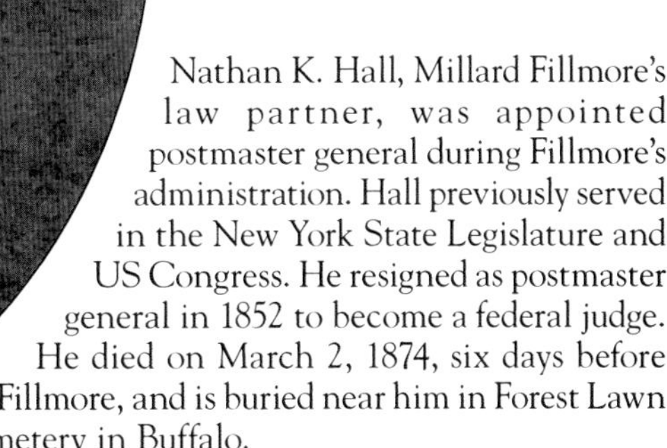

Nathan K. Hall, Millard Fillmore's law partner, was appointed postmaster general during Fillmore's administration. Hall previously served in the New York State Legislature and US Congress. He resigned as postmaster general in 1852 to become a federal judge. He died on March 2, 1874, six days before Fillmore, and is buried near him in Forest Lawn Cemetery in Buffalo.

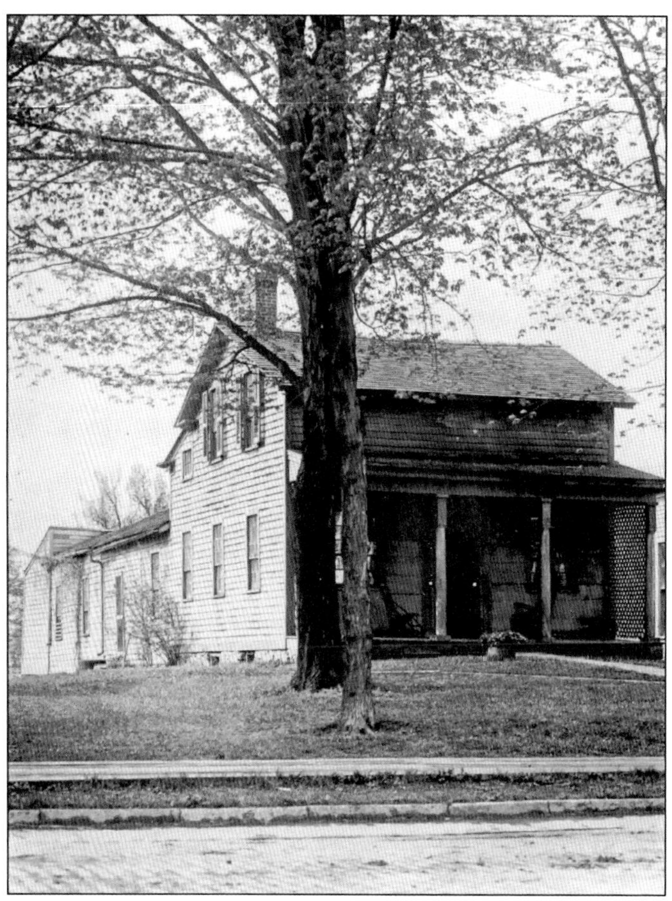

Millard Fillmore's home, built for his new bride in 1826, once stood on Main Street, just east of where the Aurora Theater now stands. An early view, shown at left, shows the rooms that were added to the back of the house. The house was moved twice; first, it was moved a short distance south to what later became Millard Fillmore Place. In 1930, artist Margaret Evans Price moved the home down Main Street to a new location on Shearer Avenue, where she used it as a studio. Shown below is the house after the move, when Margaret added a long window to the north side to provide proper light for painting portraits. She also replaced the fireplace on the opposite side of the house. The home, a National Historic Landmark, is now a museum operated by the Aurora Historical Society.

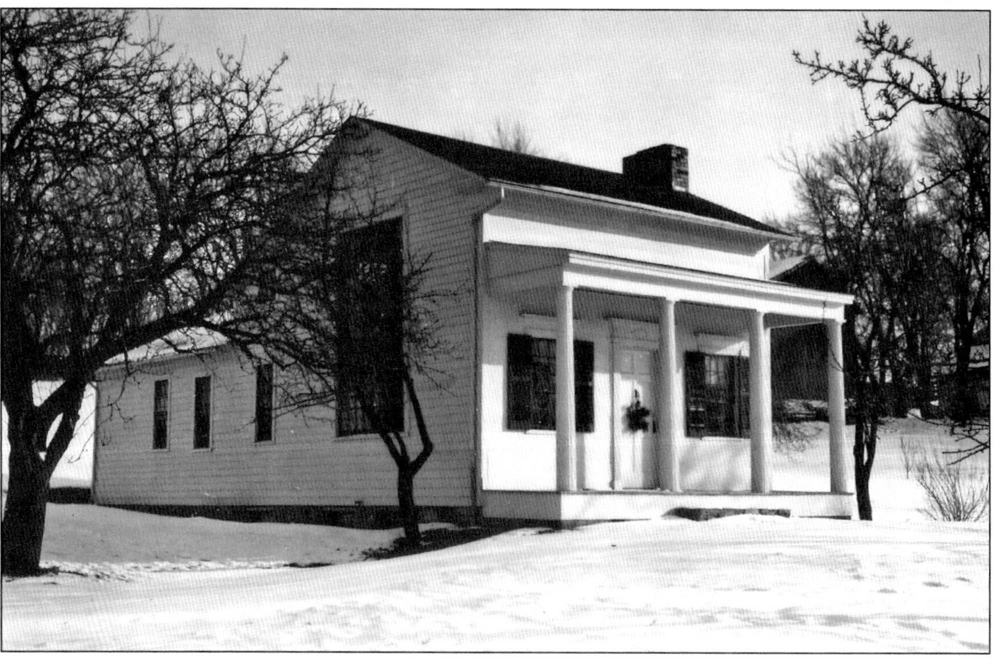

Mary Abigail, Millard and Abigail Fillmore's only daughter, was an accomplished musician and artist. She spoke five languages, including French, Spanish, German, and Italian. Due to her mother's ongoing illness, Mary Abigail served as hostess at the White House during her father's presidency. While visiting her grandparents in Aurora in July 1854, she developed cholera and died. Her bachelor brother Millard Powers Fillmore followed in his father's footstep and became a lawyer.

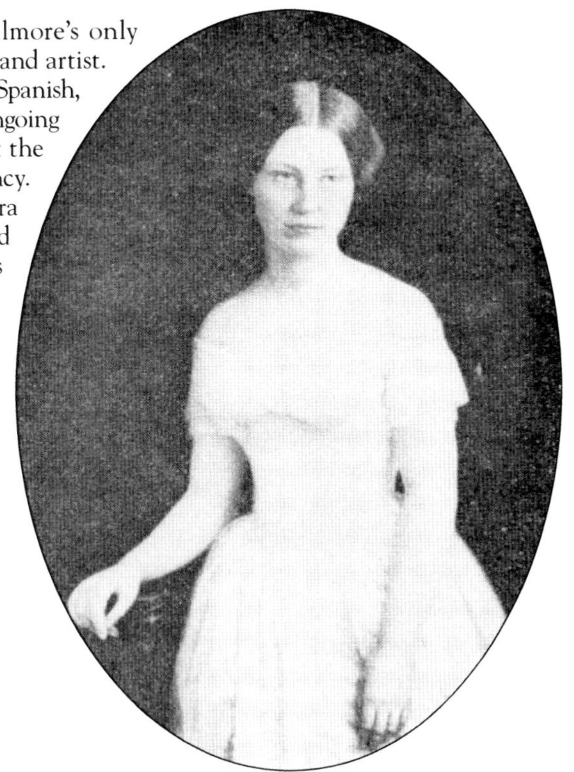

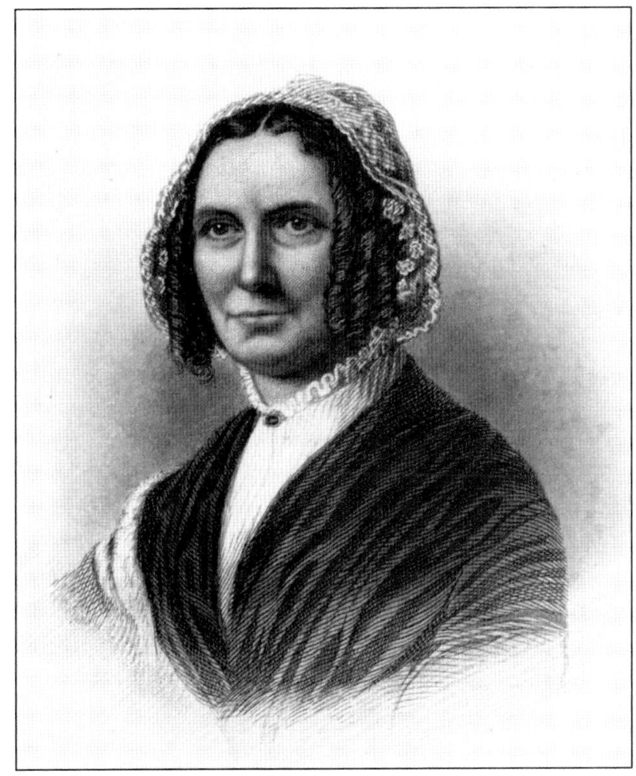

Abigail Powers Fillmore taught school in her Aurora home as her husband launched his law career across the street. When she became first lady in 1850, Abigail was appalled to find no books in the White House. She convinced Congress to provide the funds to establish the first White House library. As a result of attending Franklin Pierce's outdoor inauguration in March 1853, she caught pneumonia and died a few weeks later.

$25 Reward

The Store of the subscriber was broken open on Thursday night last, and Robbed of the following Property :--

1 piece brown figured Silk, 1 piece plain green Silk, (20 to 30 yards) 1 piece brown plain Silk, 1 piece lead colored plain Silk, and others. 1 piece invisible green Broadcloth, 1 piece olive Broadcloth, 1 piece black (super) Broadcloth, 1 piece brown Broadcloth, a quantity of Sewing Silk.

The Cloths were all of good quality.

The above Reward will be paid for the detection of the Thieves, and recovery of the goods. or a propotionate part for either.

Erie County

JOSEPH RILEY.

Aurora, Oct, 13, 1843.

Aurora did not see much crime in the early days, but it did happen from time to time. Joseph Riley offered a $25 reward, a handsome sum in those days, for the successful apprehension of the burglars who stole silk and cloth from his store in October 1843.

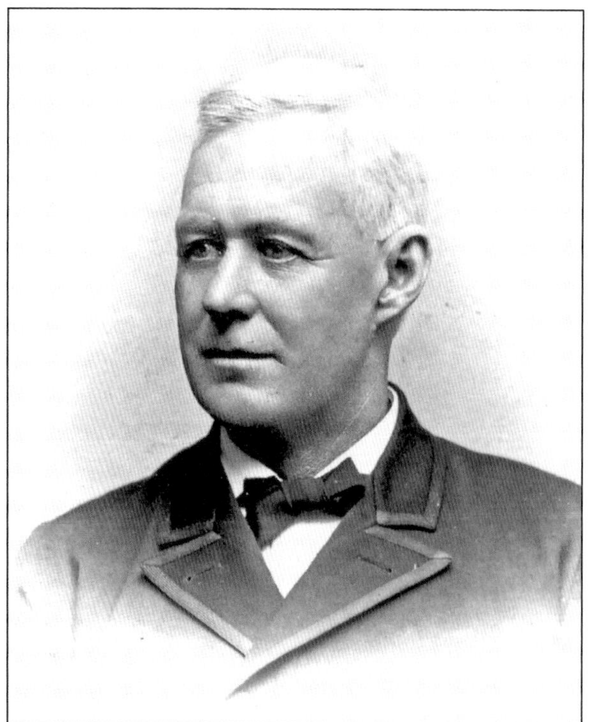

Horace E. Boies, born on Boies Road near Griffins Mills on December 7, 1827, was elected 14th governor of Iowa in 1889. A lawyer and state assemblyman before moving to Iowa after the Civil War, he declined an invitation from Pres. Grover Cleveland to become secretary of agriculture and his name was mentioned for president at the Democratic National Convention in 1896. He died on April 4, 1923, and is buried in Waterloo, Iowa.

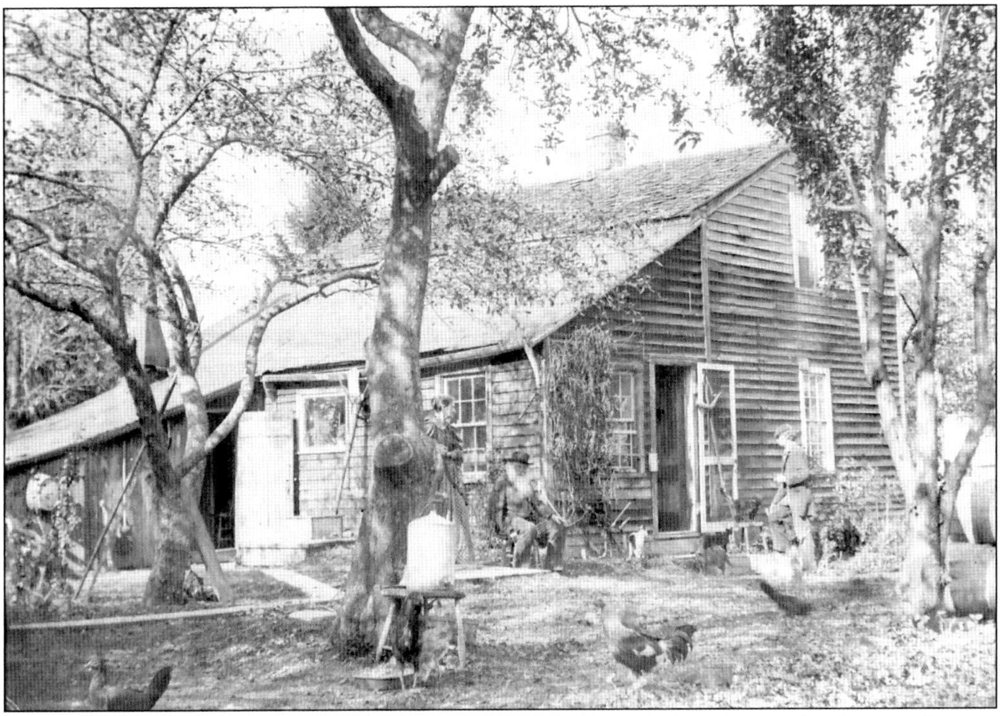

Timothy Paine sits in the chair at the center of this photograph that shows what became known as the Paine house at the end of Temple Place, next to the Pioneer Cemetery. Gail Borden is climbing the steps. Chickens can be seen roaming the yard. The house was built in 1840 for Timothy's mother, Betty. It was later demolished.

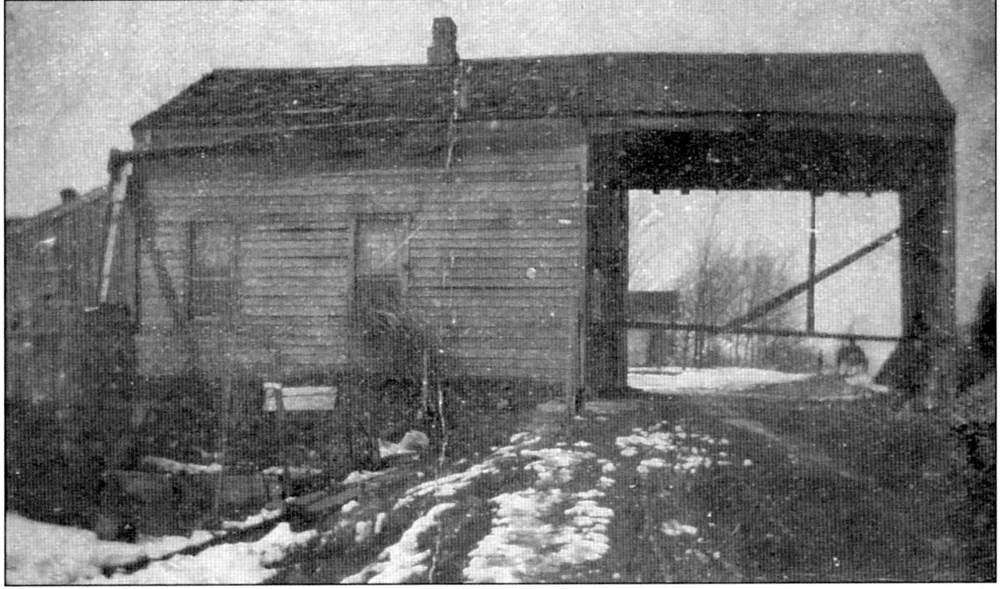

Many residents and business owners of the town became quite familiar with the tollgate just outside the town limits, located on Buffalo Road at Jamison Road. Through the efforts of Aurora businessman Gen. Aaron Riley, a plank road was completed around 1848 to provide smoother travels to Seneca and Elk Streets in Buffalo. There were three tollbooths between Aurora and Buffalo.

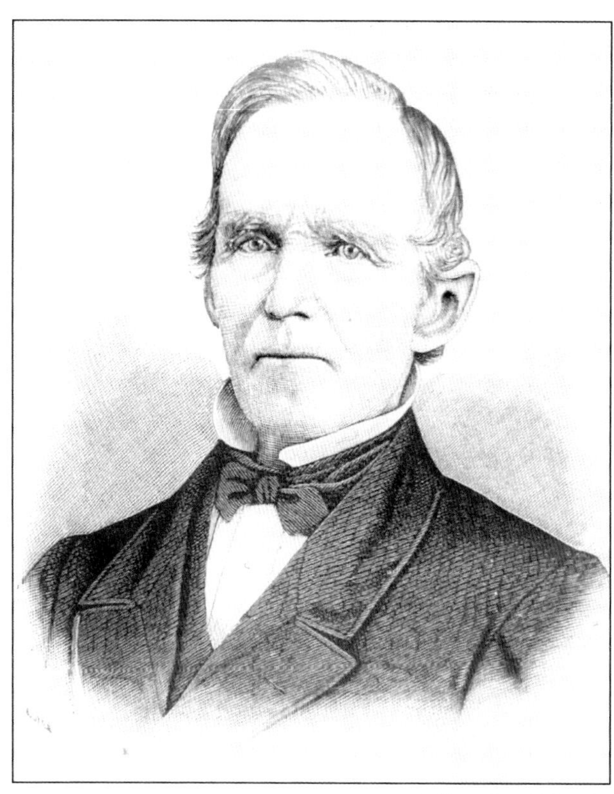

Gen. Aaron Riley was perhaps the most prominent businessman in Aurora in the 19th century. Born in Connecticut on November 11, 1806, he arrived in Aurora about 1825 and learned the mercantile trade from Joseph Howard Jr., who owned a store at the corner of Main and Pine Streets. Preferring the business world, he gave up an opportunity to become a lawyer in Millard Fillmore's practice. Riley, who later served in the Civil War, purchased Howard's store in 1828. He and his brothers Joseph and John also opened a store in Griffins Mills. In addition to organizing the formation of the Buffalo Aurora Plank Road, Riley lobbied for a railroad through Aurora and served as a trustee of the Aurora Academy. Some criticized him for having too much control over Aurora's real estate and business. He died on June 24, 1900.

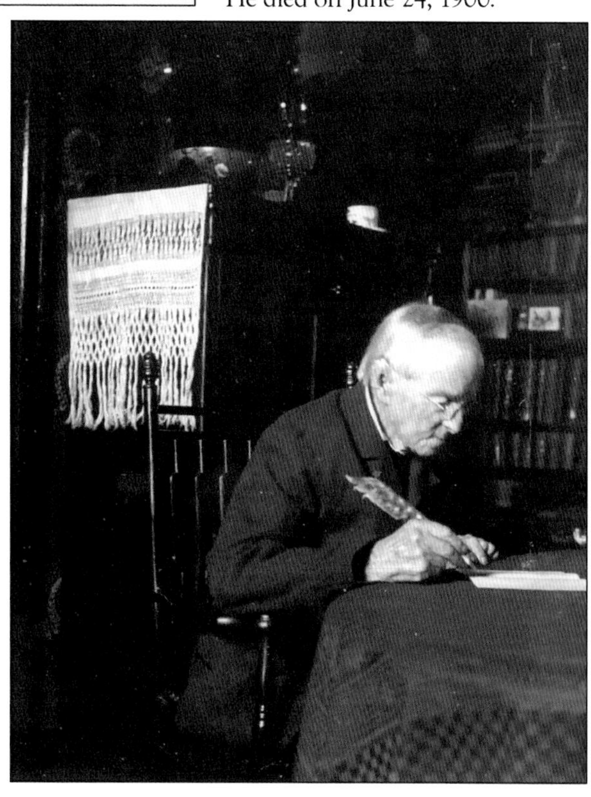

The Osborn family was one of the pioneering clans of the southwestern part of the town in the mid-1800s. Anner Haynes Osborn and her husband, James, resided on a small farm across from the railroad station in Jewettville, a hamlet at Mill and Davis Roads. Her children were born in the home, shown below in October 1914. She died in 1889 and is buried in Griffins Mills Cemetery.

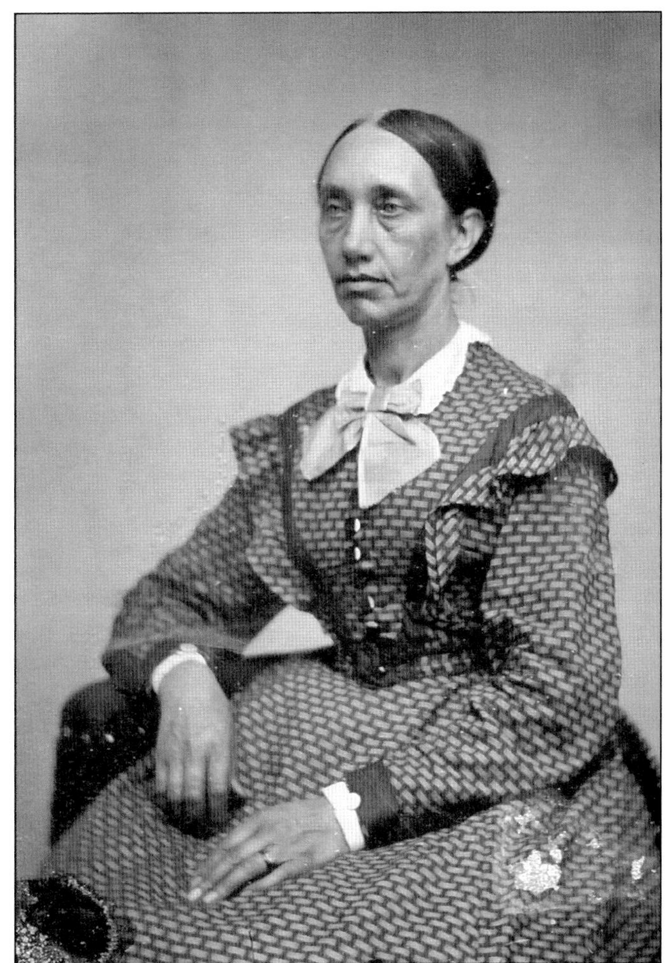

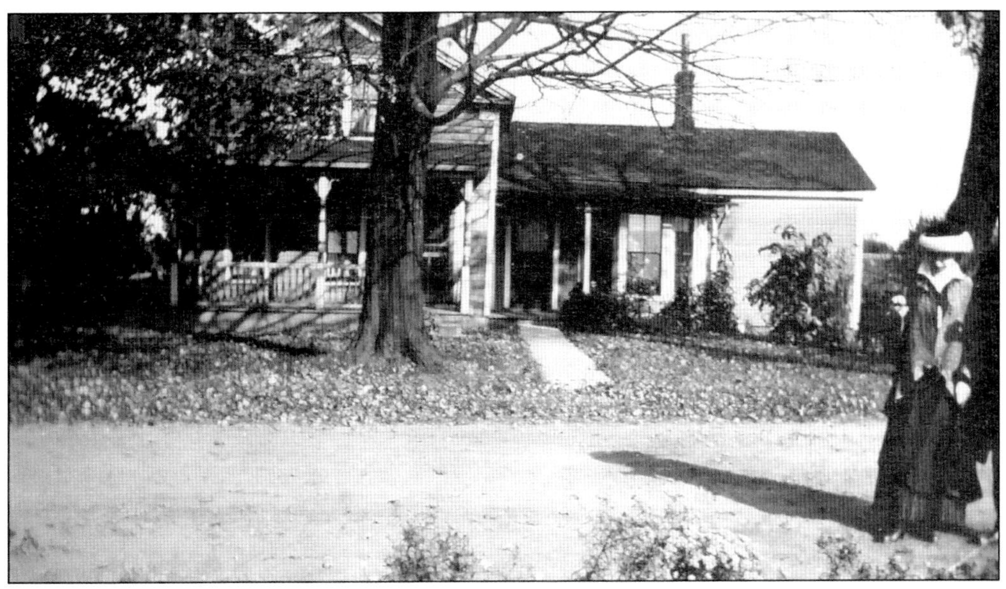

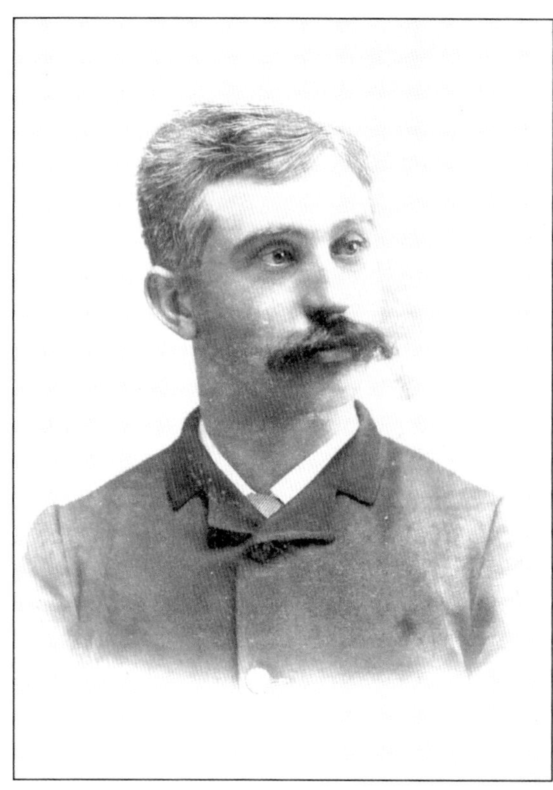

George A. Osborn, born to James and Anner Osborn on Christmas Eve 1859, was president of the Griffins Mills Cemetery Association at the time of his death in 1938, when he suffered a heart attack while driving on Main Street. He married Anna Marshall on April 10, 1890, and their three daughters are shown below. Though the order that the daughters appear in this photograph is unknown, their married names were Mary E. Little, Ethel Wittkas, and Margaret Heins. A longtime member of the Baker Memorial Methodist Episcopal Church, George Osborn was the last of his family remaining in the area. His siblings had moved to Washington state. He is buried in Griffins Mills Cemetery.

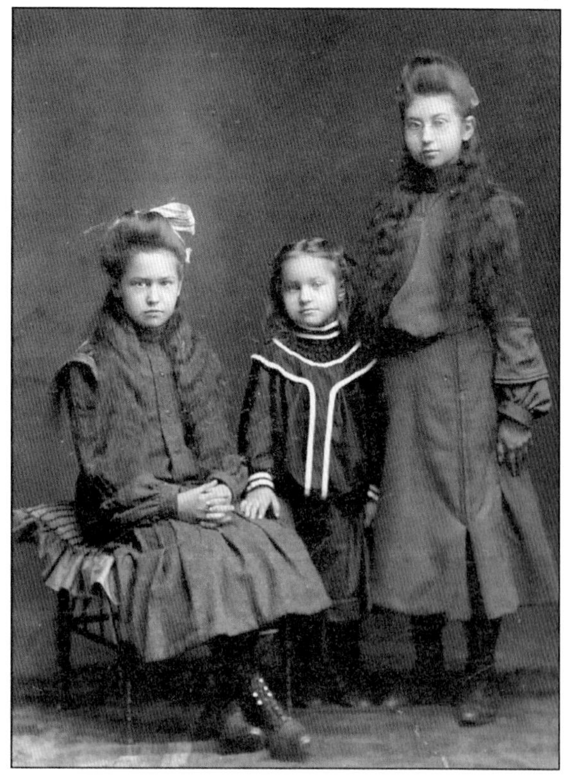

Two

The Town Grows
1861–1879

After the Civil War, Aurora experienced one of its biggest periods of growth. The community received a welcomed Christmas present when the first train traveled along the new tracks on December 25, 1867. The railroad connected local farmers and industries to the growing city of Buffalo and points beyond.

Main Street also evolved. The Eagle Tavern at the circle, which burned to the ground in 1869, was replaced within a year by the Hammond Hotel. At the other end of town, Byron D. Persons built a three-story hotel, the Persons House, on the site of the Aurora Theater. It was a massive structure and became even more prominent when a fourth floor was later added.

A new newspaper for the community was founded during this time. C.C. Bowsfield published the first edition of the *Erie County Advertiser*, now known as the *East Aurora Advertiser*, on August 9, 1872. Several other newspapers have been attempted in the community, but the *East Aurora Advertiser* has the distinction of being by far the longest-lived.

The most notable change during this time period was the name of the town's principal village. Two settlements had formed before the Civil War, one at the west end near the circle and another, known as "the upper village," near Main and Pine Streets. The west end officially incorporated as the village of Willink on December 28, 1848. It went as far east as Park Place. Over the next few decades, the two settlements grew closer together. The residents first voted in January 1874 to extend the village to include both settlements, but there was no consensus on what to call it. Some wanted to continue with the name Willink, which honored Wilhelm Willink, one of the original agents of the Holland Land Company. Others, none too pleased with the financial hold Willink and his company had on local settlers, preferred the less controversial name East Aurora. The split was evident in a special election on June 2, 1874, when the name East Aurora narrowly beat out Willink with a vote of 122-103.

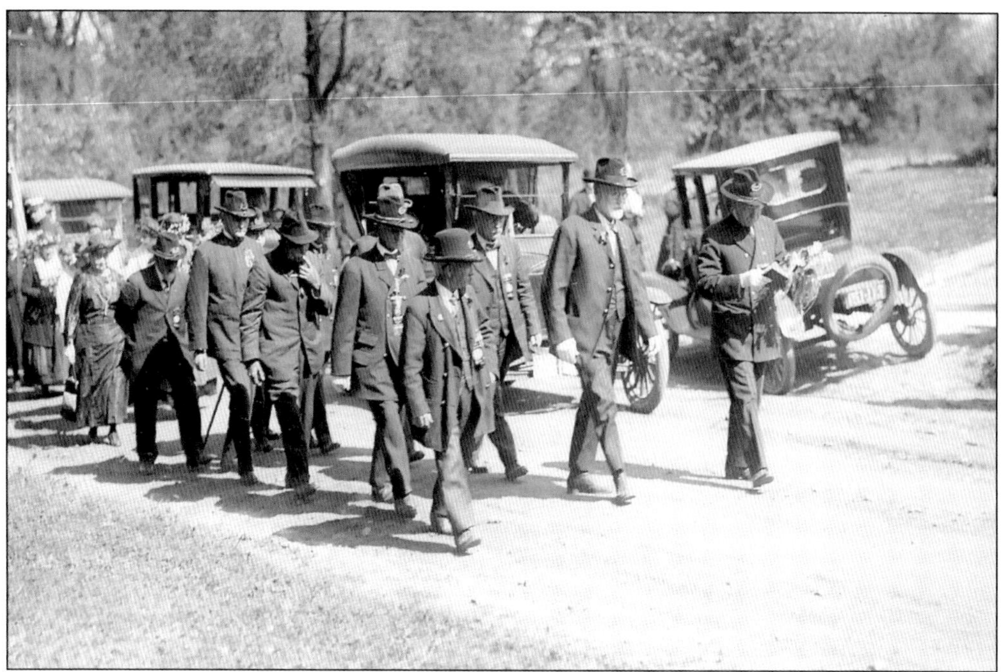

A total of 154 men from Aurora served in the Civil War. In 1923, nearly 60 years after the battles ended, some of the surviving veterans march toward Oakwood Cemetery for Decoration Day (Memorial Day) ceremonies. A monument was erected in the cemetery to honor those who served in the Civil War and has been the site of Memorial Day services each year since.

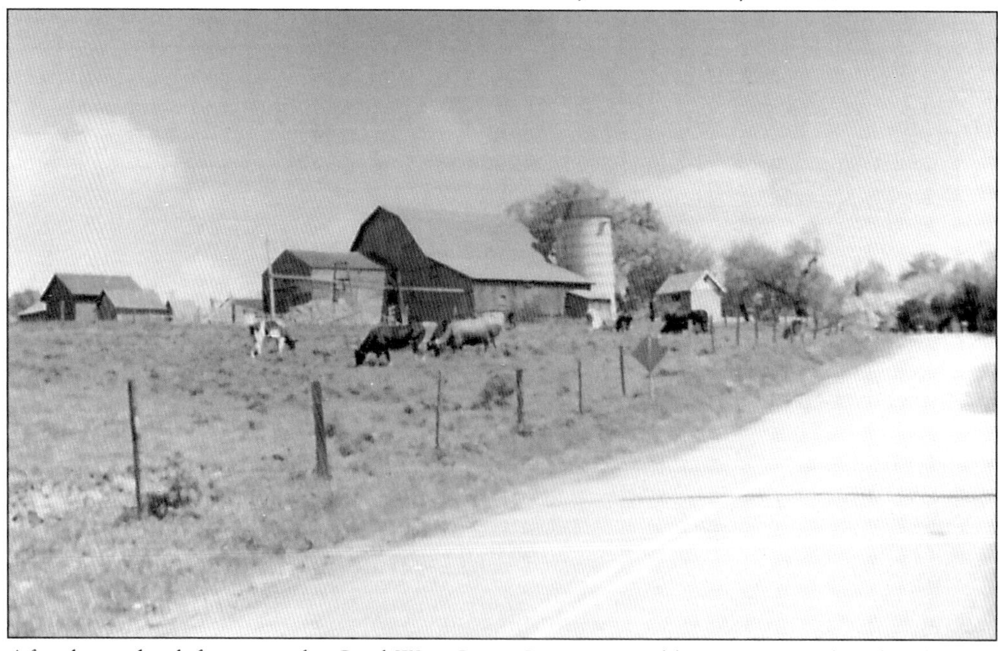

After losing his left arm in the Civil War, Gerrit Looman used his pension to buy farmland at Blakeley and Centerline Roads in 1871. In 1881, he built a new farmhouse, moving the original house to the back of the property. Three generations of the family operated the dairy farm. Looman died in 1921 and is buried in Oakwood Cemetery.

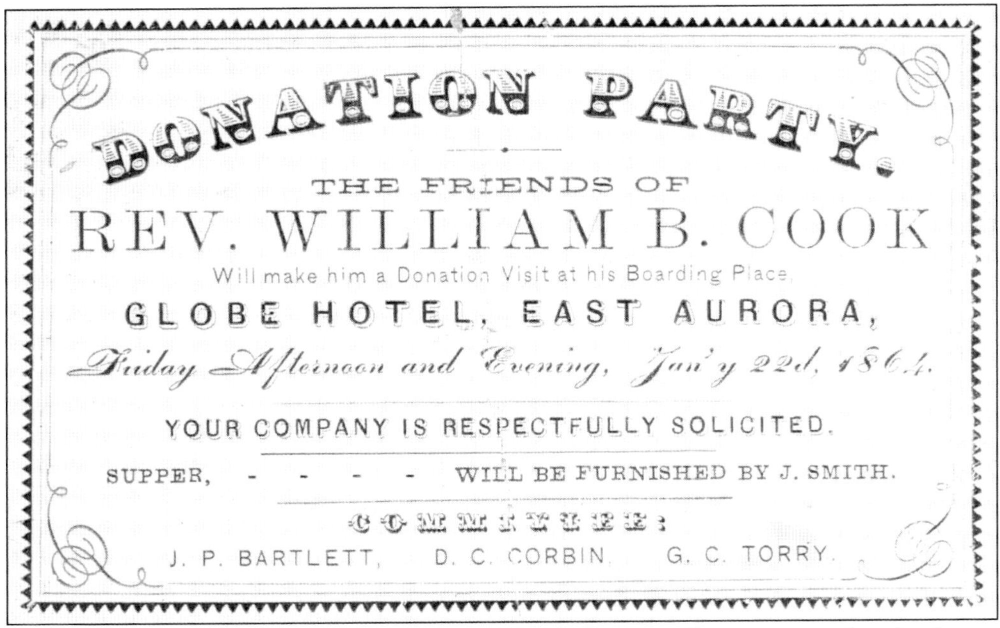

DONATION PARTY.

THE FRIENDS OF

REV. WILLIAM B. COOK

Will make him a Donation Visit at his Boarding Place,

GLOBE HOTEL, EAST AURORA,

Friday Afternoon and Evening, Jan'y 22d, 1864.

YOUR COMPANY IS RESPECTFULLY SOLICITED.

SUPPER, - - - - WILL BE FURNISHED BY J. SMITH.

COMMITTEE:

J. P. BARTLETT, D. C. CORBIN, G. C. TORRY.

The Globe Hotel on Main Street hosted numerous social affairs as well as serving as a boardinghouse. Friends of the Reverend William B. Cook hosted a party for the minister in 1864. He was staying at the hotel at the time.

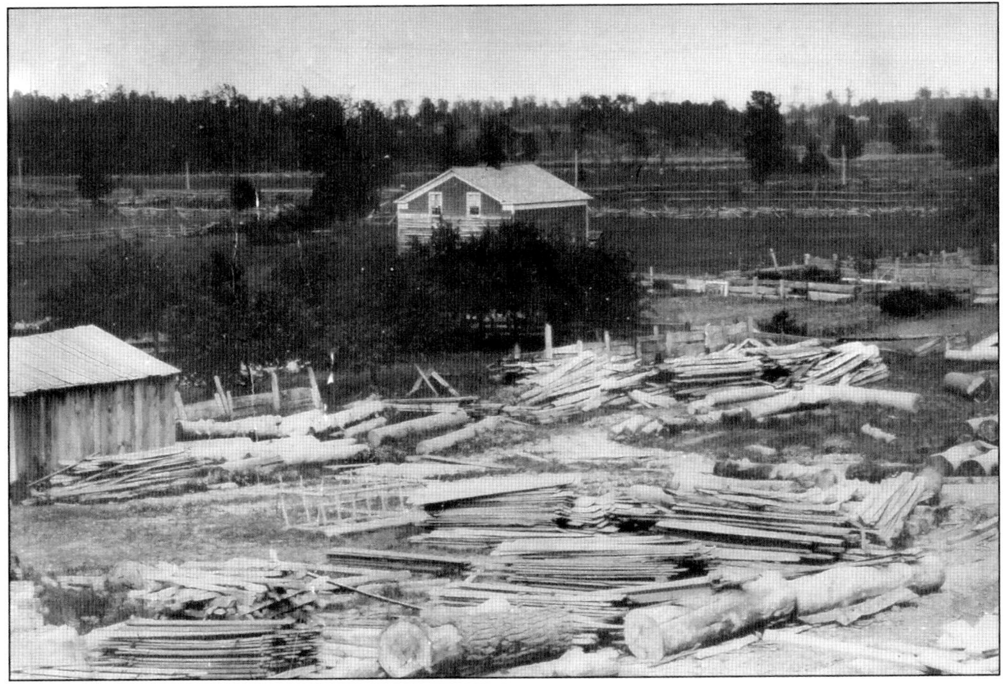

A lumberyard dominated the landscape north of the Main Street business district, between what is today Pine and Church Streets. With its rich forests, Aurora was home to many lumber companies that benefited from the arrival of the railroad. The Zapf Lumber Company owned property in the area and maintained headquarters on the east side of Elm Street, a site that later became home to Tenney Lumber Company.

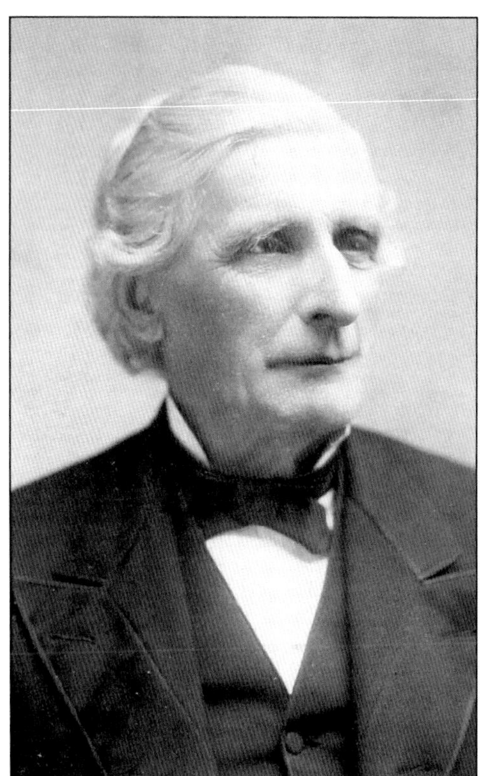

The Reverend Richard Marsh Sandford was a minister in Griffins Mills for 20 years before he also became the pastor of the First Presbyterian Church between 1865 and 1887. For nearly 10 years, he was pastor of both churches, traveling from his home in Griffins Mills to the church in the village. He became known as the marrying minister, and copies of his detailed marriage log are in the town historian's office.

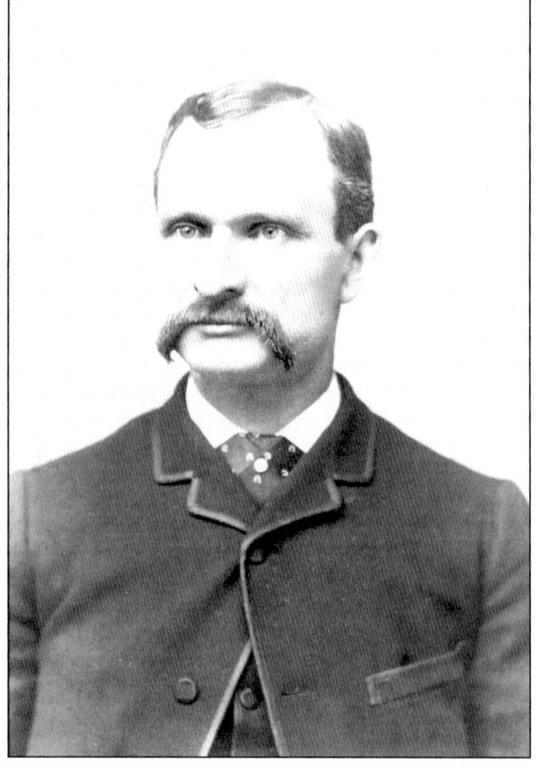

Miles Randall Williams of Blakeley Corners married Mary Follett Paine of the prominent Paine family of East Aurora on October 18, 1871. They had three children, one of whom, Alice May Williams, married into another prominent local family when she wed Frank O. Persons.

The Reverend J. Ward Stone was pastor of the First Baptist Church of East Aurora from 1870 to 1874. The Baptists began holding meetings shortly after the first settlement. They used the homes of early settlers Joel Adams and Jabez Warren. In 1810, David Irish, a Baptist missionary, officially organized the group into a church. In 1828, they built a wood-framed church on the southeastern corner of Main Street and Temple Place.

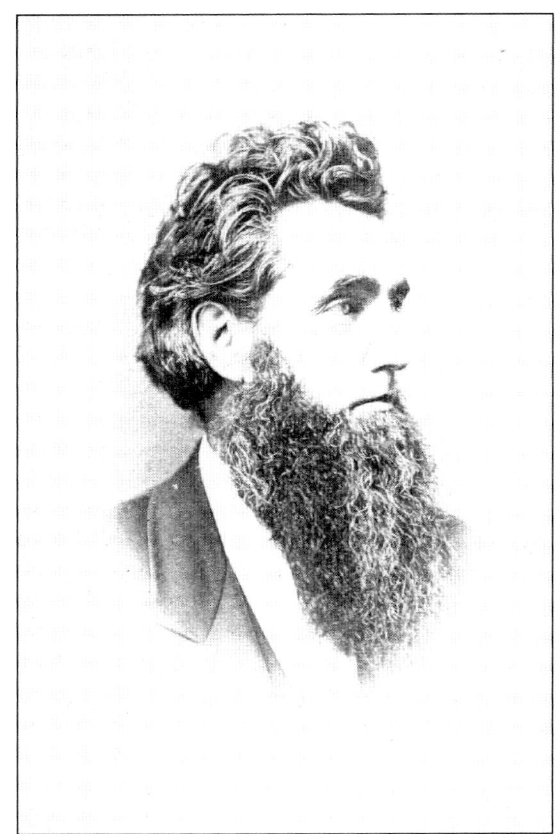

Though Willink ceased to be an incorporated village in 1874, a post office remained at the west end of the new village of East Aurora until 1913, when it was consolidated with the East Aurora Post Office. This unique wooden postcard was sent to Willink in June 1911.

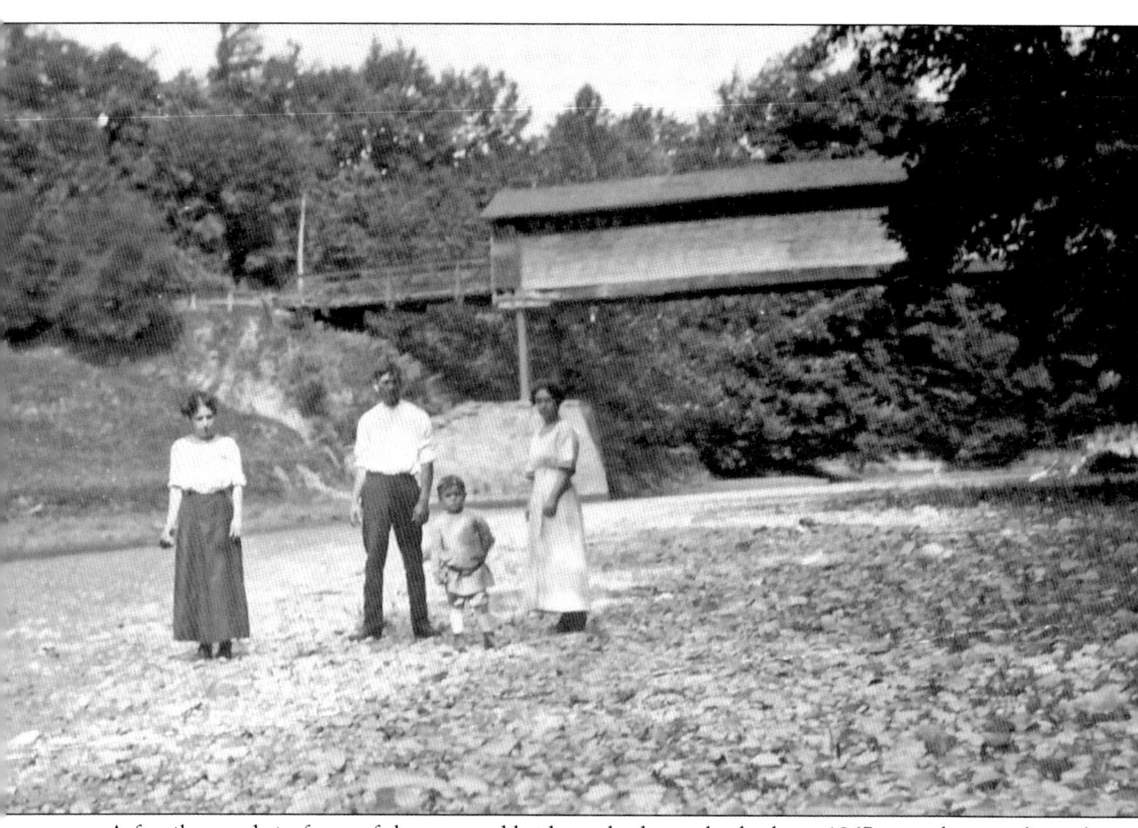

A family stands in front of the covered bridge, which was built about 1867 over the west branch of Cazenovia Creek in Griffins Mills. The red bridge was repaired in 1901. A more modern span later replaced it. Aurora was home to a handful of covered bridges, which are all long gone.

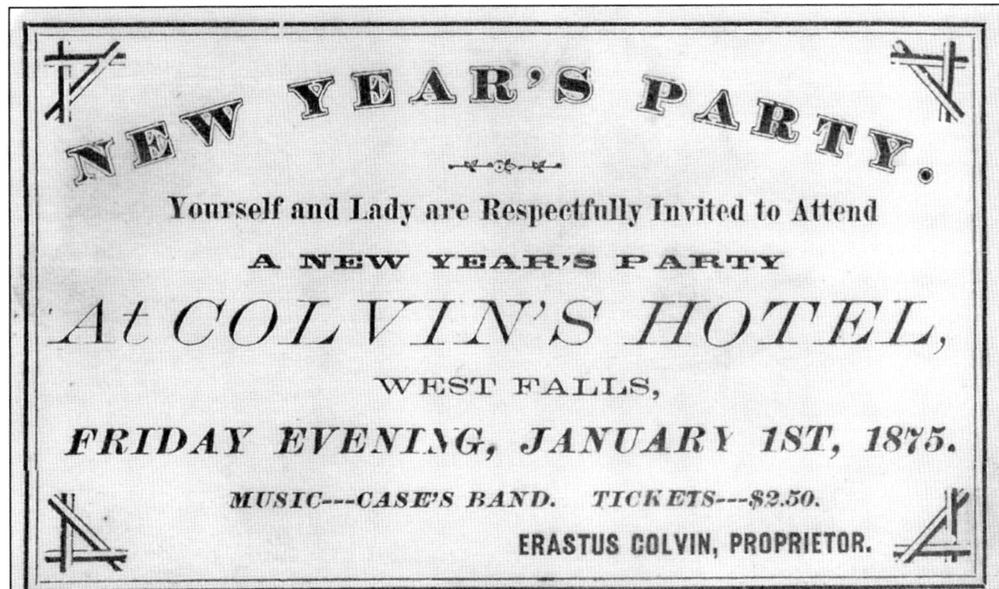
NEW YEAR'S PARTY.

Yourself and Lady are Respectfully Invited to Attend

A NEW YEAR'S PARTY

At COLVIN'S HOTEL,

WEST FALLS,

FRIDAY EVENING, JANUARY 1ST, 1875.

MUSIC---CASE'S BAND. TICKETS---$2.50.

ERASTUS COLVIN, PROPRIETOR.

There was no ball drop, but residents of West Falls rang in 1875 just the same with a New Year's Day party at Colvin's Hotel, operated by Erastus Colvin. The invitation promised music and fun for all. Note that tickets were $2.50, a hefty sum in those days.

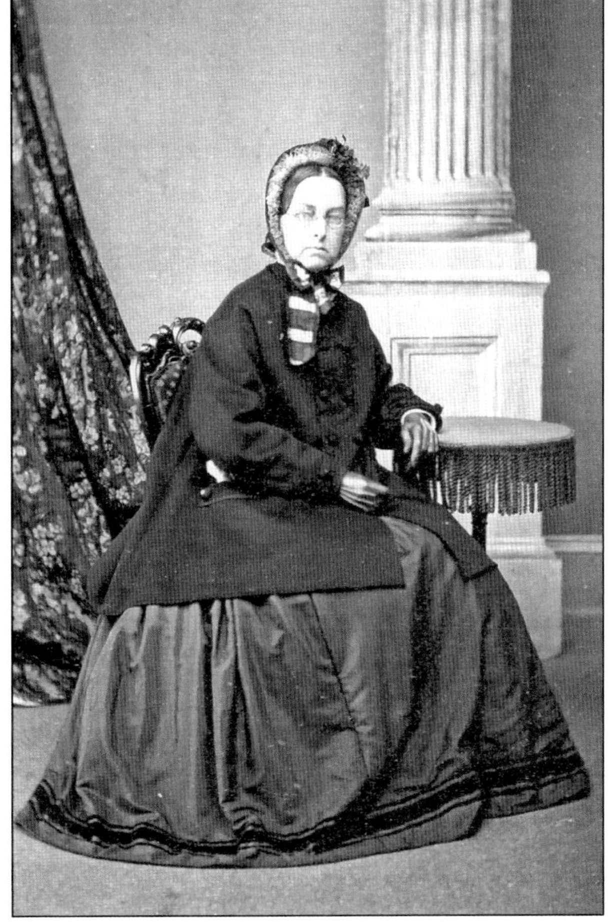

Electa Pratt Bond shows off the fashion of the day in this photograph taken by famed Boston photographer William H. Getchell, who ran a solo photography studio in the 1860s and 1870s. Electa was the daughter of Levi Pratt of East Aurora and the wife of William Bond. Levi Pratt built a handsome home on Main Street that for many years housed the library. It was demolished to make room for the modern library that replaced it.

Exhibition

ACADEMY LYCEUM,

ACADEMY HALL, FRIDAY EV'G.,

FEBRUARY 28, 1873.

PROGRAMME.

1. Darling Minnie Lee, Solo and Chorus,
R. Kelsey, F. Kelsey, Palice Dirstin, Anna Stillman.

2. CURE FOR THE FIDGETS,

Finniken F.zzleton	Mr. D. Phelps.
Hercules Sparks	Frank Kelsey.
Mr. Watkins Walkerjohn	Silas Person.
Jack Johnson	John Miller.
Seraphina	Jennie Rosier.
Miss Cecelia Walkerjohn	Ruby Metcalf.
Biddy	L. Holmwood.

3. Speed Away, Speed Away,
R. Kelsey, F. Kelsey, Geo. Hildreth, E. Darbee.

4. Pantomime,
Schwarzwald Wedding, - A Scene From Real Life.

5. Solo, Janet's Choice,
Annie Peek

6. THE DUTCHMAN'S GHOST.
A Farce in Five Acts.
Hans Barth - W. A. Day.

The Aurora Academy Lyceum, known originally as the Willink Lyceum, was founded in October 1866 to attain "the highest degree of literary knowledge." The group met in an office at Main Street and Buffalo Road (the present location of the circle) and Willink's schoolhouse at Hamburg Street and Douglas Lane before moving to the Aurora Academy Hall at Main and North Grove Streets. Their programs included poetry readings, music, and discussions. This poster for the February 28, 1873, lyceum advertised musical solos, comedies, and farce. Admission was 25¢.

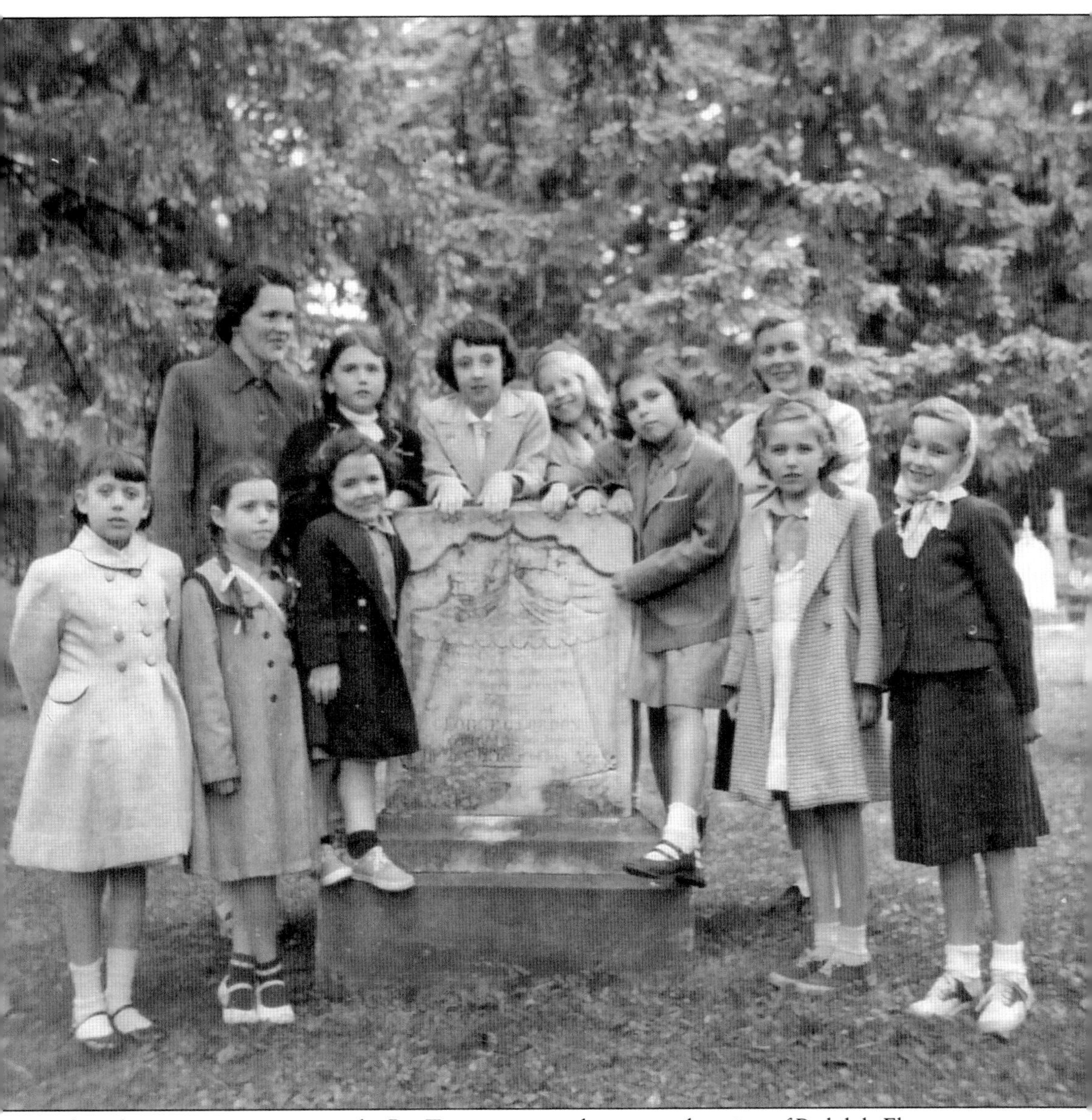

When the circus came to town, the Big Top went up at the present location of Parkdale Elementary School, where on June 11, 1872, thirty-one-year-old performer George G. Gordon died. According to one local legend, he fell off a horse, but a more reliable account indicates that he was foreman of the tent crew and collapsed of a heart attack while raising the Big Top. A gravesite in Oakwood Cemetery was donated, and the management of the Great Central Park Menagerie and Circus later provided a tombstone with an engraving of a circus tent. In this photograph, Girl Scouts visit the grave in the early 1960s. A circus lady, feeling bad that she had to leave her colleague behind in an unfamiliar town, asked the children gathered at Gordon's funeral to make sure wildflowers were placed on his grave each Memorial Day. The tradition carried on for decades. Many children have taken field trips to the cemetery to see the interesting grave marker and learn the story of the circus man who, with no permanent home of his own, became an adopted citizen of Aurora.

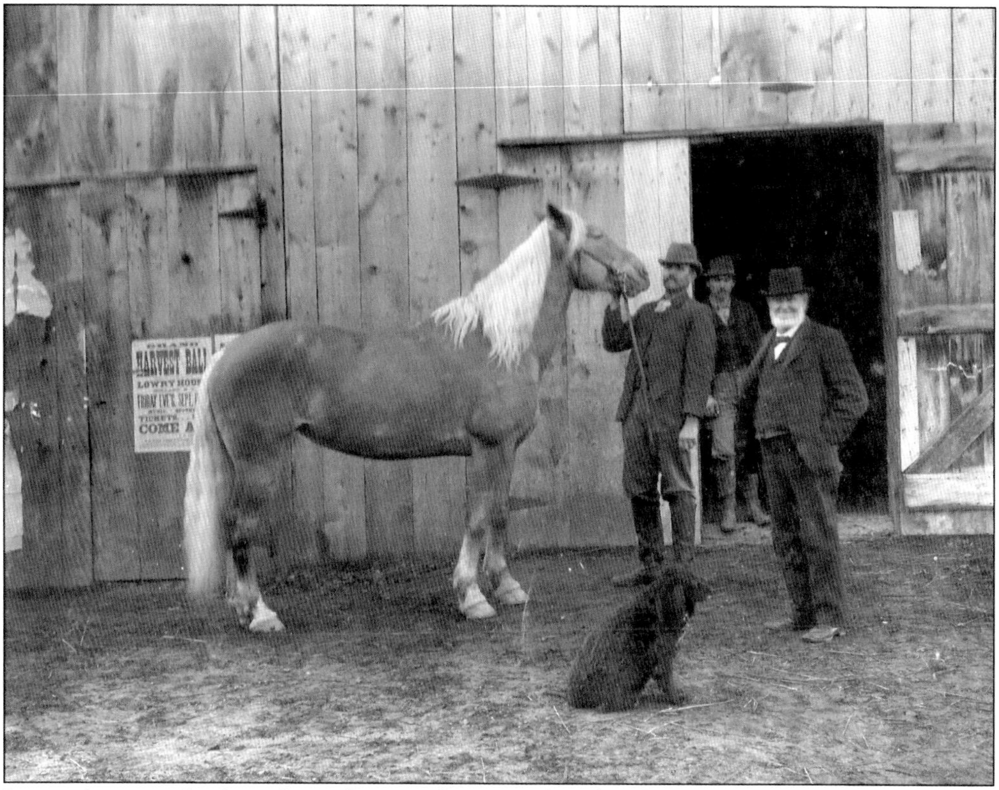

It is unclear exactly where these photographs were taken, but the posters on the barn door in the background advertise a Harvest Ball and circus in East Aurora. Perhaps these farmers are preparing their livestock for the upcoming Erie County Fair. The fair has been held in the nearby town of Hamburg since the 1860s, but Aurora hosted the event in both 1850 and 1854.

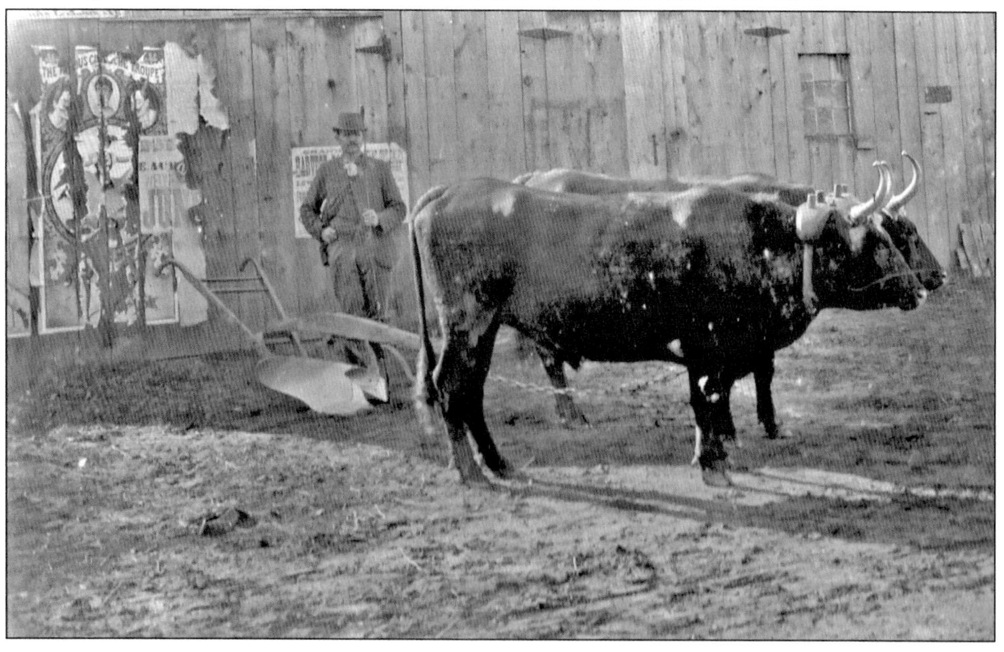

Three

Horse-Racing Capital 1880–1889

The 1880s were a decade of transformation in Aurora. With the establishment of a second world-class horse breeding and racing farm, the community became known as the "horse-trotting capital of the world."

Cicero J. Hamlin planted the seed when in 1855 he purchased more than 60 acres on the north side of Main Street between Buffalo Road and Tannery Brook. Hamlin, who later donated the land on the south side of the village for the park that now bears his name, built stables on the Village Farm for more than 700 horses. It became the "world's greatest trotting nursery." Visitors came from around the globe to get a glimpse of Mambrino King and the other champions at his farm.

In 1878, the Jewetts purchased land near Grover Road and established their own horse farm. Their claim to fame was the construction in 1885 of the world's largest indoor horse track, which allowed for races during the winter months. It was 30 feet wide with windows on both sides. The track was dismantled in 1918, and many of the windows were saved and used in various homes around town.

Horses also were the attraction on South Street, where the village had established the East Aurora Driving Park in 1877.

The 1880s were also a time of economic growth in Aurora. Richardson, Beebe & Company was converting cream from area dairy farms into world-famous cheese; Sylvester Griggs opened his flour and feed business on Main Street, which later became the locally famous Griggs & Ball; Adam Wallenwein built a three-story hotel at 584 Main Street; and Henry Z. Persons and his son Henry H. Persons founded East Aurora's first bank in 1882.

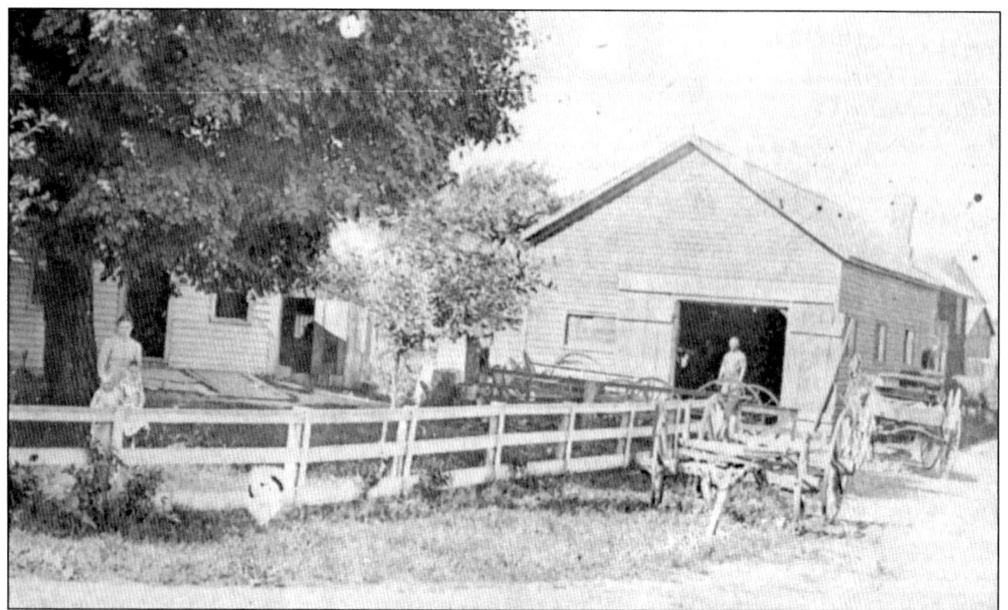

William Scott Lipsett operated his blacksmith shop on Mill Road near Quaker Road in the 1880s. His homestead can be seen directly behind the large tree on the left side of the photograph. Just like cars need service today, horse carriages and buggies were "in the shop" from time to time. Lipsett's daughter Mary later ran the subscription department at the Roycroft. (See page 73.)

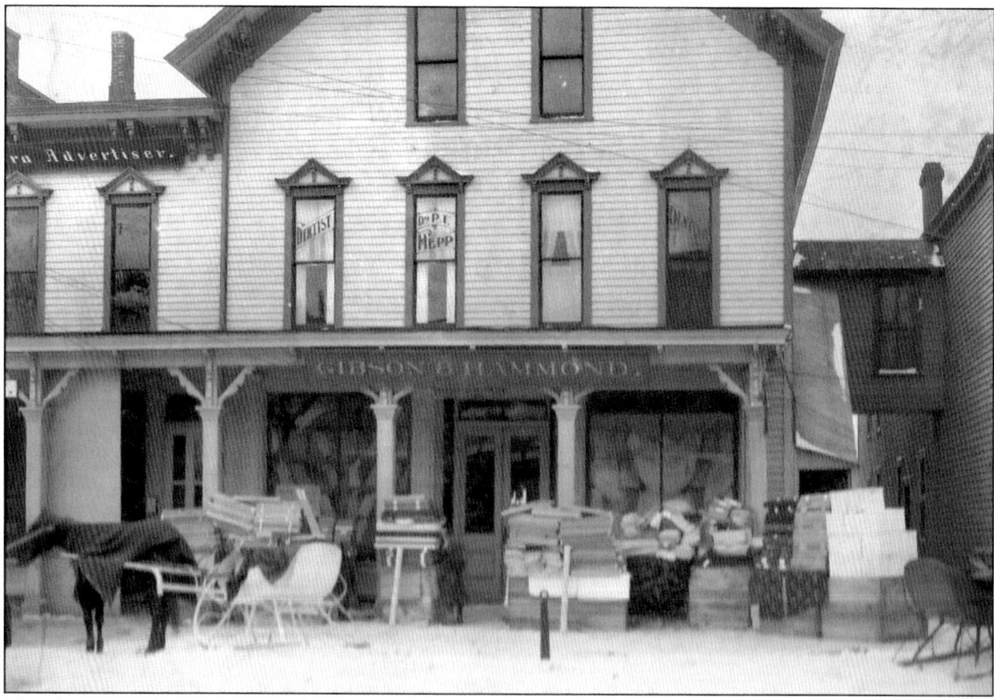

Sleighs await their owners, who are busy shopping inside the Gibson and Hammond store, built on the north side of Main Street in 1880 to replace a previous general store across the street. The business was later purchased and became Kent and Roat. Note the *East Aurora Advertiser* sign to the left and the passage over the alley from one building to the other on the right.

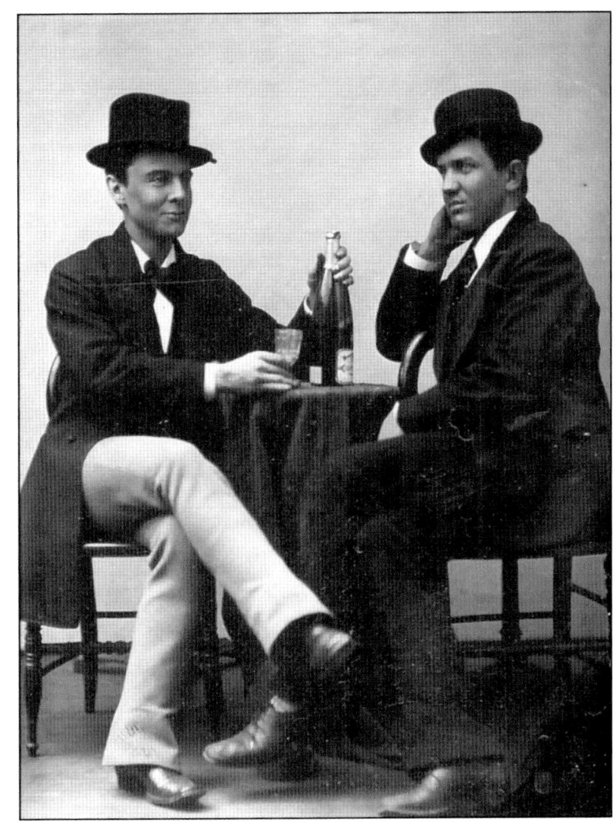

The man on the left is believed to be Clarence Lamb, who went on to become East Aurora's oldest active fireman. He started his career as a jeweler but later became a real estate agent. Lamb married his wife, Louise D. Bodiner, amid great fanfare in front of 15,000 witnesses at East Aurora's Village Fair in 1887. He died in July 1940 at the age of 87. The other man is unidentified.

Grace Fuller, right, with her daughters Beata and Eloise, was the wife of F. Henry Fuller, whose father, Turner Fuller, opened a general store west of the Globe Hotel shortly after moving to the village in the early 1870s. F. Henry Fuller and his son-in-law Harrison Hall, Beata's husband, later ran the business.

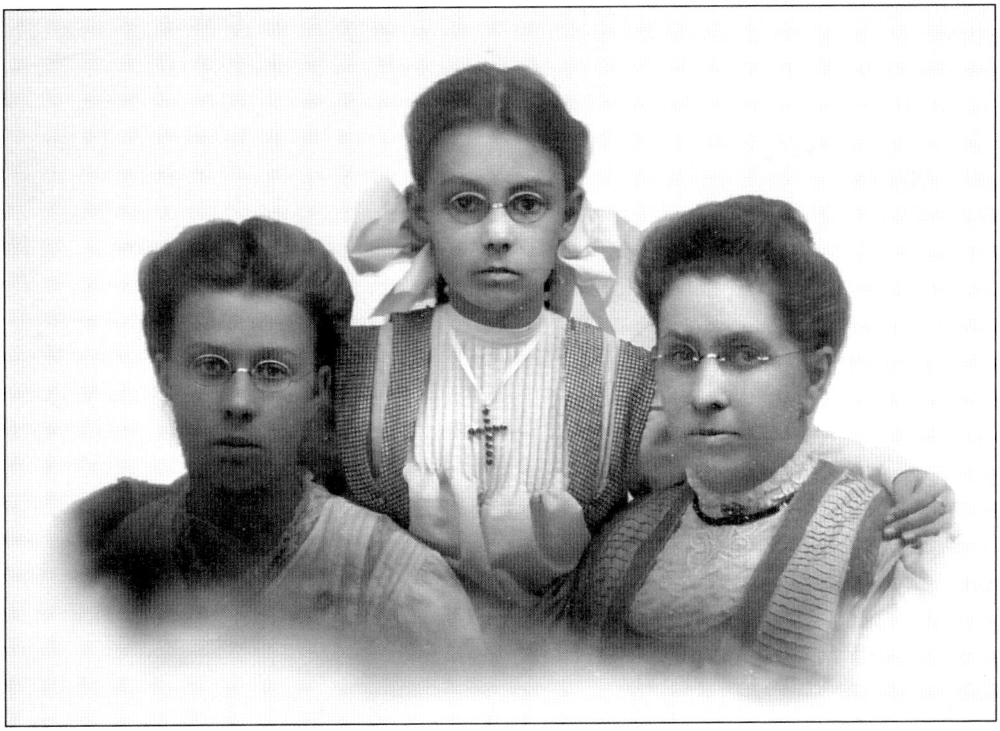

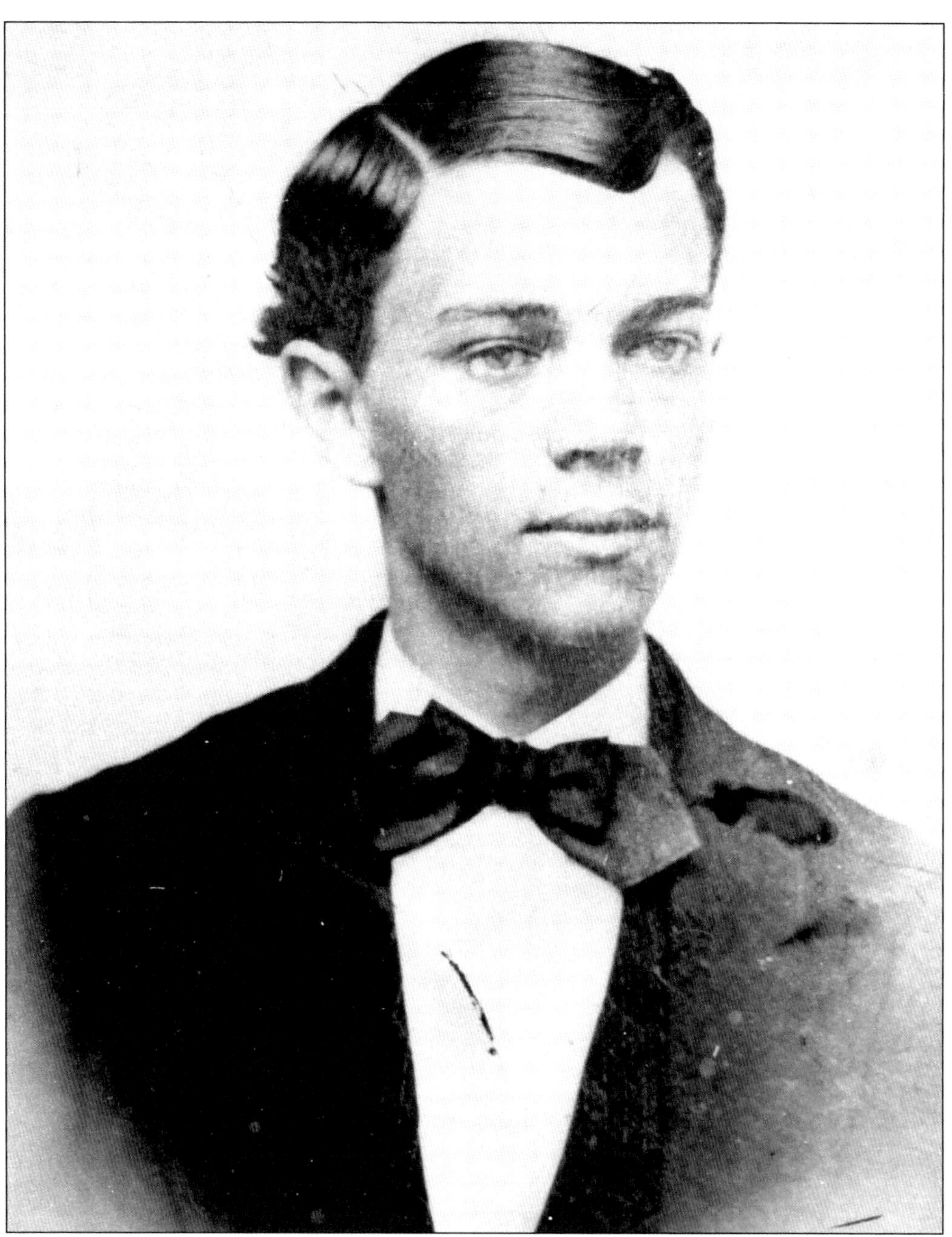

At the age of 35, Frank H. Paine, son of Timothy Paine, died at sea on June 29, 1884, aboard the ship *Dakota*. After practicing medicine and dentistry in Paris and the East Indies, failing health induced him to take the ship back home, but he died en route and was buried at sea. His short life was quite eventful. According to one family history, he was on his way to Washington, DC, in 1874 to accept his Signal Service appointment when, on a stop in New York City, he was drugged and taken to Havana, Cuba. Paine, the story goes, escaped on a vessel bound for Florida but, due to bad weather, he ended up in North Carolina. He was arrested as a Marine deserter when he returned to Washington. When the truth was discovered more than a year later, Paine was accepted back into the Signal Service and began studying medicine.

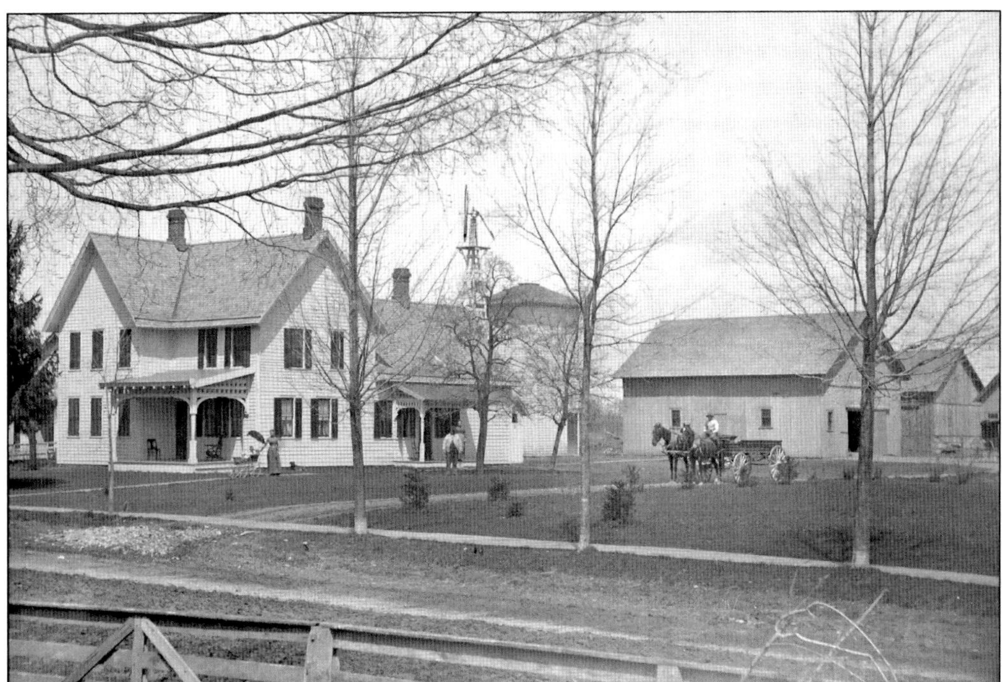

The Green family homestead was built at 494 Main Street in 1831. This photograph was taken in the late 1880s or early 1890s. Alice Conser Green is standing with the baby carriage next to the porch. The home still stands directly across from Park Place but has been remodeled.

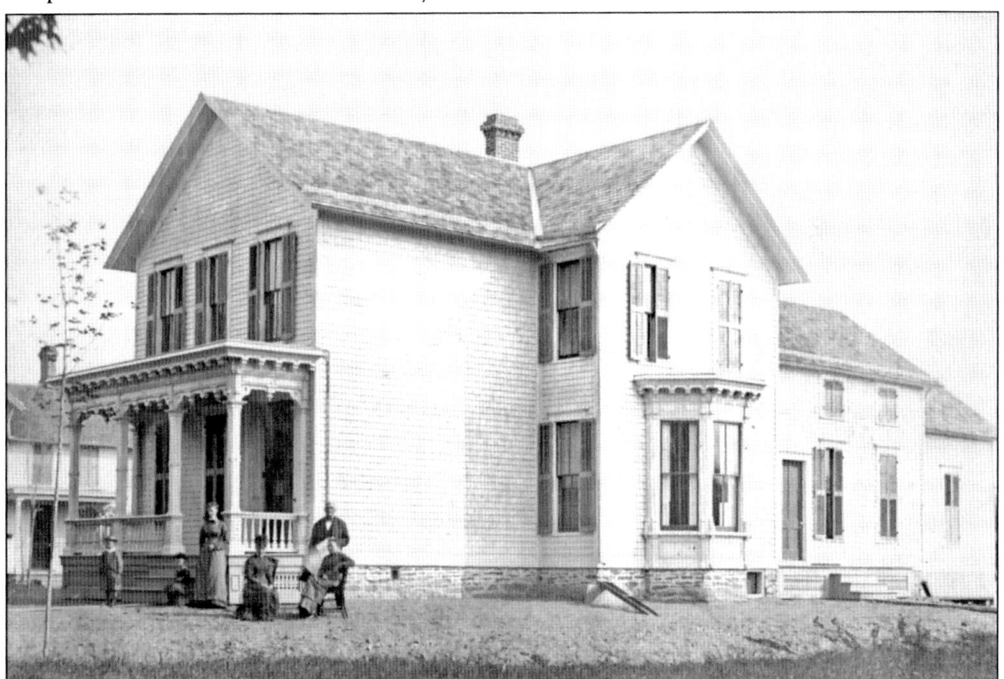

A number of Aurora's houses were built following the Civil War. The Dwight Spooner house was built at 110 Pine Street in the late 1870s. The cellar was started on June 5, 1878. The house was completed and occupied in early 1879.

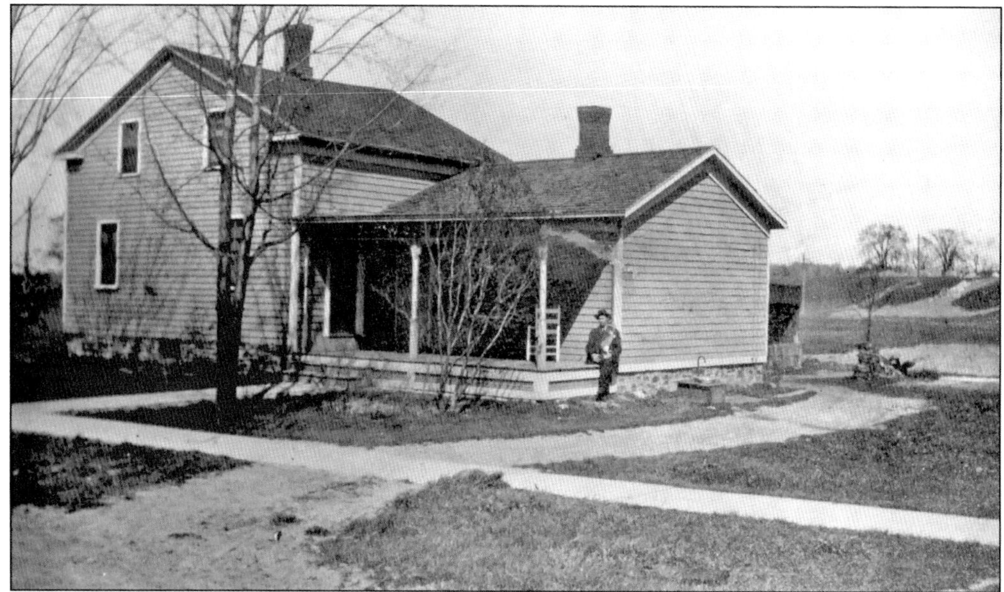

This house once stood on the east side of Pine Street, right around the corner from Main Street. The site is now the location of an insurance office.

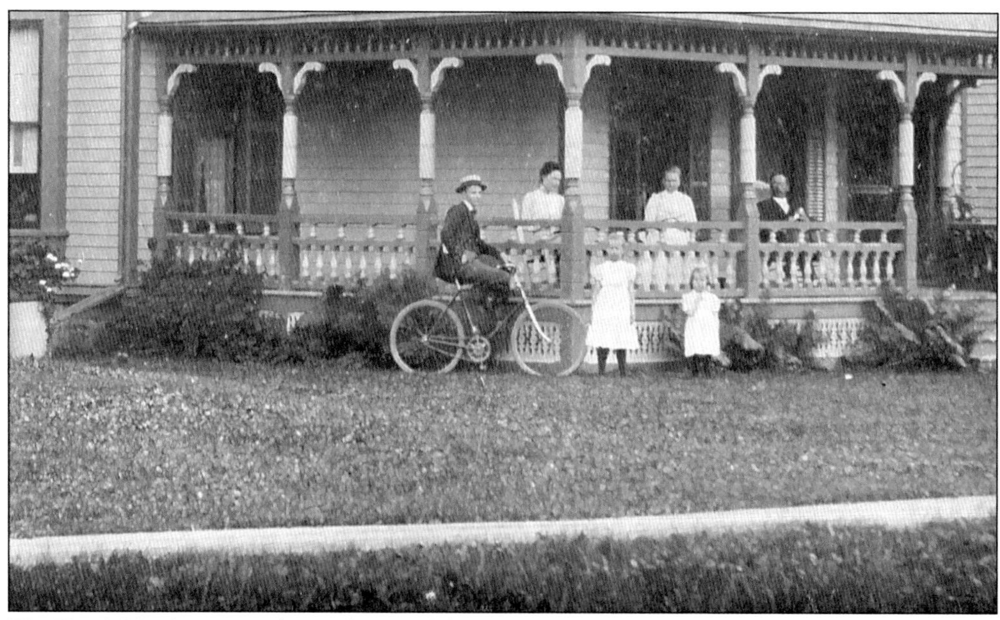

The Frank Nye home was located west of the Presbyterian church near Main and Paine Streets. The land is now a car dealership. Pictured are, from left to right, (first row) Wells Parker (on bike), who married Ella Nye and went on to become a prominent local attorney, and Ella's sisters Florence and Evelyn; (on porch) Ella Nye, mother Louise, and father Frank.

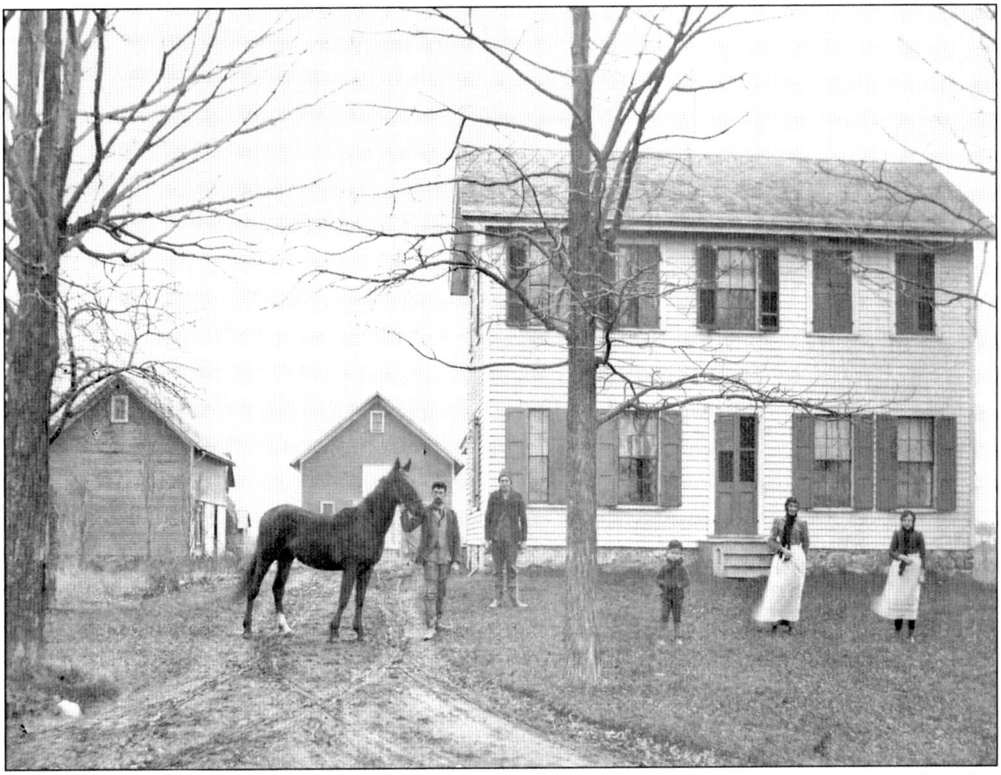

Imagine the mud the women had to keep out of the farmhouse during the early spring months! The family poses for a photograph on the Williams farm. The date of the photograph is unknown, but it is known that the Williams family owned a great deal of land on Girdle and Maple Roads on the border of Elma and Aurora. In fact, Maple Road in Elma was once known as Williams Road.

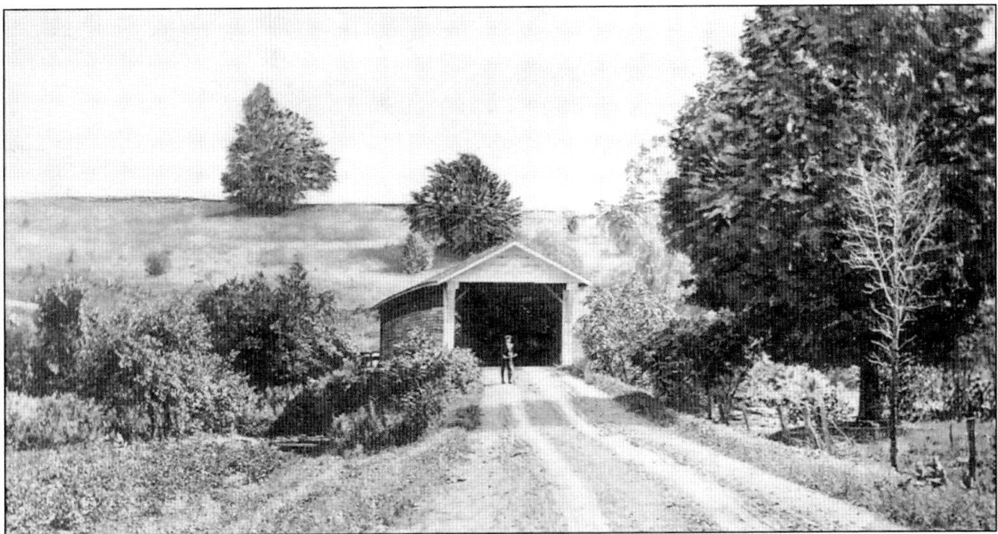

Covered bridges, built in the late 1800s, existed in Aurora's more rural areas well into the 1900s. This covered bridge went over Cazenovia Creek on Jewett Holmwood Road near Grover Road. The photograph appears on the front of a postcard that was sent from Aurora to Buffalo in February 1908.

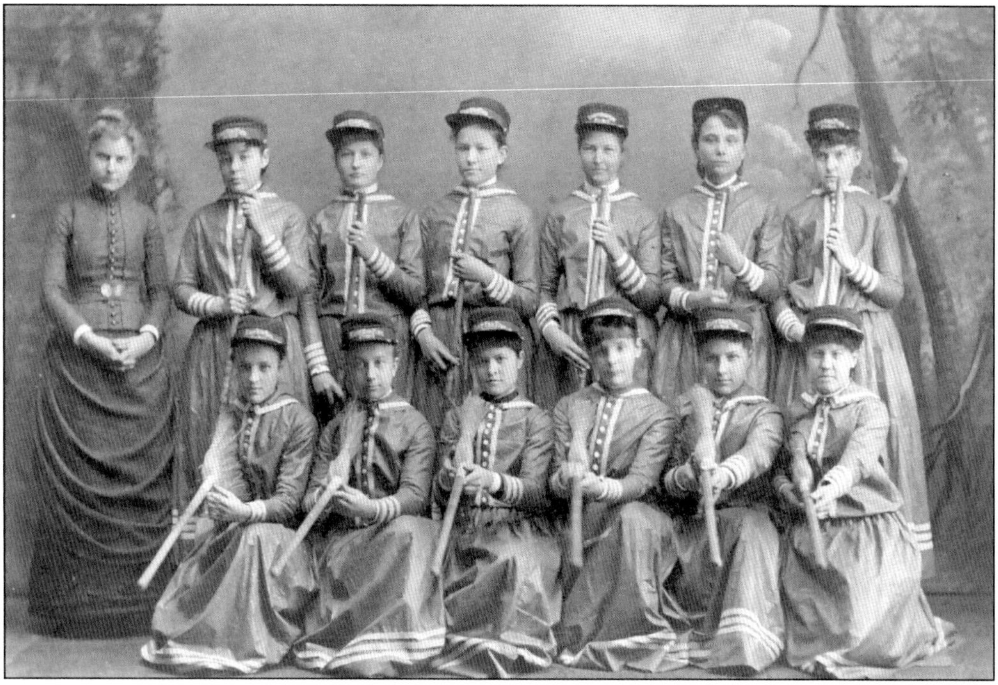

The women of the East End Fire Company No. 1 prepare for a broom drill in the mid-1880s. Not all the women in the photograph are identified, but the group does include Catherine Pratt, Mary Hitchcox, and Lillian Bradburn.

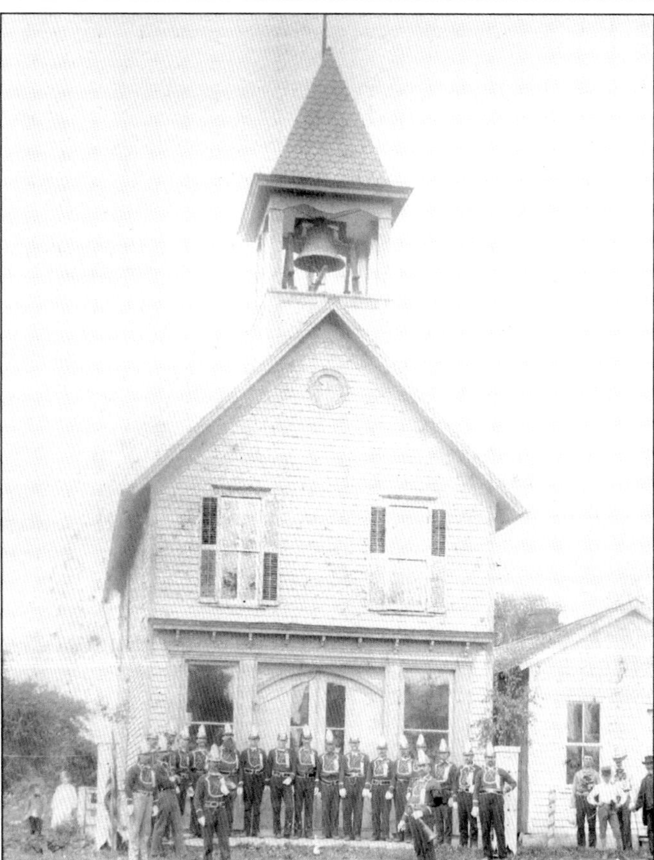

Firefighters pose in their formal uniforms outside the fire hall at the circle in Willink sometime in the late 1800s. The building was vacated after the community's four fire companies combined into a central fire hall on Oakwood Avenue. It has been renovated and now serves as a financial services office. The bell was removed and taken to the new fire hall.

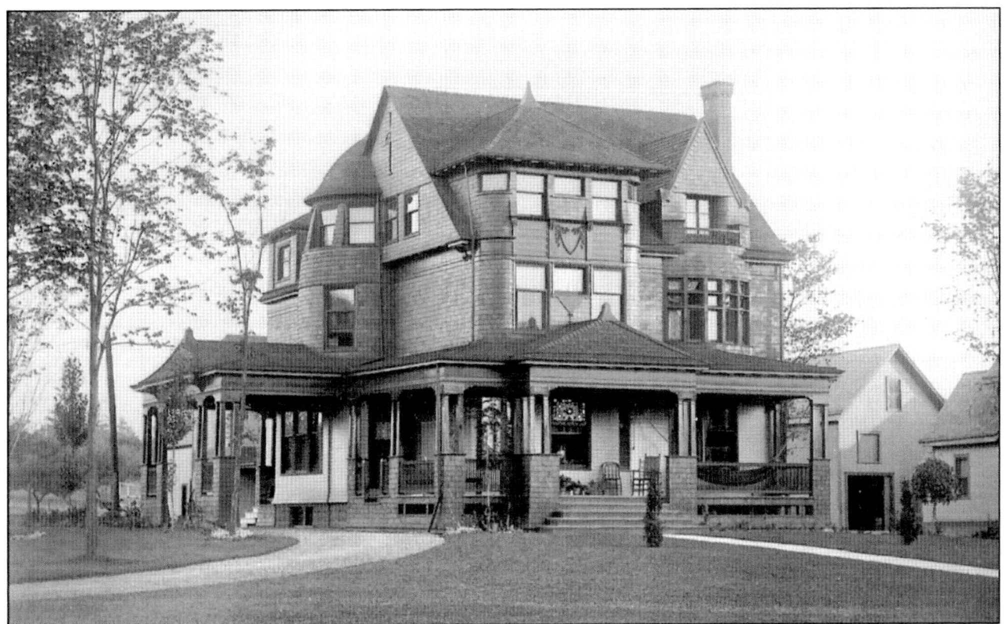

One-time East Aurora president Abbott Griggs built the Griggs mansion. Located at East Main Street and Elmwood Avenue, the home fell into disrepair before Elmer and Sharon Pisle purchased the property in 2004 and restored it for a bed and breakfast. It was among several mansions built in the 1880s and 1890s along East Main Street in the village.

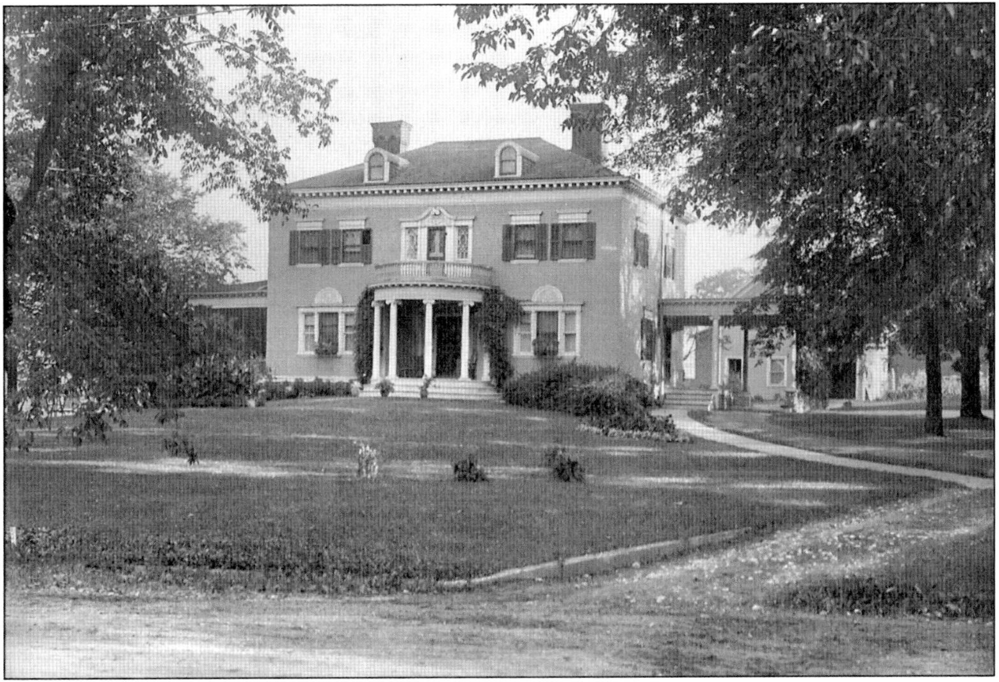

The 19th-century home of Horace B. Taber at 905 Main Street is shown before the East Aurora Chapter of the Loyal Order of the Moose acquired it in 1947. It is one of the many large homes that still remain on East Main Street. Note the dirt road that was Main Street at the time. The building has been remodeled.

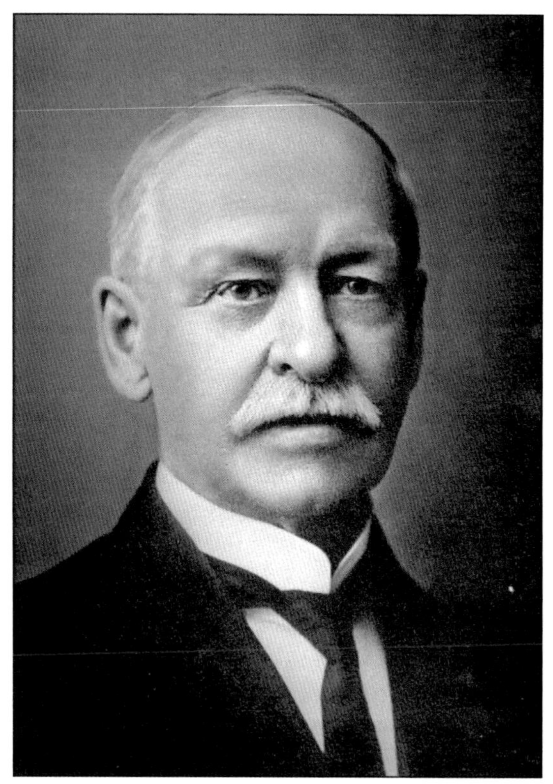

Harvey W. Richardson, left, and Wellington Beebe, below, made it big in the cheese business, taking advantage of the cream produced by area dairy farms. Their operation was headquartered next to the railroad tracks on Elm Street. In September 1885, the firm claimed to produce the largest block of cheese ever pressed up until that point. It weighed a reported 3,300 pounds. The *New York Times* even mentioned it, calling the block "the immense cheese." Richardson was a prominent Democrat, serving on committees at the state and national levels. He also played a part in bringing electricity to East Aurora. He was president of the First Spiritualist Society of East Aurora and held the mortgage when the members of the congregation purchased land on Temple Place and constructed a church in 1911.

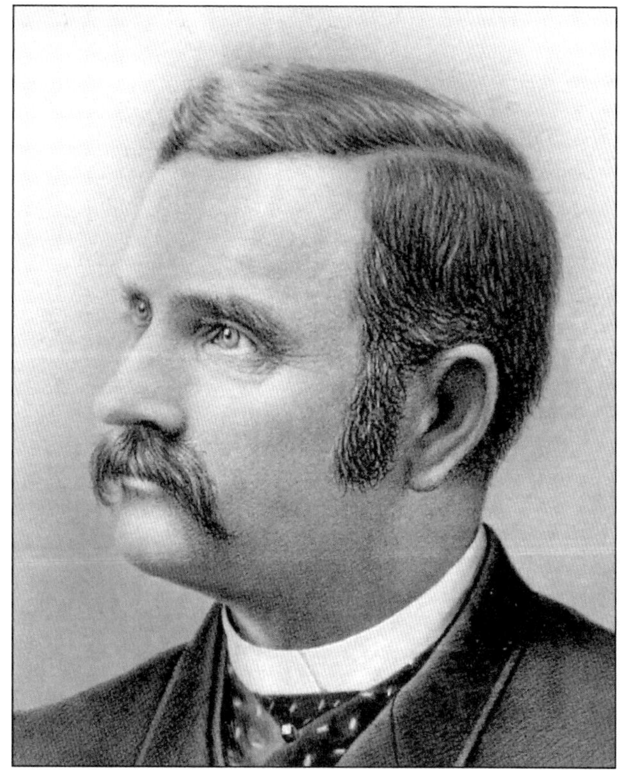

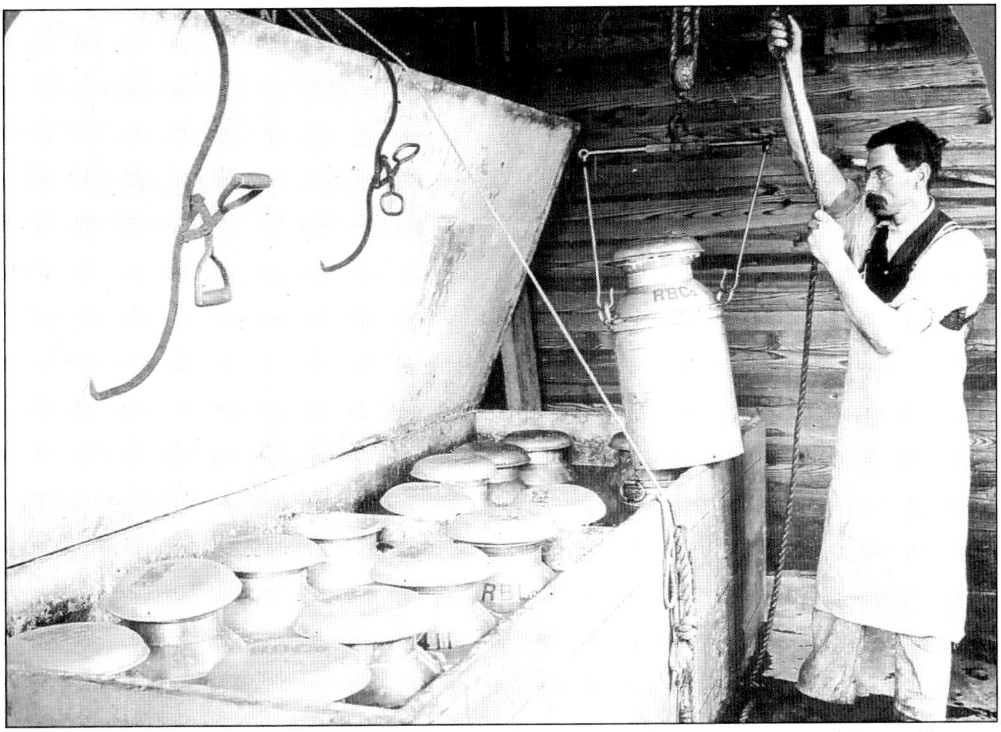

A worker at the cheese factory in East Aurora places cans of cream into vats of ice-cold water before the cream is churned in preparation to make cheese. Some of the old-fashioned milk cans are now used to decorate community porches as relics of days gone by.

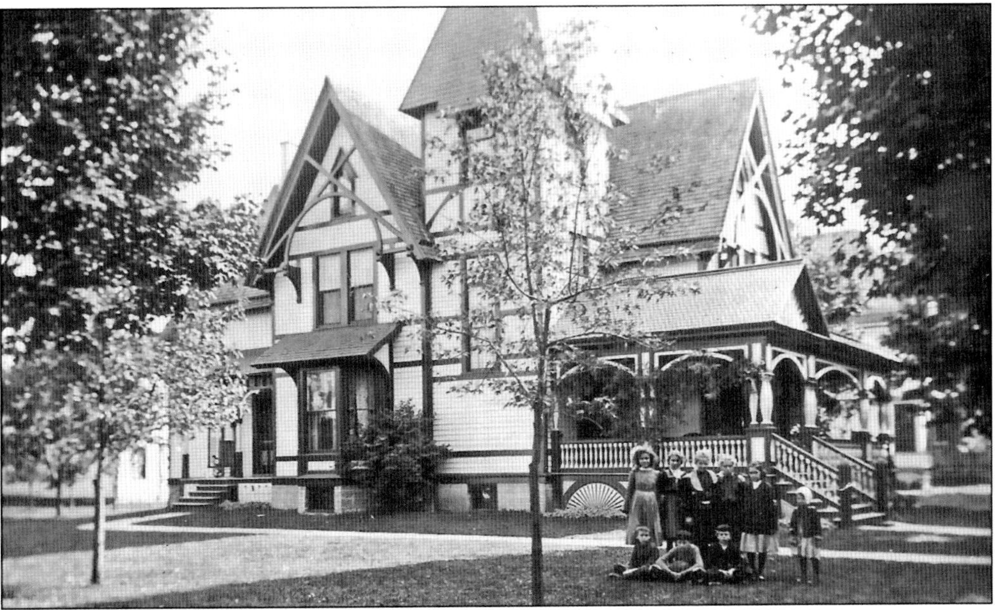

Wellington Beebe lived in this house at 50 Park Place from 1890 until he died in 1905. Christopher Peek, a local businessman who owned a great deal of village property and served as town supervisor from 1871 to 1873, built the home. It was demolished in September 1973 to make room for the Immaculate Conception Church's parking lot.

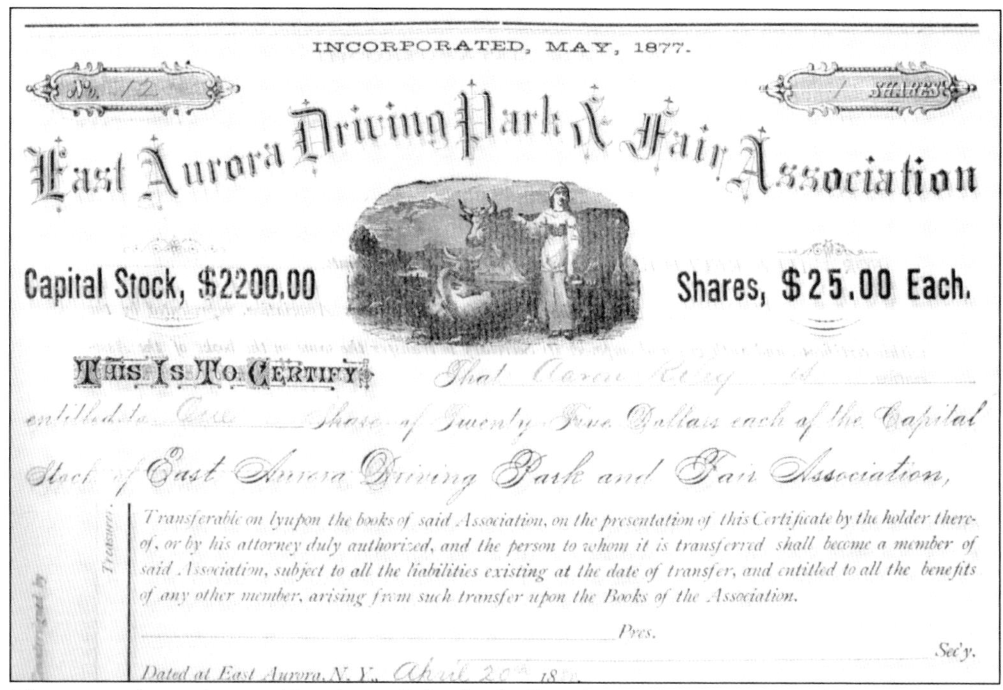

INCORPORATED, MAY, 1877.

No. 12 — 1 SHARES

East Aurora Driving Park & Fair Association

Capital Stock, $2200.00 — Shares, $25.00 Each.

This Is To Certify That Aaron Riley is entitled to One Share of Twenty Five Dollars each of the Capital Stock of East Aurora Driving Park and Fair Association,

Transferable on lyupon the books of said Association, on the presentation of this Certificate by the holder thereof, or by his attorney duly authorized, and the person to whom it is transferred shall become a member of said Association, subject to all the liabilities existing at the date of transfer, and entitled to all the benefits of any other member, arising from such transfer upon the Books of the Association.

Treasurer.

Pres.

Sec'y.

Dated at East Aurora, N.Y. April 20th 18

This is a stock certificate sold to Aaron Riley for the East Aurora Driving Park and Fair Association. The organization was formed in May 1877, and the fairgrounds were located on South Street. The organization folded, and the property was sold at public auction in February 1889.

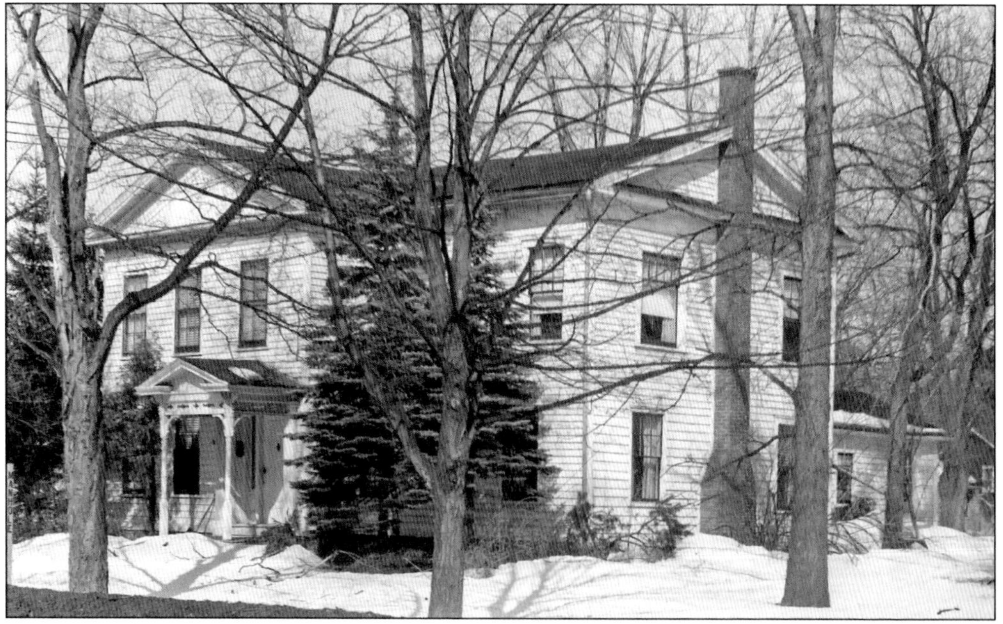

Cicero Hamlin's famous Village Farm was located on the north side of Main Street, from Buffalo Road to Tannery Brook. One of the buildings that remained from the old horse farm was the c. 1890 home of the farm superintendent, at the northeast corner of Main and North Willow Streets. The house was demolished in the mid-1960s to make way for a gas station. It is now the location of Pasquale's restaurant.

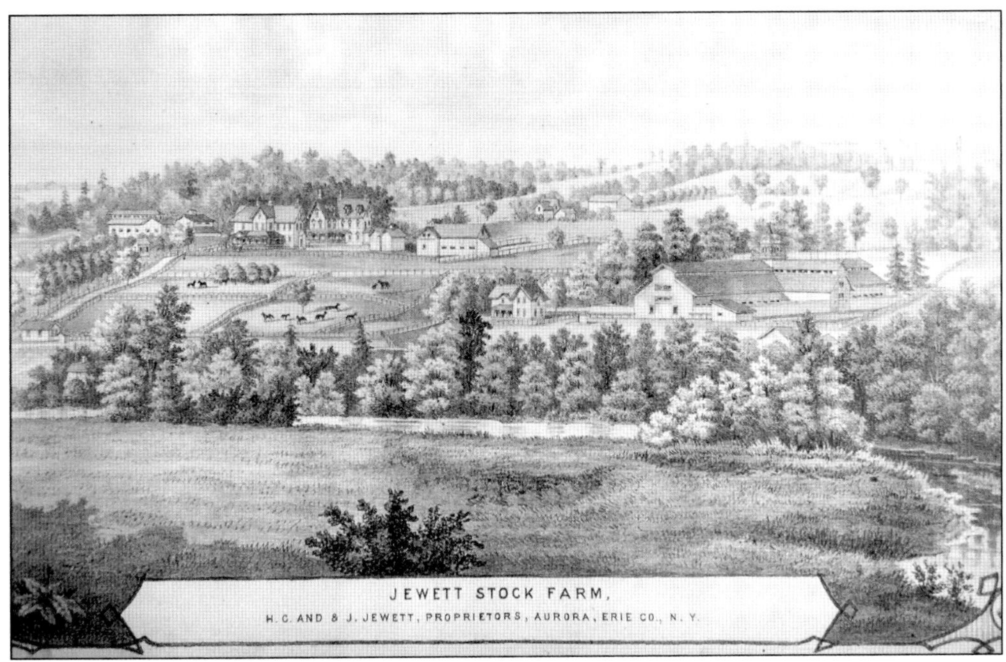

Henry Jewett purchased 400 acres of land off Grover Road in 1878 to raise horses. Seven years later, Jewett put his farm on the horse-racing map when he constructed the famous mile-long, covered racetrack, the only indoor racetrack of its kind in the world. Horses could be trained and raced in the winter months. The famous racetrack, which was later featured in the "Ripley's Believe It or Not!" newspaper column, is shown below in the background of a rare photograph. It was dismantled in 1918, and some of the windows were preserved and used in area homes.

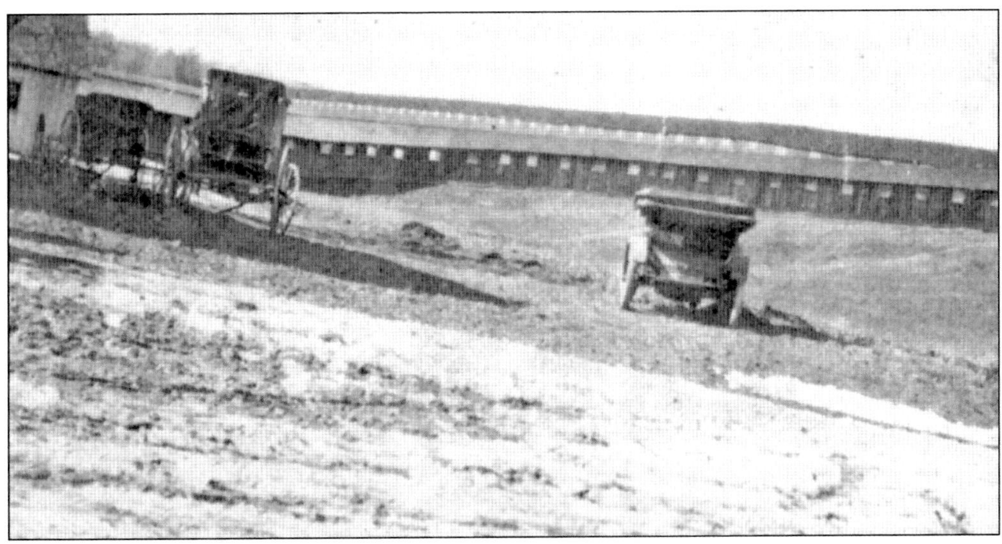

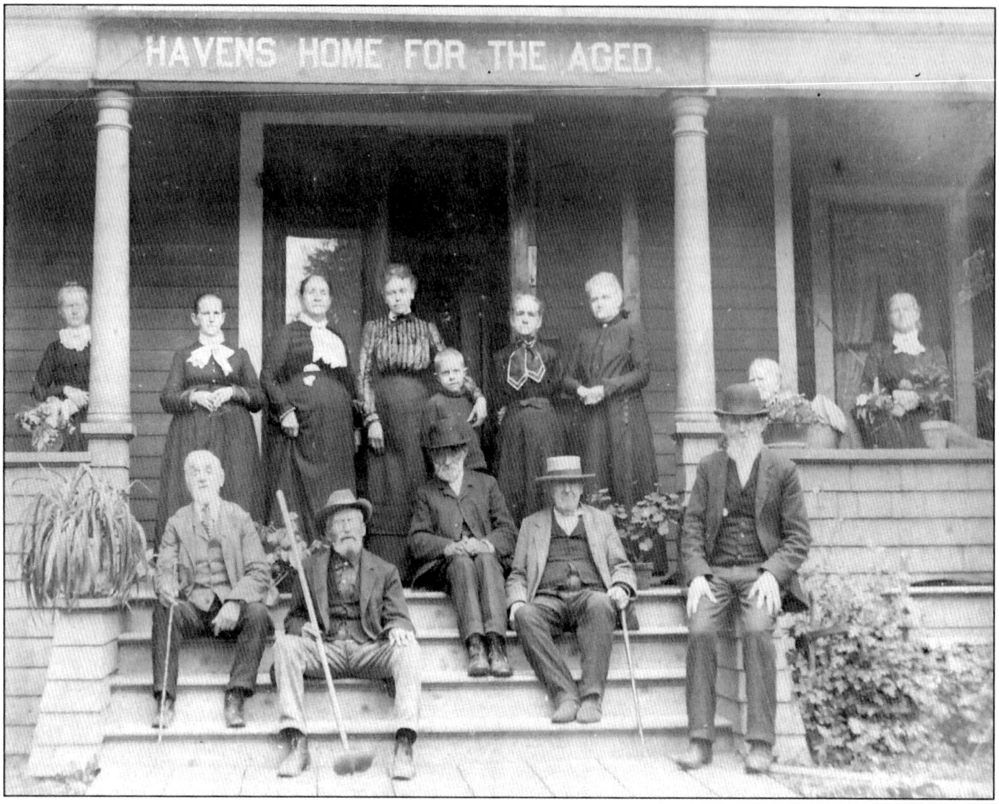

Ursula Havens realized a dream when she opened a home for older citizens to live out their lives in dignity. The Havens Home for the Aged opened at the northwestern corner of Center Street and Prospect Avenue in 1887. A decade earlier, she had purchased the land amid an apple orchard and constructed the large, frame house. There were rooms for about 35 people, who often sat on the porch and invited members of the community for lawn parties. Children were invited for Christmas parties. Ursula Havens died just four years after the home opened, but her husband, Alonzo, continued the effort. Other charitable organizations ran the home between 1894 and when it closed in 1923. Oakwood Cemetery, a block away, contains a section for those who spent their final years at the Havens Home. The house is now a private residence.

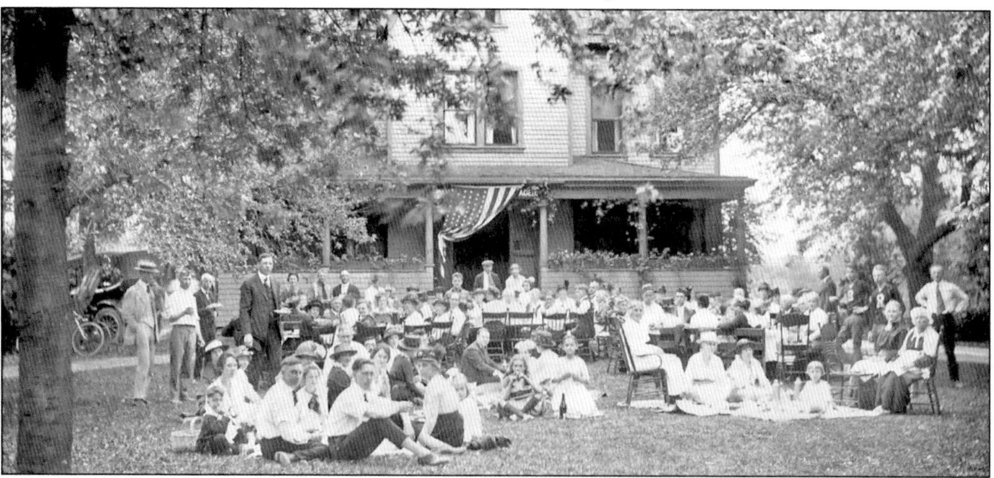

Four

Lights, Water, and Roycroft 1890–1915

The lights came on in East Aurora in the 1890s. So did the water and the telephones. East Aurora built its first power plant on Elm Street to generate electricity for streetlights. This building still stands today. The switch was turned on January 21, 1891, but some Aurorans were only moderately impressed. While the local newspaper touted the brightness of the lights, some residents complained that the new electric lights were considerably dimmer than the kerosene lamps that lit up the streets since 1879.

Also in 1891, water was first pumped from springs near Cazenovia Creek through more than 14 miles of pipes in the village. In 1893, the first telephone was installed in the Globe Hotel, and a short time later, about 25 residents had phones installed in their homes as well.

As the community's need for electric power expanded, a new power plant was built on Mill Road in 1903. The new decade also brought new roads. Erie County took over the old plank road in 1904, and a new brick road was laid between East Aurora and Buffalo. In 1912, the brick road was extended south on Olean Road to South Wales.

However, the biggest turn-of-the-century change for Aurora was Roycroft, an Arts and Crafts community launched by former soap salesman Elbert G. Hubbard. He had already been constructing his medieval-looking buildings at the corner of Main and South Grove Streets when his essay "A Message to Garcia," published in his magazine *The Philistine*, catapulted him into worldwide fame. Fans came from around the world to meet the man behind the magazine, and craftsmen journeyed to East Aurora in search of a place on his campus of artisans and philosophers.

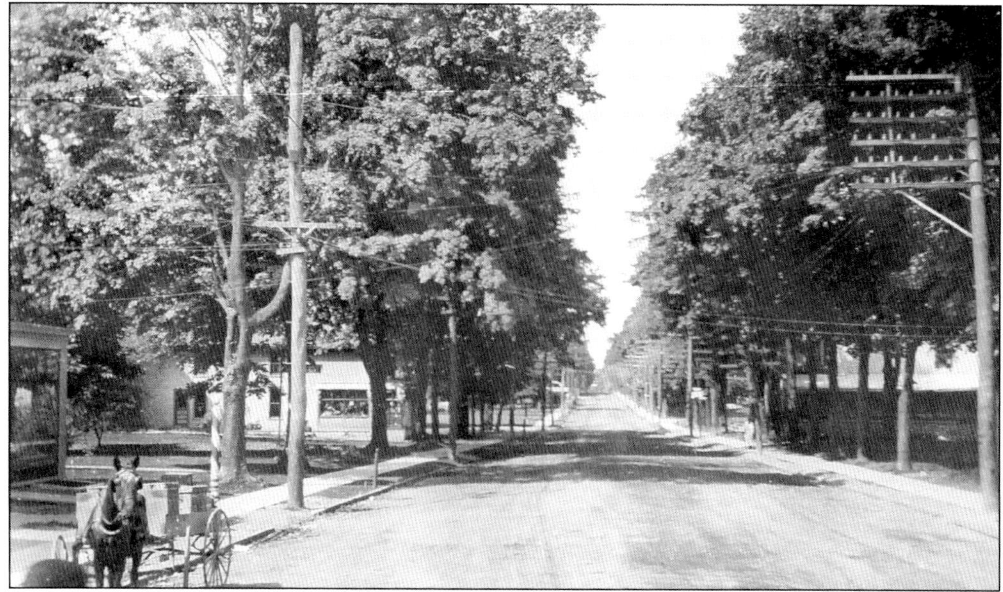

Utility poles line East Aurora streets around the 1890s, the decade that saw the introduction of electricity, telephone, and public water services in the village. Local residents were willing to put up with the poles, perhaps overwhelming and unsightly by today's standards, in exchange for the modern convenience of electric light and telephone.

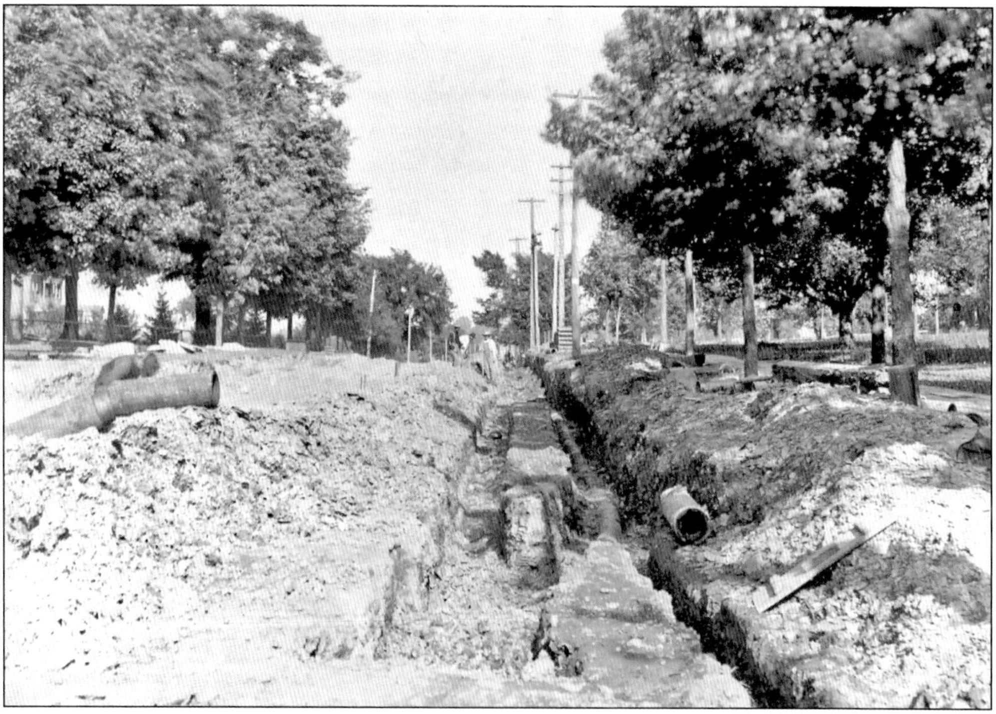

A labor force of 70 men was hired in 1890 to begin digging trenches for water mains on Main Street. The village originally used a variety of water sources, including pumping stations at the foot of Pine Street and at the current location of American Legion Post 362 on Center Street. There were also wells at Sinking Ponds and natural springs off Center and South Streets.

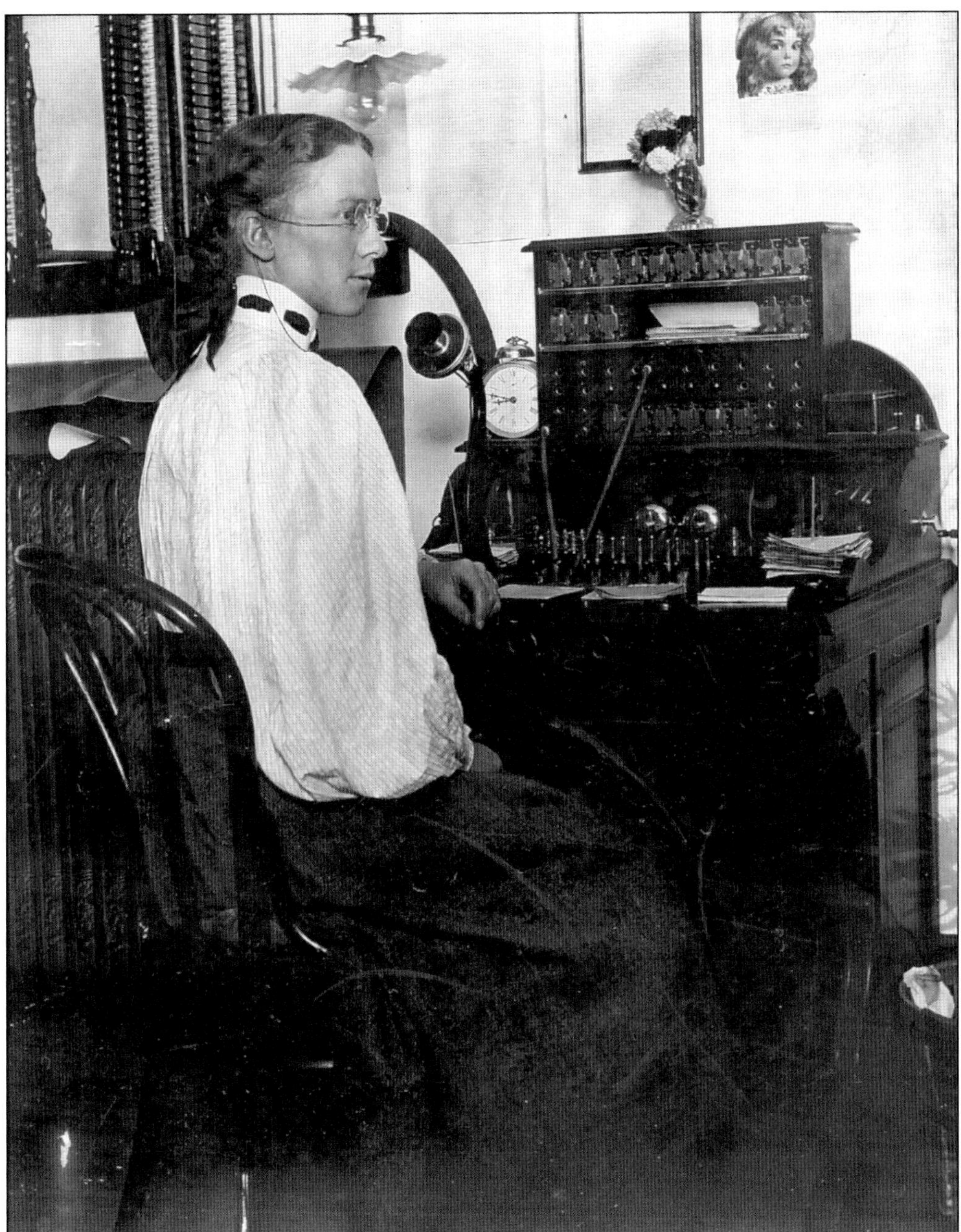

East Aurora's first telephone operator, Harriet L Persons, is shown in front of the relatively small switchboard around 1895 or 1896. Note the electric light above her head. The Globe Hotel had the first telephone in the community, but not too many businesses and homes had their own telephones at this time. That prompted Kirk's Drugstore to install the first public telephone in 1899. Early telephone operators not only connected business and social calls, but they also were in charge of sounding the alarm when an emergency call came in. In the early days, there were competing phone companies. In order to contact someone, a caller needed to subscribe to the same company as the person he or she was calling. The Village Board settled the matter in 1902 by granting a franchise to the Haines Phone Company to provide telephone service to village residents.

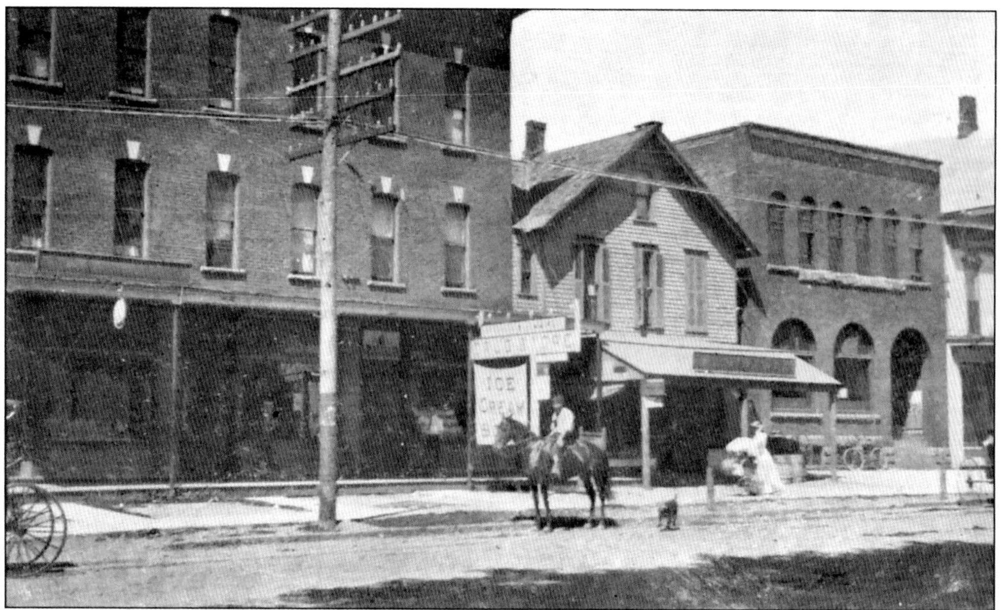

The buildings on this section of Main Street, between Church and Pine Streets, have not changed much in more than a century. Ice cream was available for 5¢ at the drugstore behind the man on his horse in this photograph from about 1905. Note the way the utility poles dominate the downtown area.

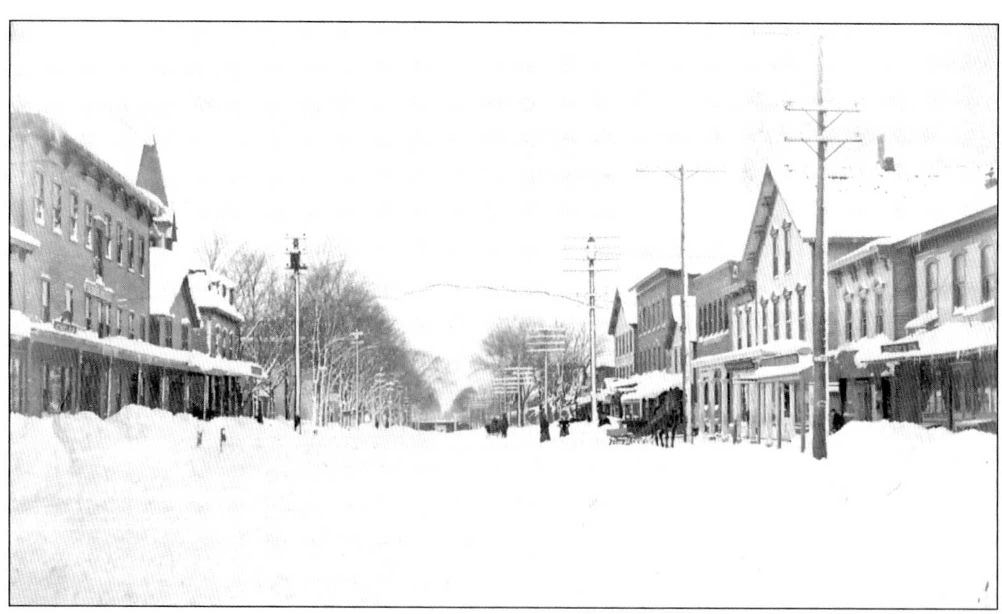

Main Street is shown looking west from Olean and Pine Streets following a winter storm. The photograph was taken sometime after 1891 and before 1904. The oldest business in Aurora, the Globe Hotel, built in 1824, is at the left side of the photograph. Streets were not plowed and salted during this time period, so Aurorans relied on sleighs and cutters to get to their destinations.

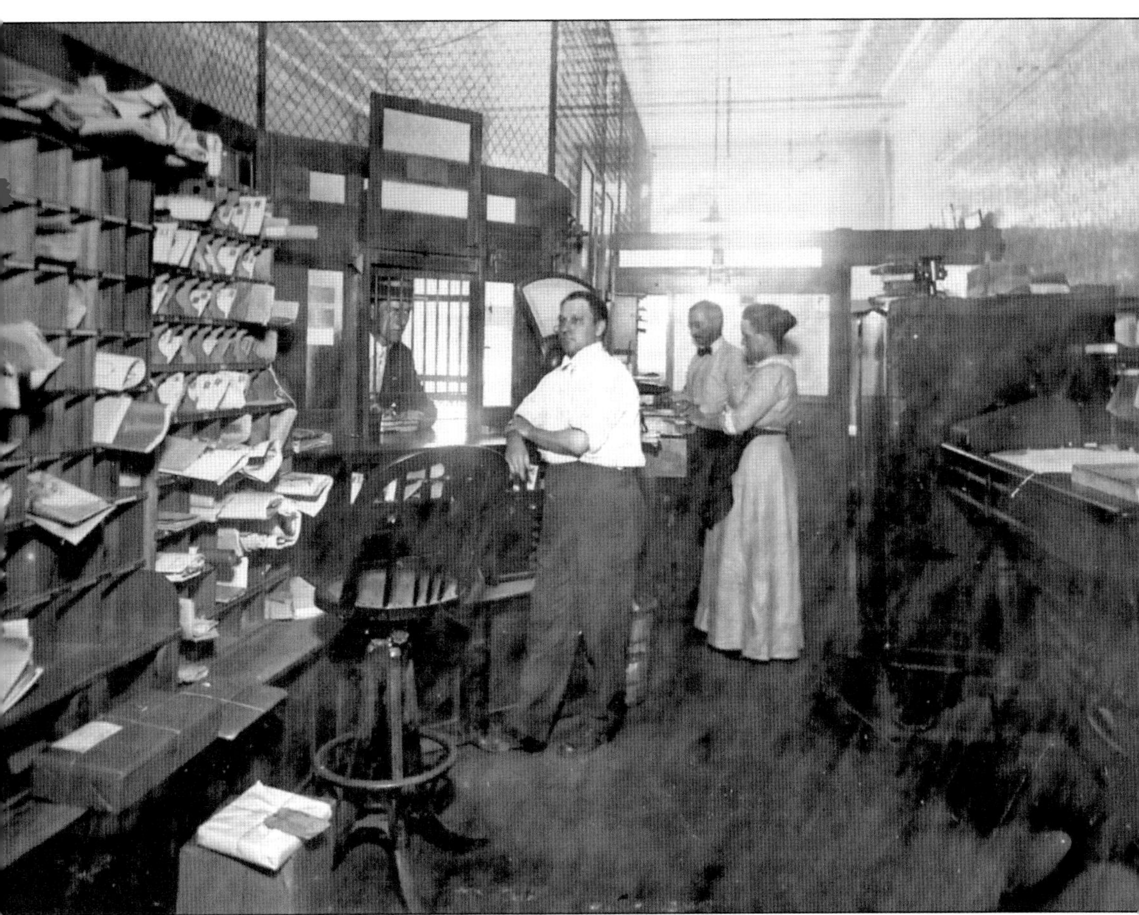

Postal employees Harry Buffum, Kate P. Mead, and Lindsay Edwards assist a customer at the window of the East Aurora Post Office, which was located at 710 Main Street, now the office of the *East Aurora Advertiser*. The customer at the window is unidentified. The East Aurora Post Office, after merging with the Willink Post Office in 1913, moved to the former First National Bank of East Aurora Building next door in 1923 and, again, to a new, brick building on the south side of Main Street near Elm Street in 1929. That building later housed Major's clothing store and the Aurora Sewing Center. In 1962, a new building for the post office was erected just west of the railroad tracks, followed by a more modern and spacious facility on Quaker Road at the western edge of the village in 1992.

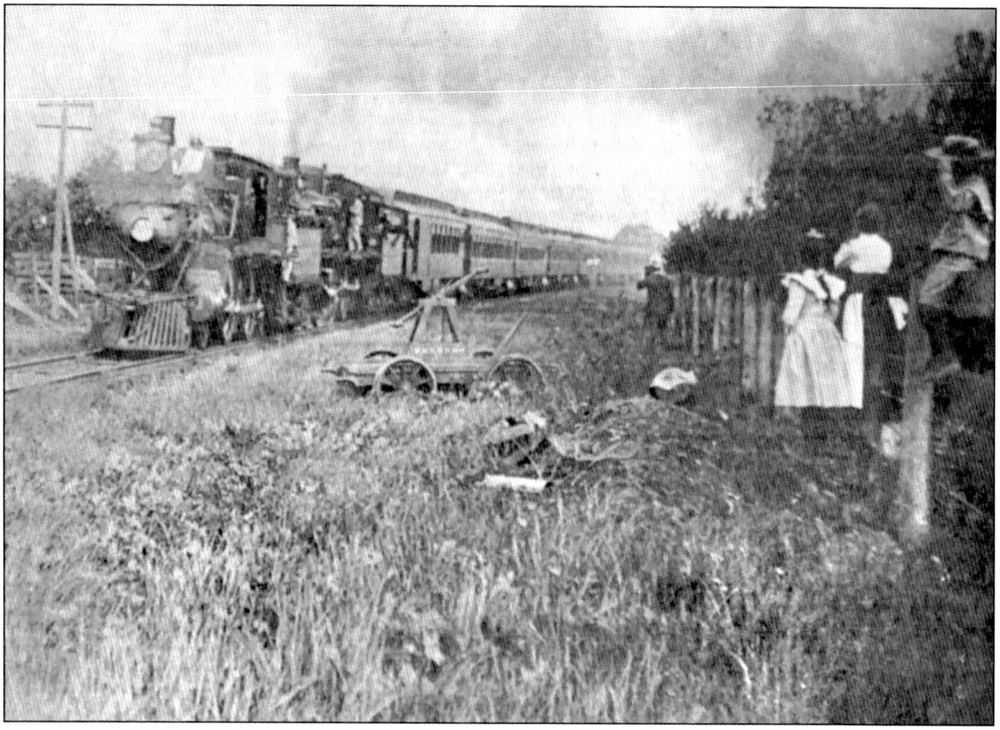

The funeral train of Pres. William McKinley passes through East Aurora on its way to Washington, DC, on September 16, 1901, after the president was assassinated at the Pan-American Exposition in Buffalo. This was not the only famous train to pass through East Aurora. In 1939, residents gathered in the middle of the night to catch a glimpse of the train carrying Britain's King George VI and Queen Elizabeth, who were on a tour of the United States and Canada.

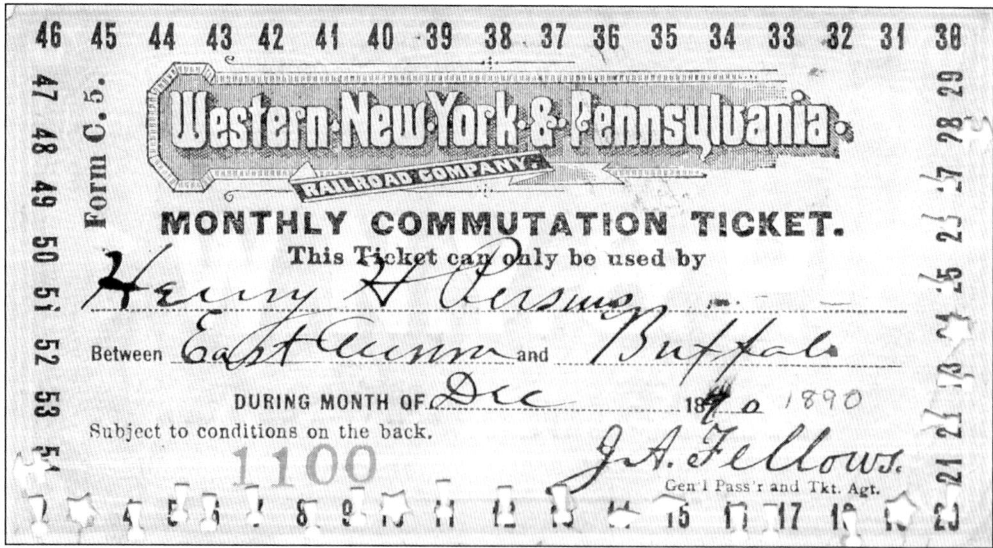

46 45 44 43 42 41 40 39 38 37 36 35 34 33 32 31 30

Form C. 5.

Western New York & Pennsylvania
RAILROAD COMPANY

MONTHLY COMMUTATION TICKET.

This Ticket can only be used by Henry H Persons

Between East Aurora and Buffalo

DURING MONTH OF Dec 1890

Subject to conditions on the back.

1100

J.A. Fellows.
Gen'l Pass'r and Tkt. Agt.

The train through the village provided an opportunity for many East Aurorans to commute daily to Buffalo for business. Banker Henry H. Persons was one of several local residents who took advantage of a commuter discount and purchased his tickets from the New York & Pennsylvania Railroad a month in advance. This is his commuter ticket from December 1890.

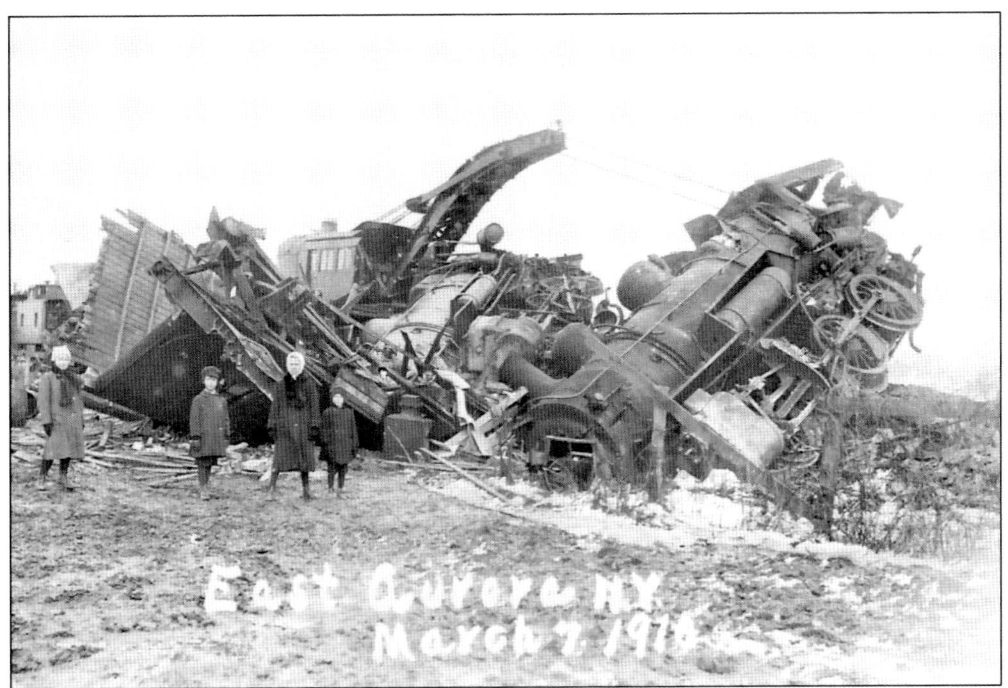

The railroad brought additional prosperity to East Aurora, but it did not come without accidents. Newspaper reports often included details of pedestrians and railroad workers being hit by passing trains. There were the occasional derailments, as well. Shown here are young children having their picture taken in front of a major derailment in East Aurora on March 7, 1910.

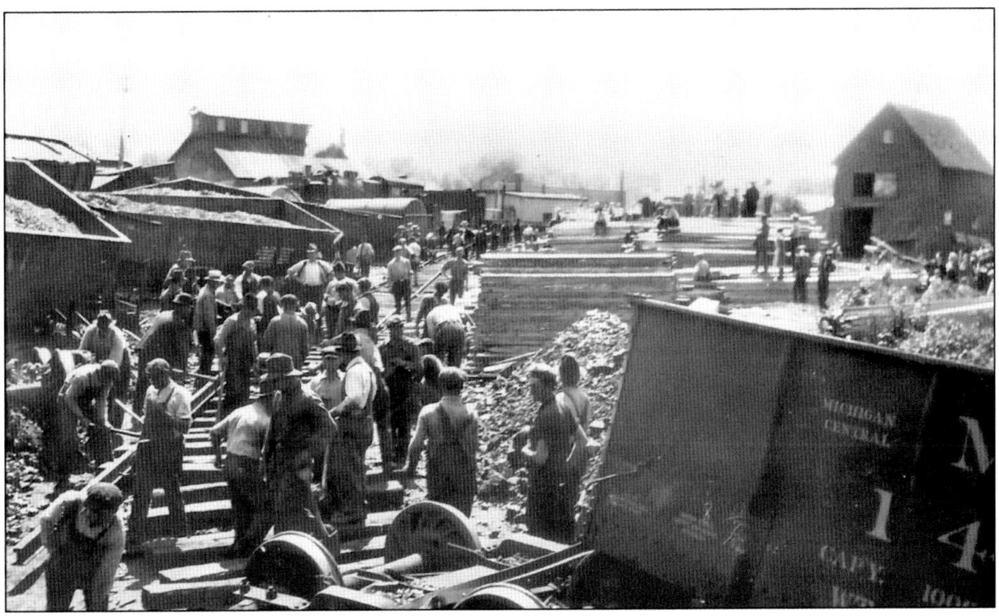

In the late summer of 1924, an open switch caused about 21 cars of a 50-car train heading northbound to derail near the Peek Lumber Mill on Oakwood Avenue. A brakeman was hurt in the accident. The accident no doubt wreaked havoc on local businesses and residents until the train cars were cleared.

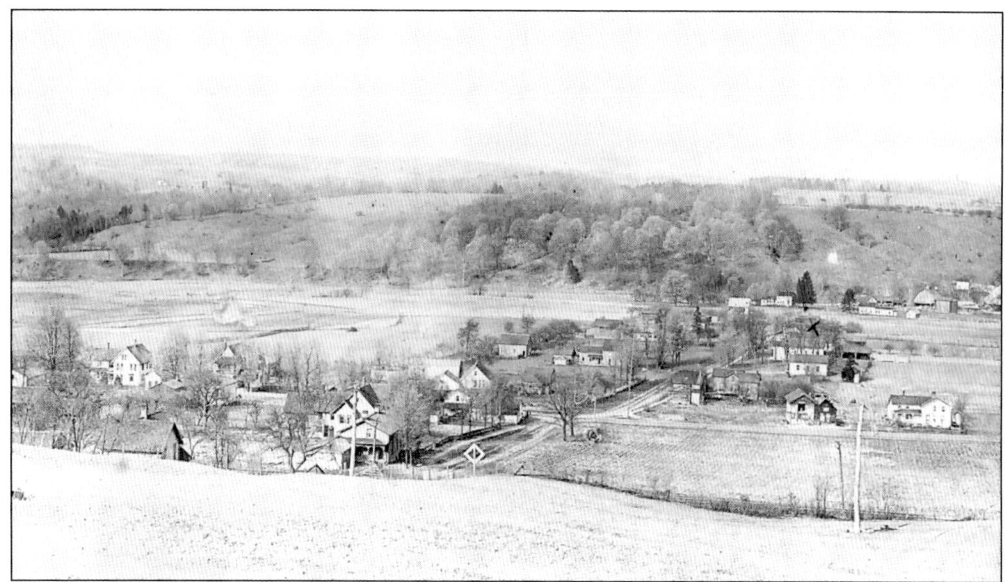

A bird's-eye view of the hamlet of South Wales was captured from the east hill in 1913. The photograph shows the intersection of Olean Road (Route 16) and Emery Road looking west. One of the houses on the left side of Emery Road became part of the Gow School, founded by Peter Gow in 1926 to help boys with dyslexia and other learning disabilities.

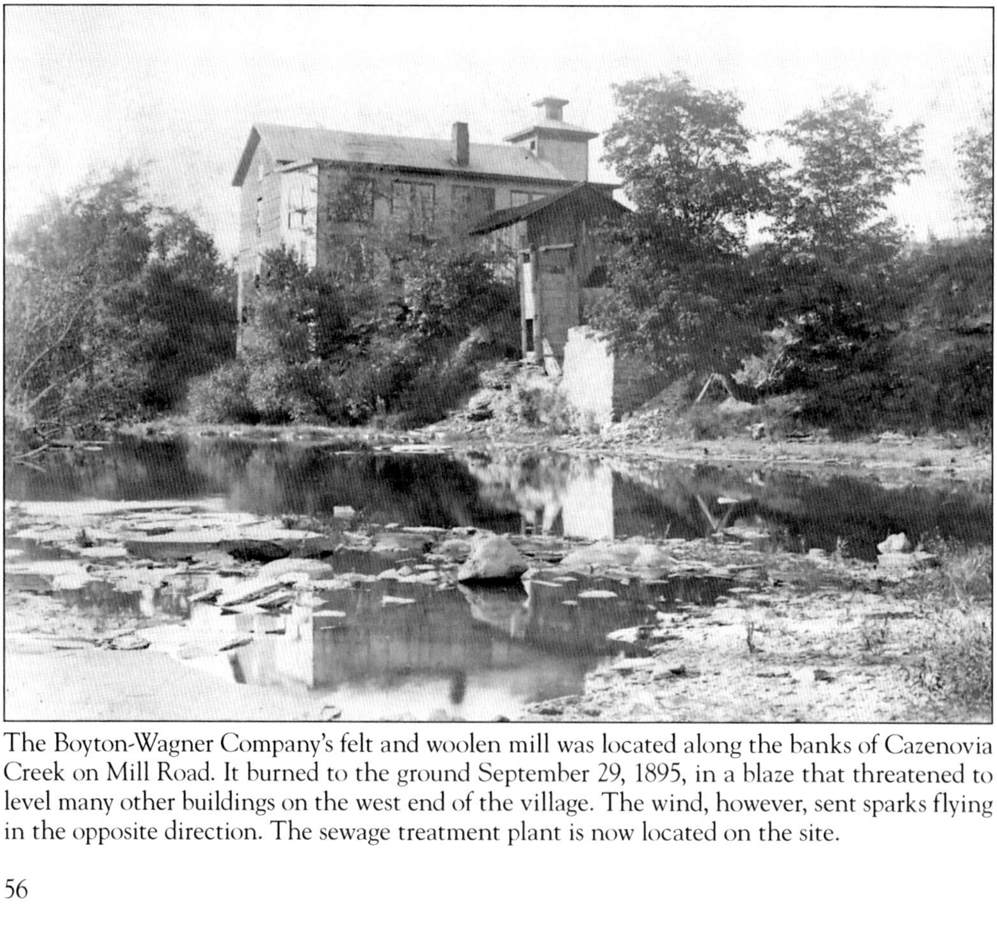

The Boyton-Wagner Company's felt and woolen mill was located along the banks of Cazenovia Creek on Mill Road. It burned to the ground September 29, 1895, in a blaze that threatened to level many other buildings on the west end of the village. The wind, however, sent sparks flying in the opposite direction. The sewage treatment plant is now located on the site.

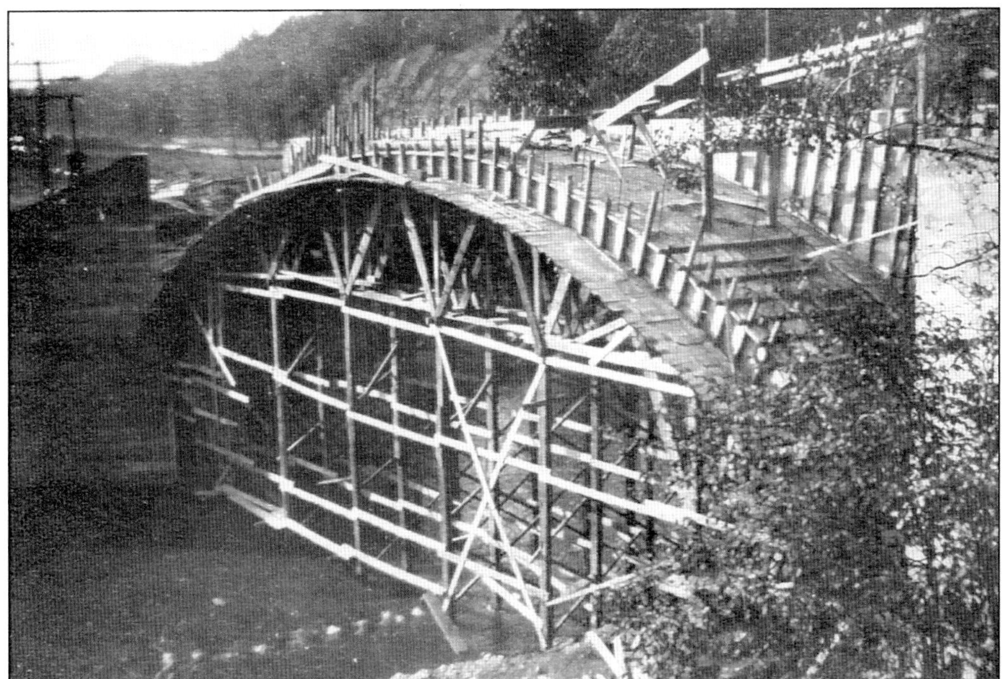

This view shows the new bridge under construction over Cazenovia Creek on Jewett Holmwood Road October 10, 1915. The bridge was located at the bottom of Reed Hill, which was named for the family that owned property near the two branches of the creek.

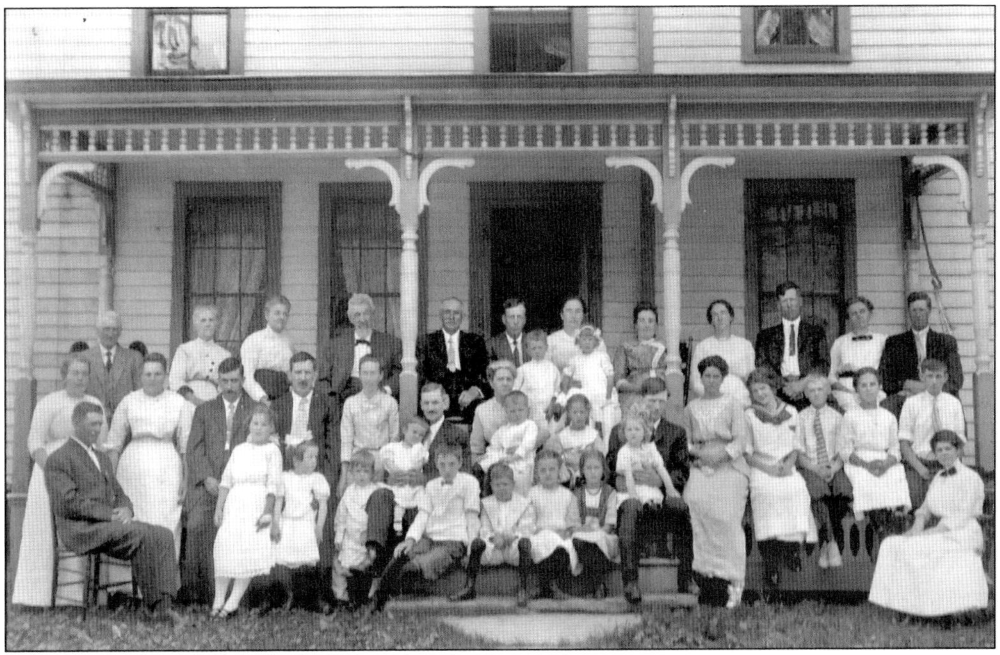

Members of the Adams and Tomlinson families gather for a family portrait during a reunion at the home of Edwin Tomlinson on Porterville Road around 1914. William and Mary Burroughs Tomlison, who came from England in the 1830s, had six children, three of whom married into the Adams family.

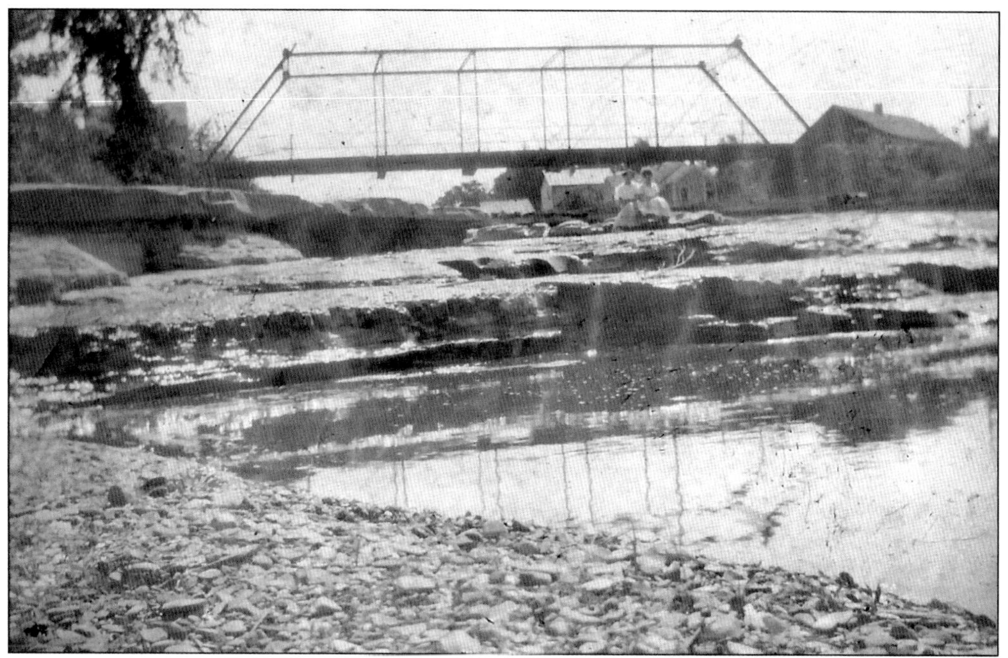

The iron bridge in West Falls can be seen in the background of this view looking south along the west branch of Cazenovia Creek. According to some older residents, West Falls children would pretend the creek was the Niagara River, with one side being the United States and the other being Canada.

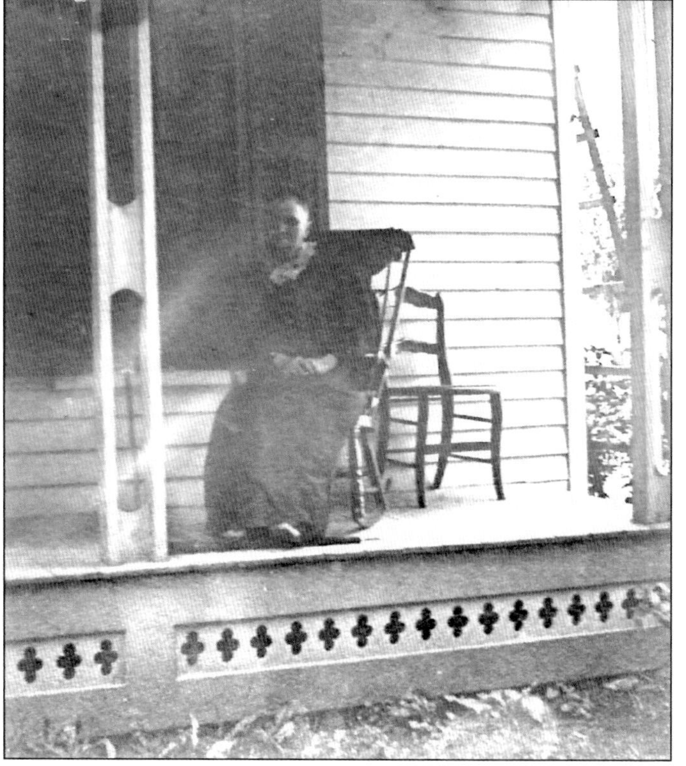

The woman relaxing on a rocker on a warm summer day is not identified, but it is known that this is the front porch of the Wood home in West Falls, which took in boarders. Perhaps it is Mrs. Wood taking a break from her daily chores.

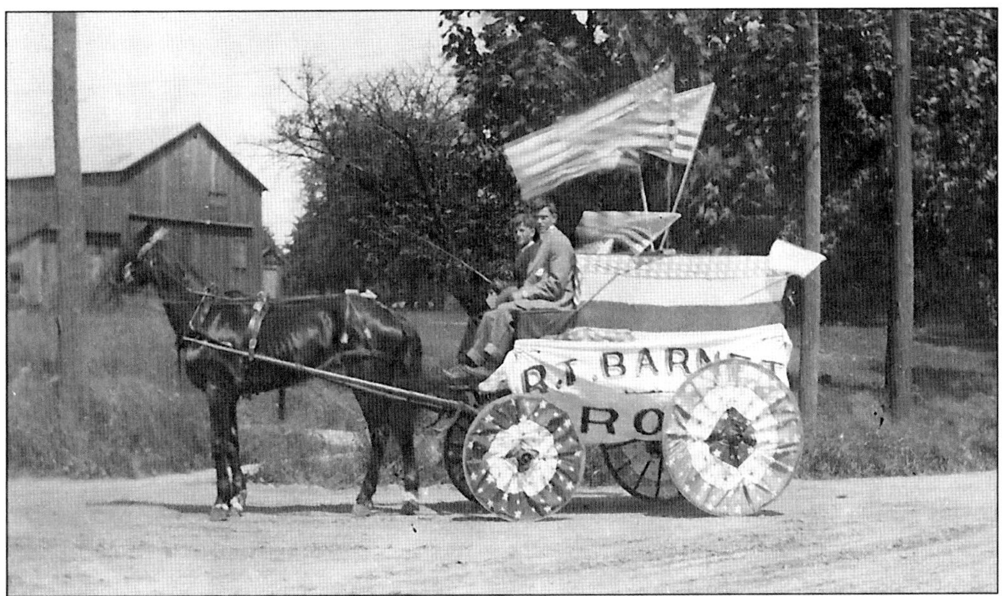

The R.T. Barnett Grocery wagon is decked in patriotic colors for a Fourth of July parade. R.T. Barnett purchased the grocery business of L.F. Persons in September 1906. It was located at 716 Main Street, which is now home to Petrocy Jewelers. According to a newspaper article written when Barnett purchased the business, he "has had many years experience in the business and proposes to keep a model, up-to-date grocery, handling only the best groceries and selling at reasonable prices."

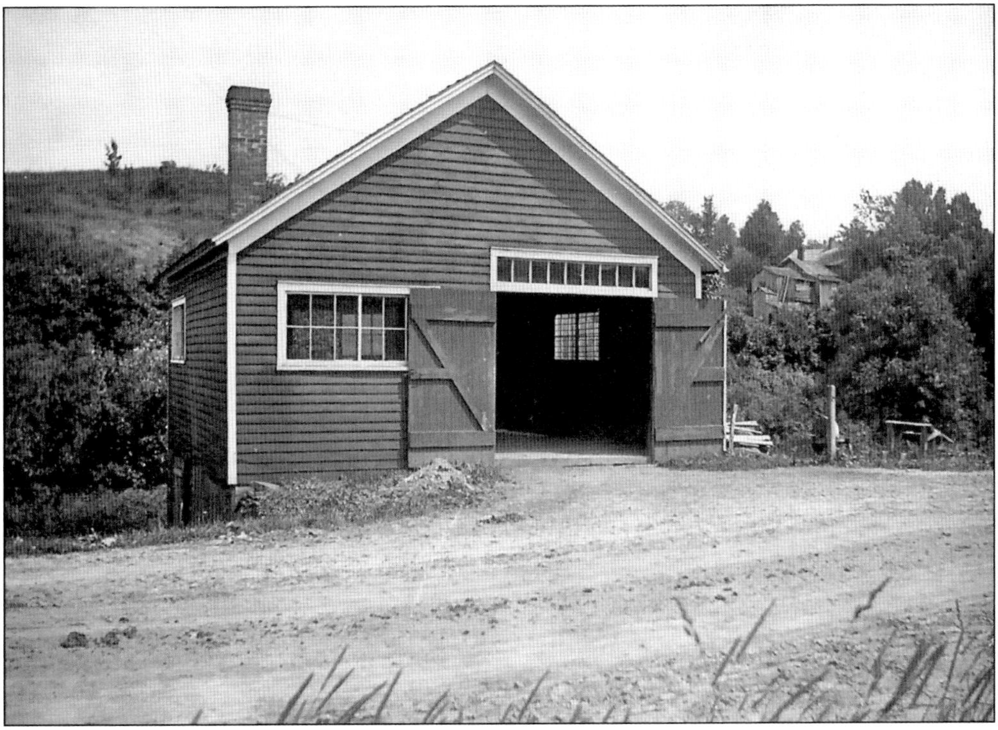

Henry Wood's blacksmith shop is shown in West Falls. Carriages could be conveniently pulled into the shop through the wide doors leading from the dirt road.

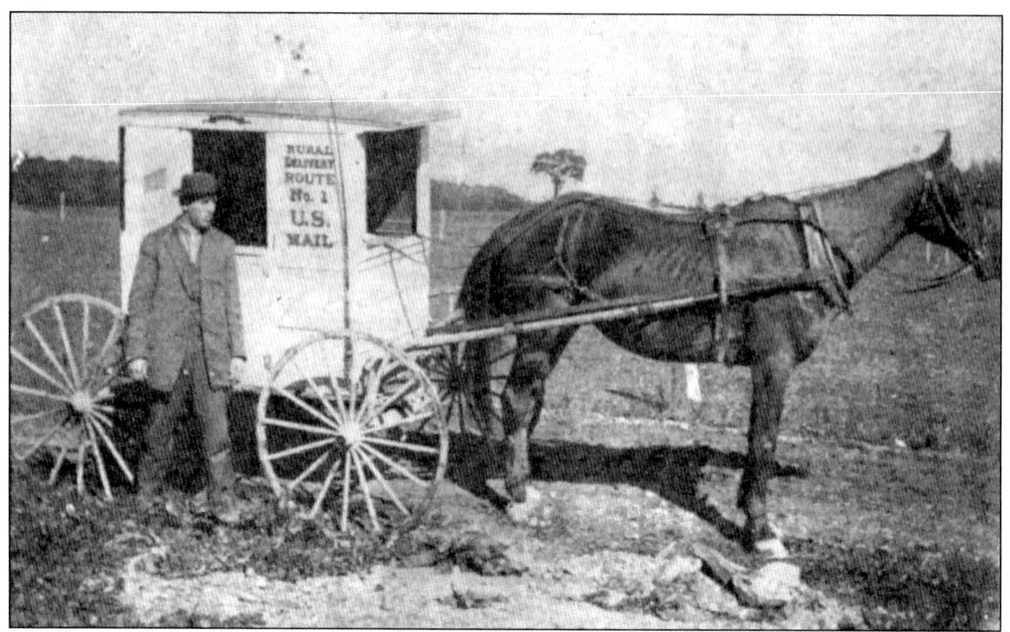

The horse-drawn mail wagon might have taken longer to get to its destination, but few letters were reported lost. This wagon, pictured in 1914, traveled from East Hamburg (now Orchard Park) and East Aurora six days a week, all year round.

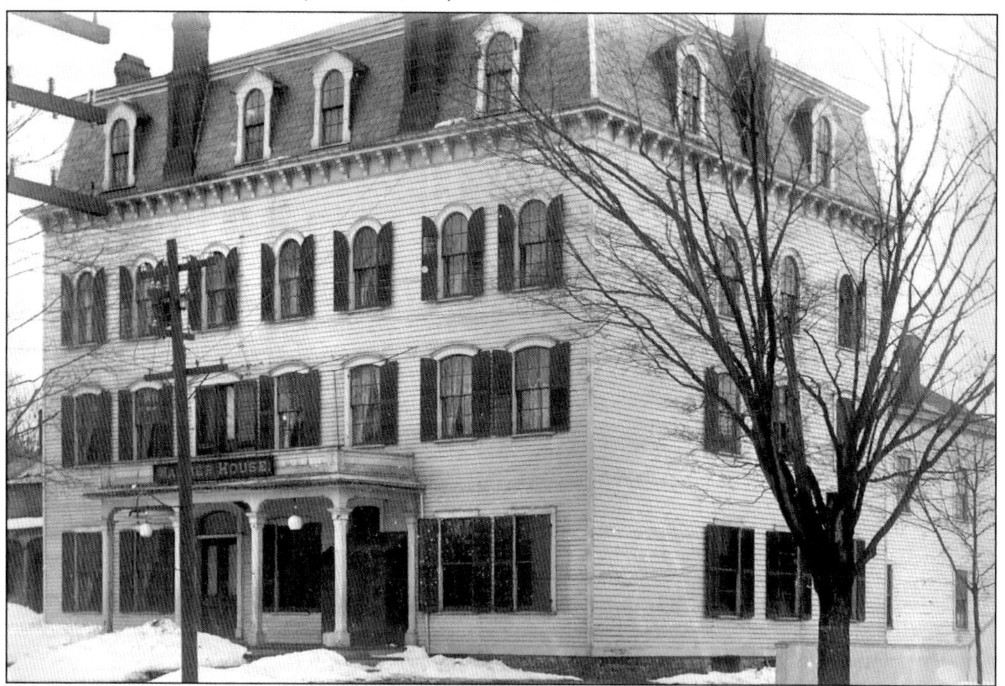
Byron Persons built the Persons House on Main Street, across from Church Street, in 1872. A.B. Warner modernized the hotel in 1897 and changed the name to the Warner House. It was also known by a handful of other names. It was named the Hotel Eulalia in the early 1890s in honor of the Spanish royalty who stayed there. The building burned October 23, 1905. (Courtesy of the *East Aurora Advertiser.*)

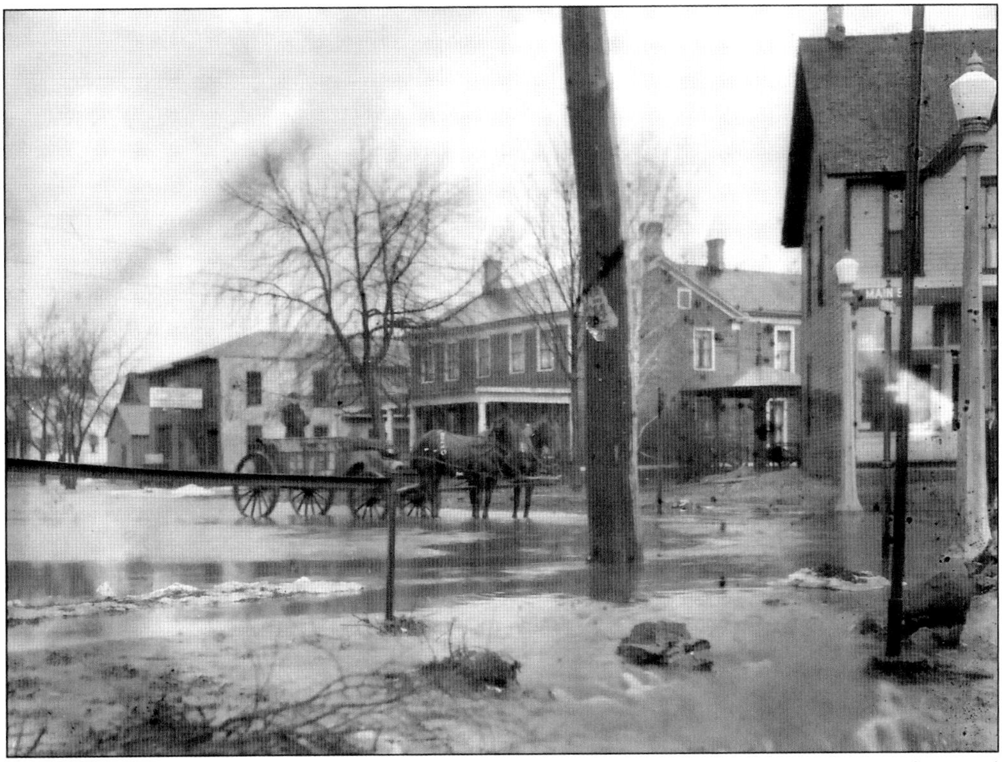

Willink Square, known today simply as the circle, is shown under water during a flood around 1904. The photograph was taken facing northwest, with Main Street at the right and Buffalo Road off to the left. Note the judge's stand from the old Hamlin Village Farm beyond and to the right of the utility pole. It was later moved to the grounds of the nearby nursing home.

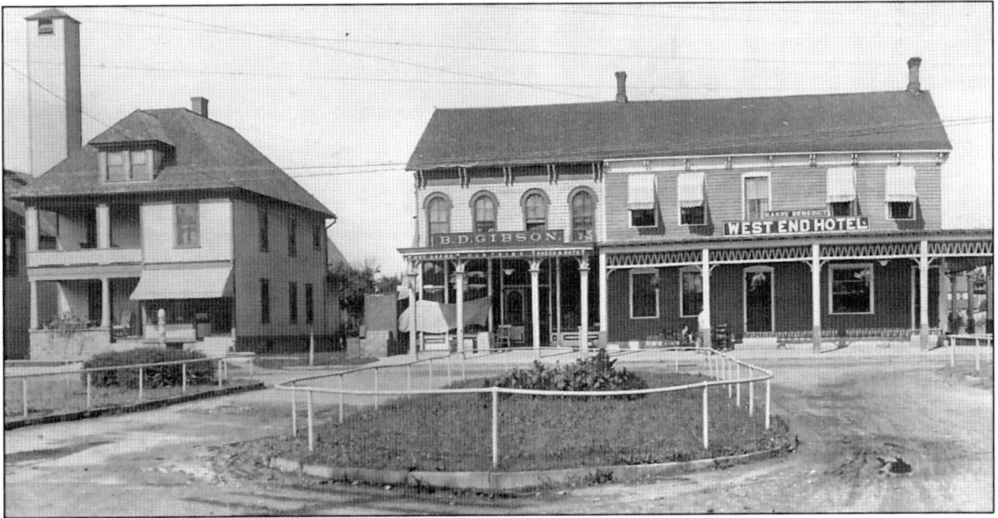

This is what the circle looked like shortly after Harry Benedict bought the old Hammond Hotel in 1909 and operated it as the West End Hotel. Byron D. Gibson was operating the business started by his father, Chisman, in 1857 to the left. This building, which replaced the Eagle Tavern that burned to the ground in 1869, survived a bad fire of its own in 1942, and another fire destroyed the building in January 1963.

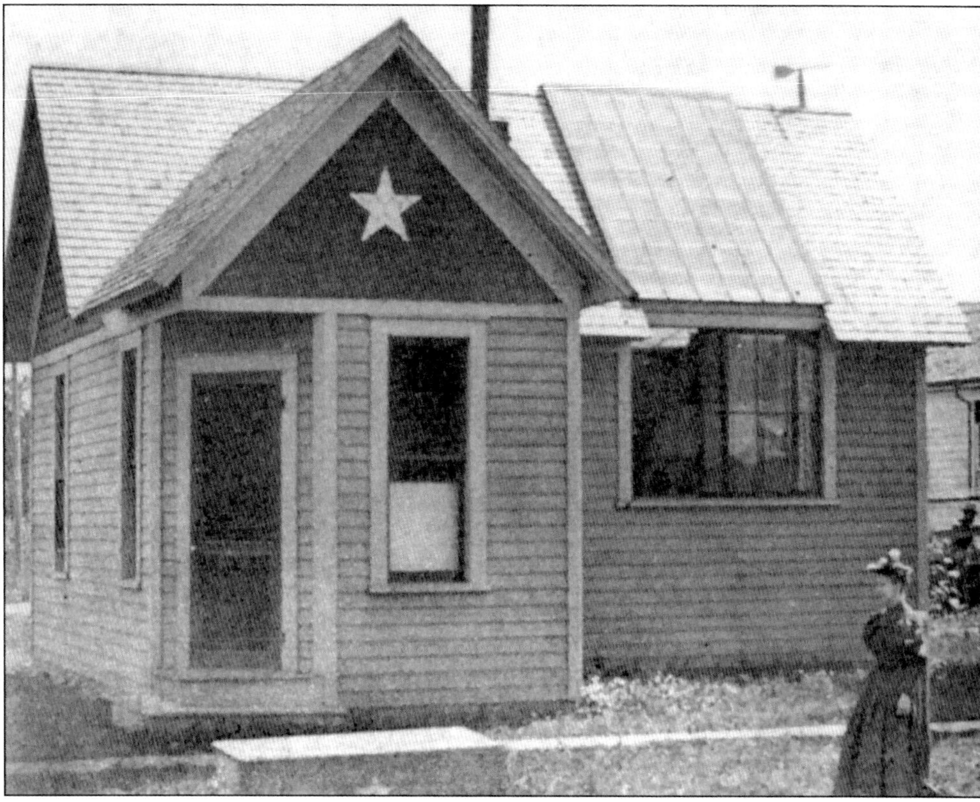

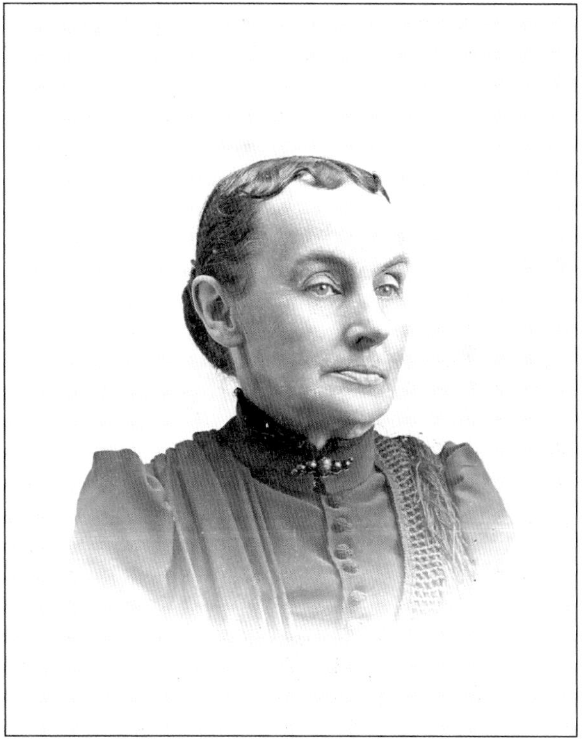

Mary Hitchcock is shown in front of the Hitchcock Star Photographic Gallery that she opened in a little building at Knox Road and Grey Street in 1890. For a short time, she was a teacher, but her real love was photography. Her portraits, many of which can be found in local family albums and archives, can be distinguished by a small gold star logo. Failing eyesight forced Mary, who never married, to eventually sell the business and property. She died in May 1958. Note the skylight on the roof of her building. One of the portraits taken by Hitchcock was of local resident Elizabeth Addington.

A banquet was held in honor of one of Aurora's most famous citizens on October 21, 1913, just as Wally Schang was beginning his Major League career. Born August 22, 1889, in the town of Wales, Schang honed his skills on the Hamlin Park baseball diamond before catching for five different Major League teams between 1913 and 1931. He is the only player to win the World Series three times with three different teams.

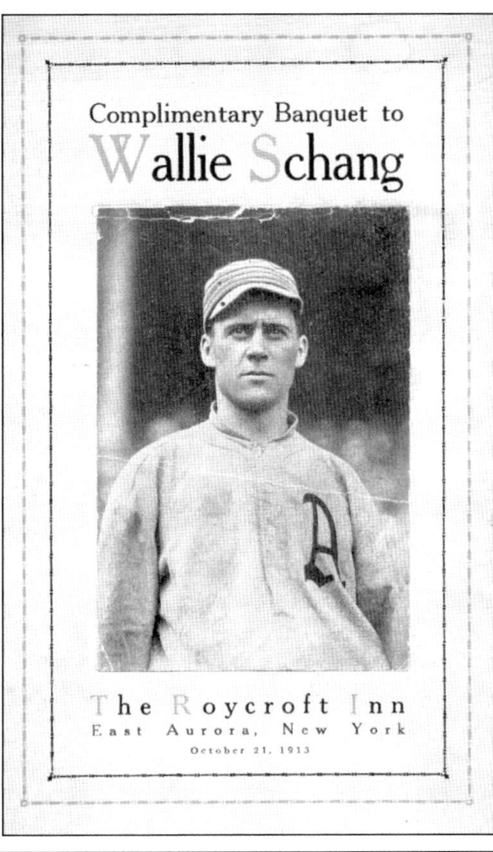

T. English purchased the home at 739 East Main Street in October 1905. In the front, his wife opened a millinery store, which provided the latest fashions to East Aurorans. Pictured are, from left to right, (on ground) T. English; (in seats) Mrs. English and Pearl Davidson.

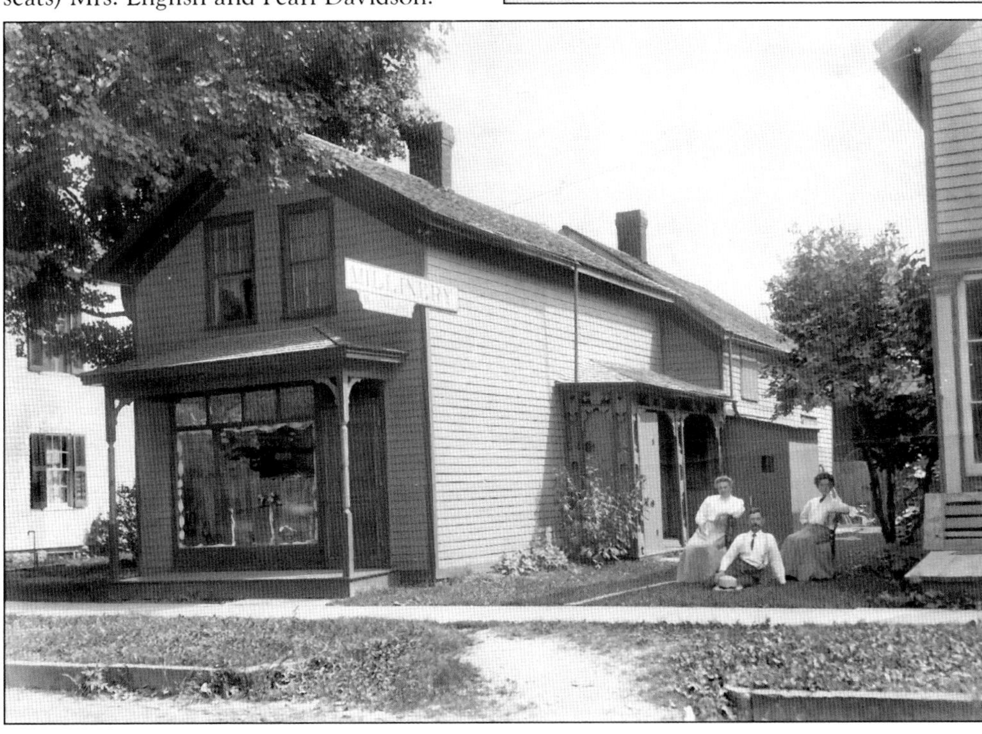

Aretus P. Burroughs was principal of the East Aurora Union Free High School for one year, in 1904. After the resignation of Charles Goldsmith in 1898, the school went through a succession of short-termed leaders. T.F. Kane served for one year, followed by Charles McGavern for three years and George M. Wiley in 1902. After Burroughs and a Mr. Klock in 1904, Harry W. Mead became principal in 1905.

Young students of the East Aurora Union School pose for a class portrait with their teacher in 1891. The students and teacher are not identified, but the class is pictured outside the school at Main and North Grove Streets. The school was expanded just four years earlier to allow the consolidation of smaller schoolhouses in the village. The brick addition to the old Aurora Academy Building cost about $15,000.

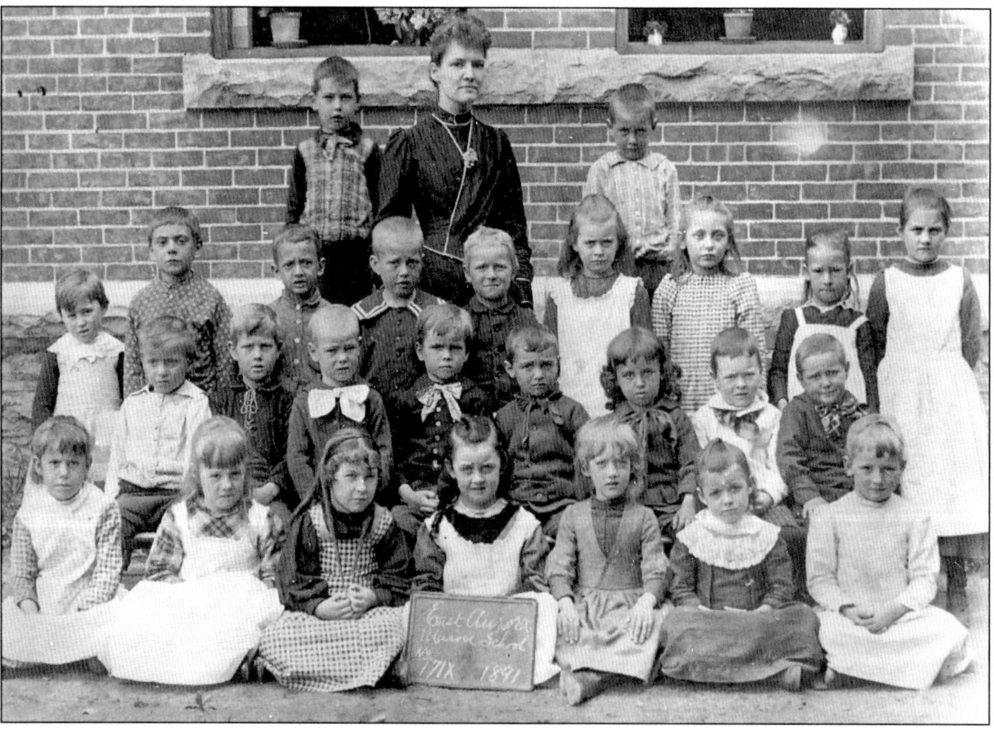

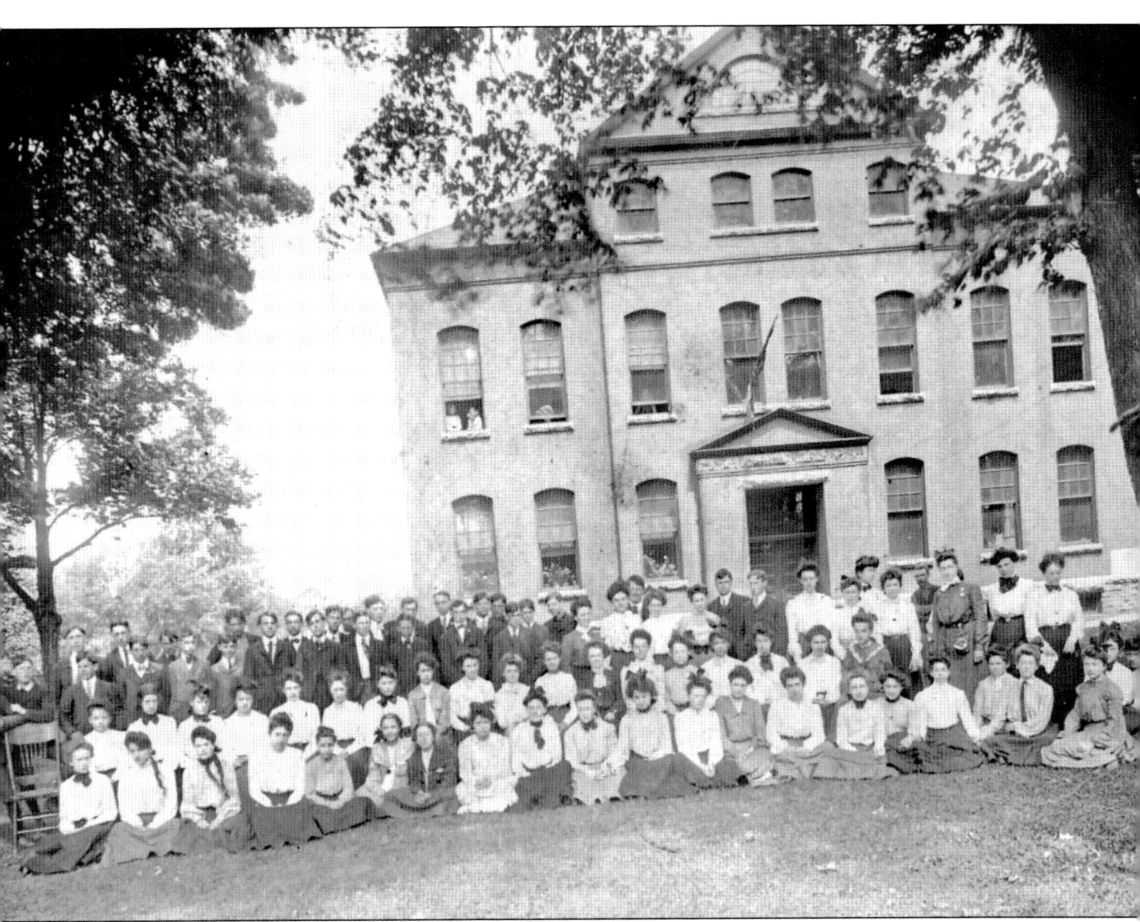

The East Aurora High School class of 1904 gathers outside the old school building at Main and North Grove Streets shortly before graduation. This building was constructed in 1887 as an addition to the front of the old Aurora Academy structure and contained spacious halls and a library that was open to the residents of the village. These students would have been looking upon a great deal of activity across the street at the time of this photograph as Elbert Hubbard was constructing the buildings for the Roycroft Campus. The Roycroft Chapel, located directly across the street, would have been completed just a few years earlier and famous visitors would have been roaming the campus, along with eccentric craftsmen and artisans.

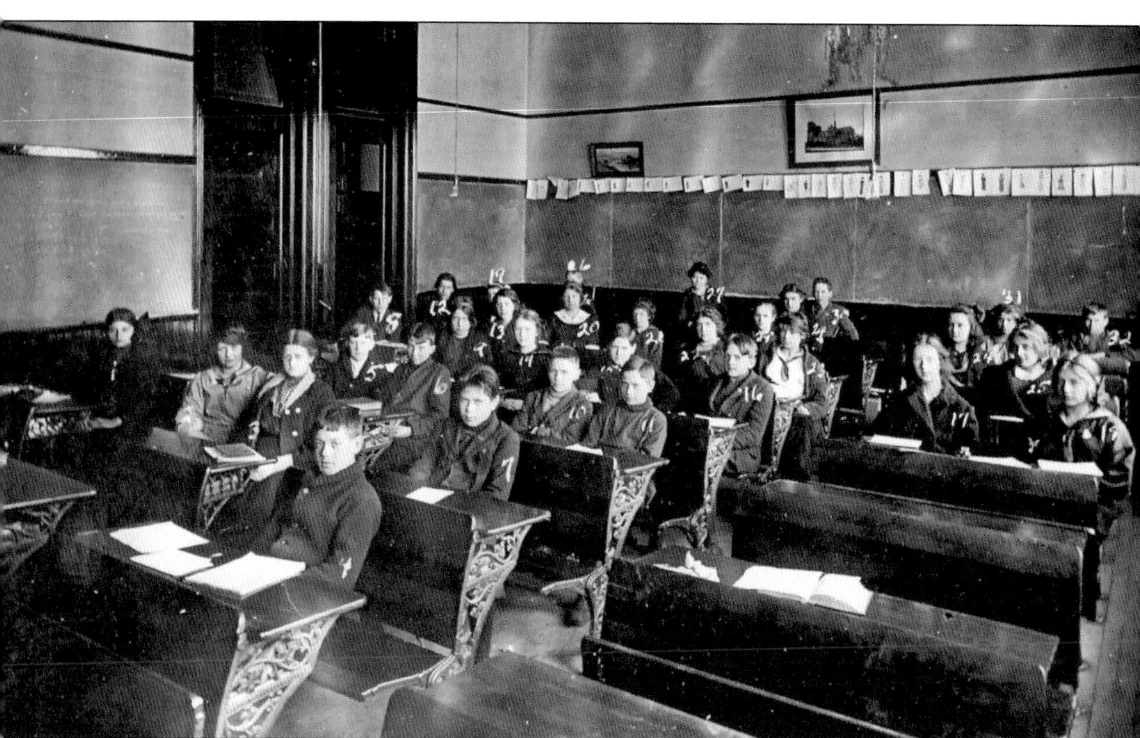

Students sit at old-fashioned desks in the old East Aurora school building in 1914. The teacher was Miss Clark, who is seated in the center of the back of the room. The students included Mildred Paul, Harriet Haskell, Julia DuBois, Glenn Foss, Harvey Burns, Harry Lippert, Ray Miller, Horatio Bangs, Grace Sly, Walton Whittemore, Clarence Hollis, Faye Newton, Elizabeth Blackmar, Bertha Mason, Edward Buffum, Willard Brooks, Marion Robertson, Lydia McCreary, Victoria Hoth, Katherine Perry, Grace Draffan, Margaret Downing, Beulah Phelps, Laura Jones, Vera Burzette, Frank Adams, Fanny Gleed, Marion Palmer, Norman Godfrey, Eva Arnholt, and Norman Heim. (Courtesy of the *East Aurora Advertiser.*)

Mary Taylor is believed to have been the first black student to graduate from the East Aurora Union School in 1901. She was a member of the Baptist church, but no other information is known about her.

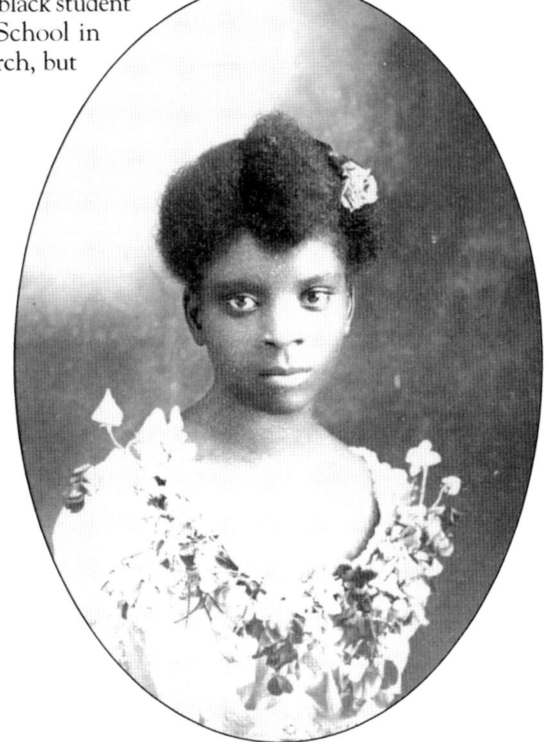

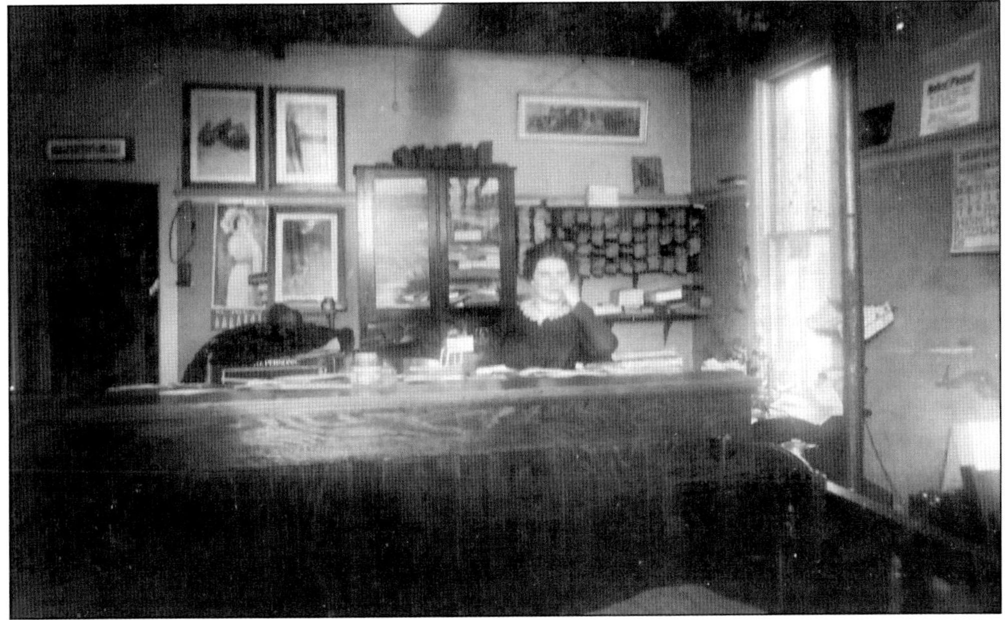

When Frank O. Persons owned the *East Aurora Advertiser* from 1901 to 1915, he moved the operations from the second floor of 710 Main Street to a house on Temple Place near Millard Fillmore Place, where this photograph was taken. The counter at which this young woman is sitting is still used by the *Advertiser*. The newspaper office moved back to 710 Main Street in 1923 and has remained there since.

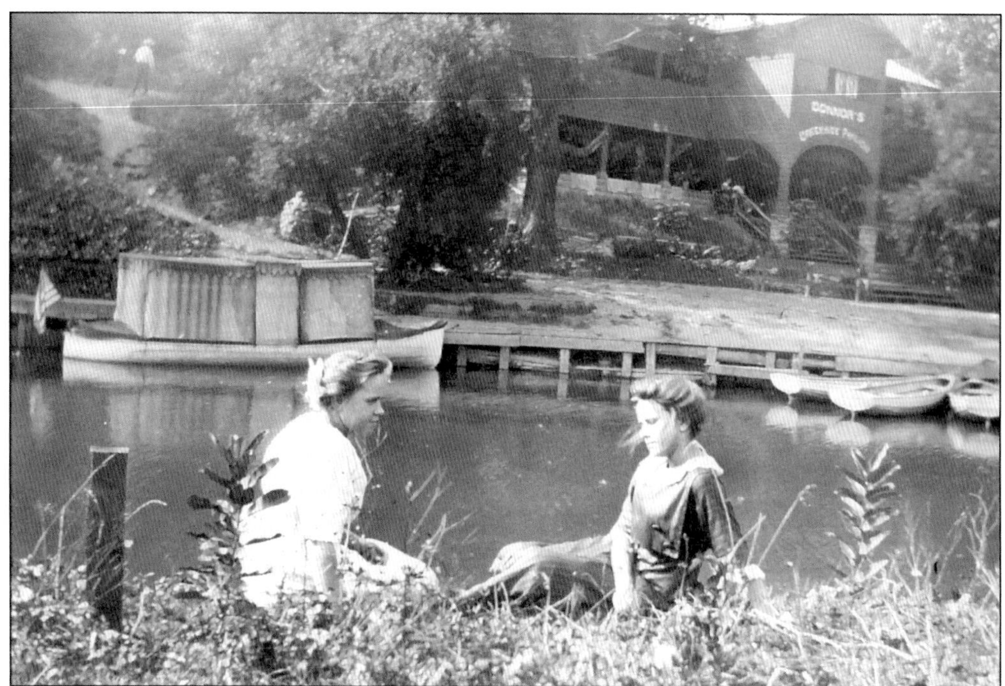

Robert J. and Emma G. Lange Donnor built Donnor's Creekside Pavilion on the banks of Cazenovia Creek near South and Center Streets in 1909. The pavilion became a popular destination for church picnics, family outings, and a leisurely ride on one of many canoes. Robert Donnor also built a motorboat; the *Arrow* seated up to 27 people. A dance floor in the pavilion was considered one of the best in the area. During the summer, the Donnors hosted up to three dances per week with live dance bands. The Donnors sold the property during World War I. After a few successive owners, the pavilion fell into disrepair and was later burned in a training exercise by the local fire department.

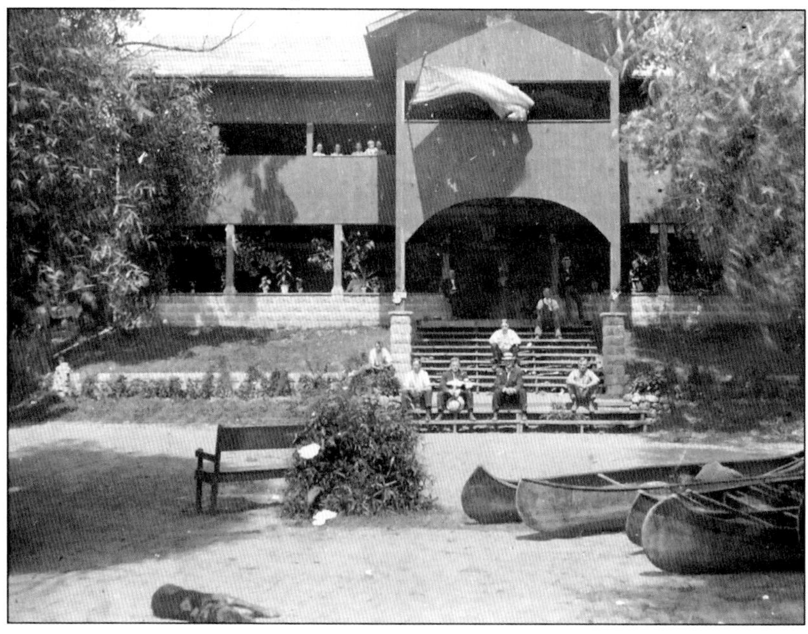

Journalist and editor Harry Persons Taber is identified as this man posing for an eccentric portrait in his younger years. Before Taber moved to Wilmington, Delaware, just prior to World War I, he had a successful newspaper career in the Buffalo area and established *The Philistine* magazine with Elbert Hubbard in the mid-1880s. Hubbard, a short time later, took ownership of the printing business and expanded it into the Roycroft Campus.

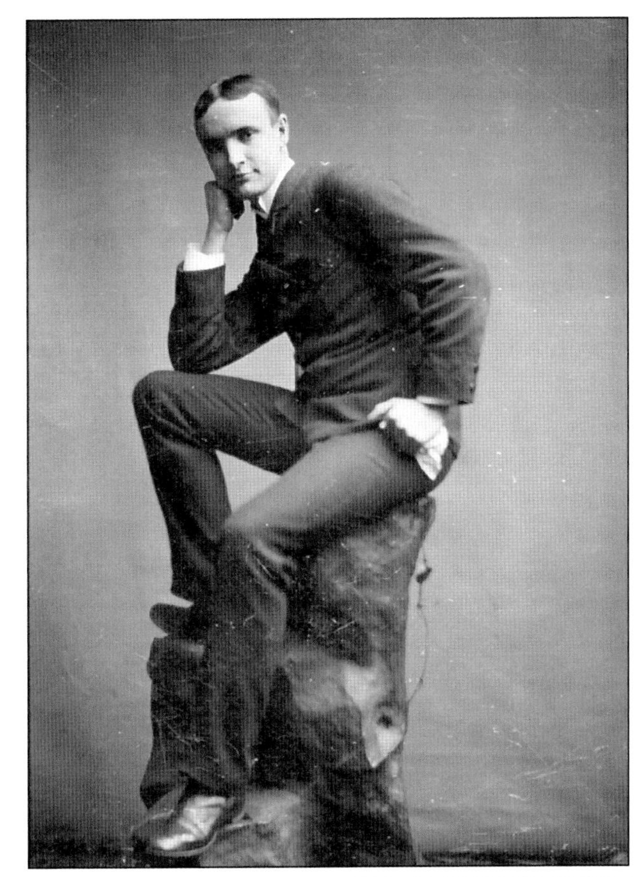

Elbert Hubbard built the Roycroft Print Shop on South Grove Street in 1898. When an expanded shop was later opened across the street, this original print shop was connected to the Roycroft Inn. Hubbard's fame and the status of the Roycroft Campus was solidified with his essay "A Message to Garcia," published in *The Philistine* magazine in 1899.

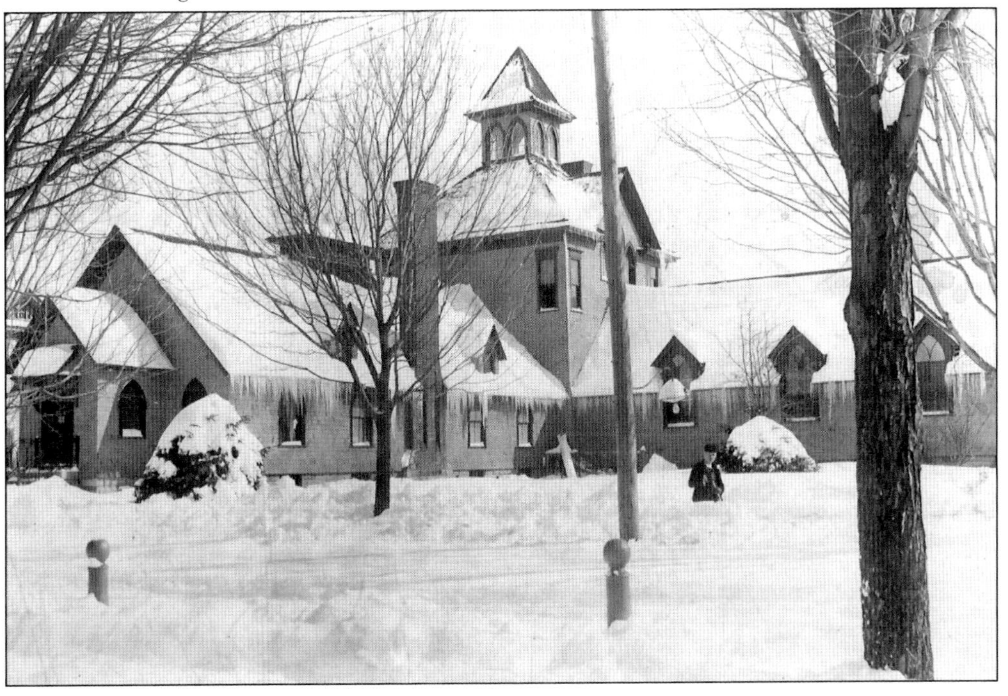

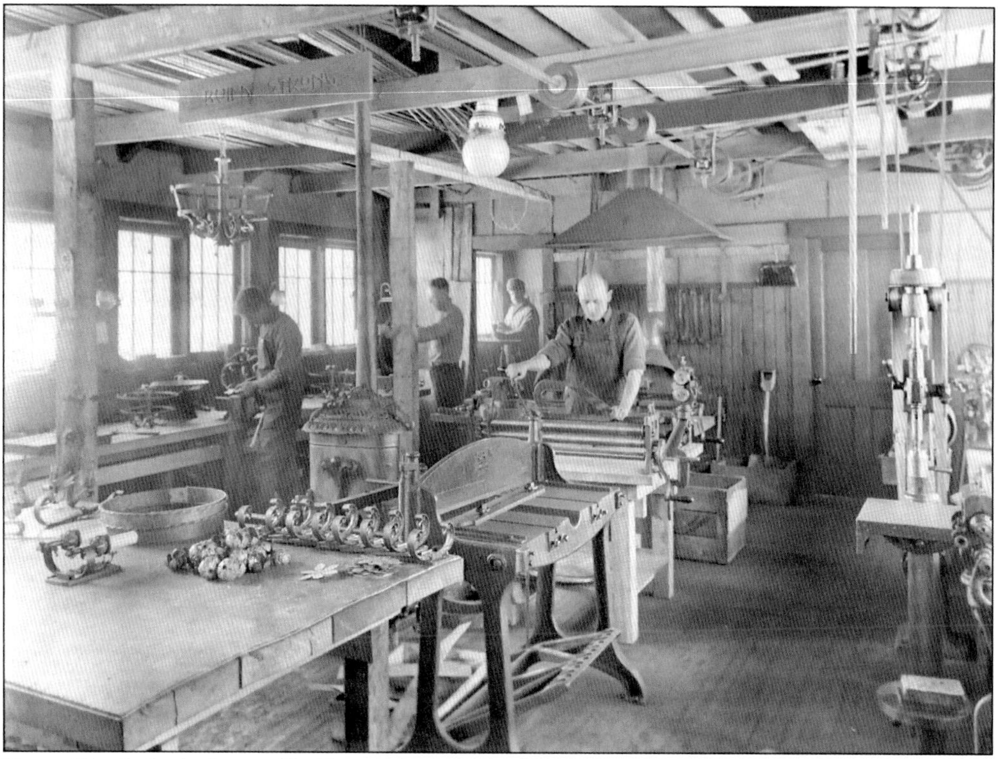

Victor Toothaker's shop at 70 Church Street, which later became the first manufacturing center for Fisher-Price Toys, is shown around 1920. Toothaker worked at the Roycroft Copper Shop before venturing out on his own.

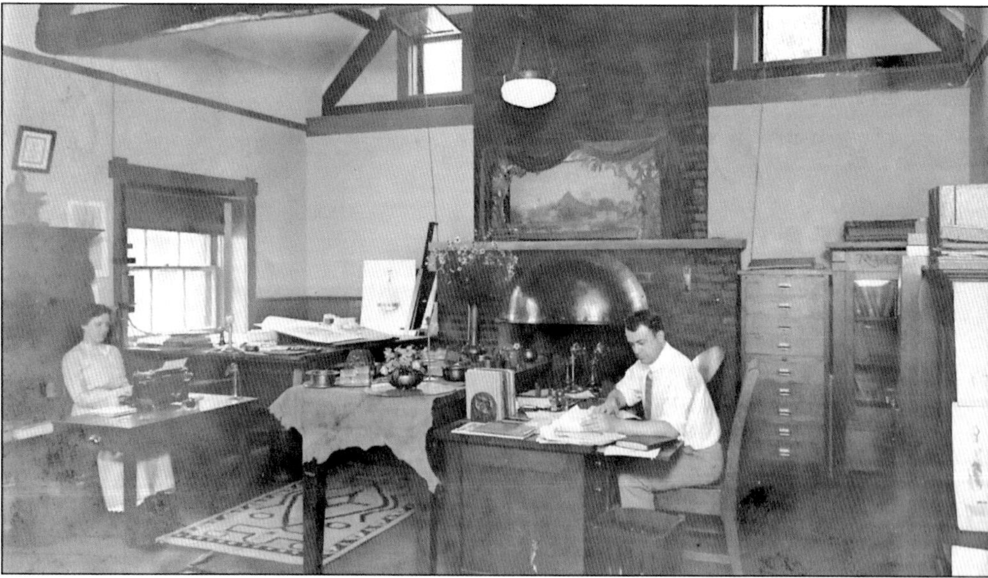

Victor Toothaker and his secretary work in the office of the Roycroft Copper Shop on the first Sunday after moving there in May 1913. After the Roycroft went out of business in 1939, the Copper Shop became a gift shop and most recently the headquarters of the Roycroft Campus Corporation, which is a group working to revitalize the national landmark campus.

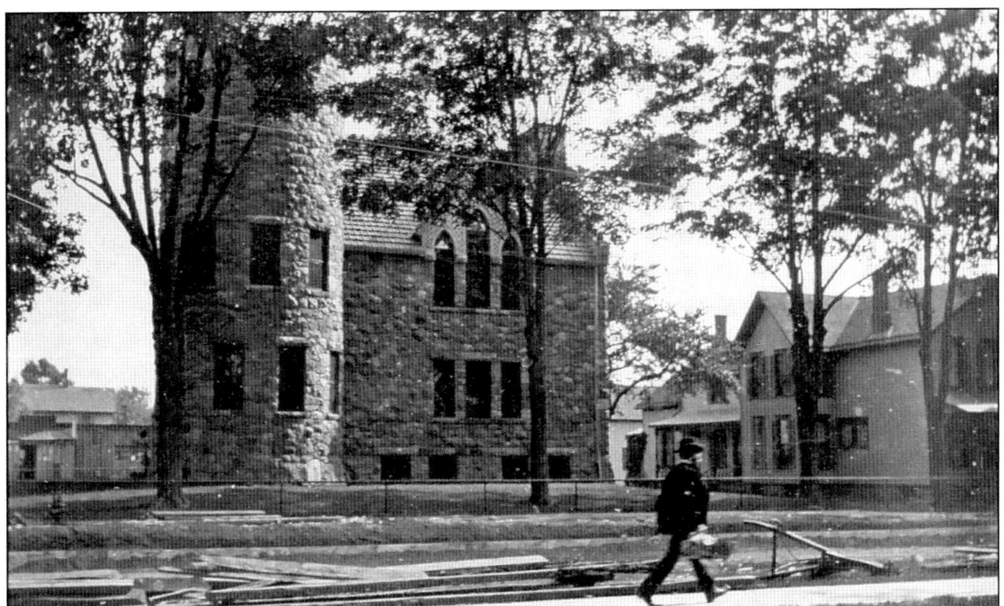

Elbert Hubbard moved a handful of houses, including the one to the right in this photograph, to build the Roycroft Chapel and other campus buildings at the corner of Main and South Grove Streets. Hubbard housed his editorial offices and an art gallery in the chapel, which was sold to the Baptist church after the Roycroft closed in 1939. It was converted to the Aurora Town Hall in 1958.

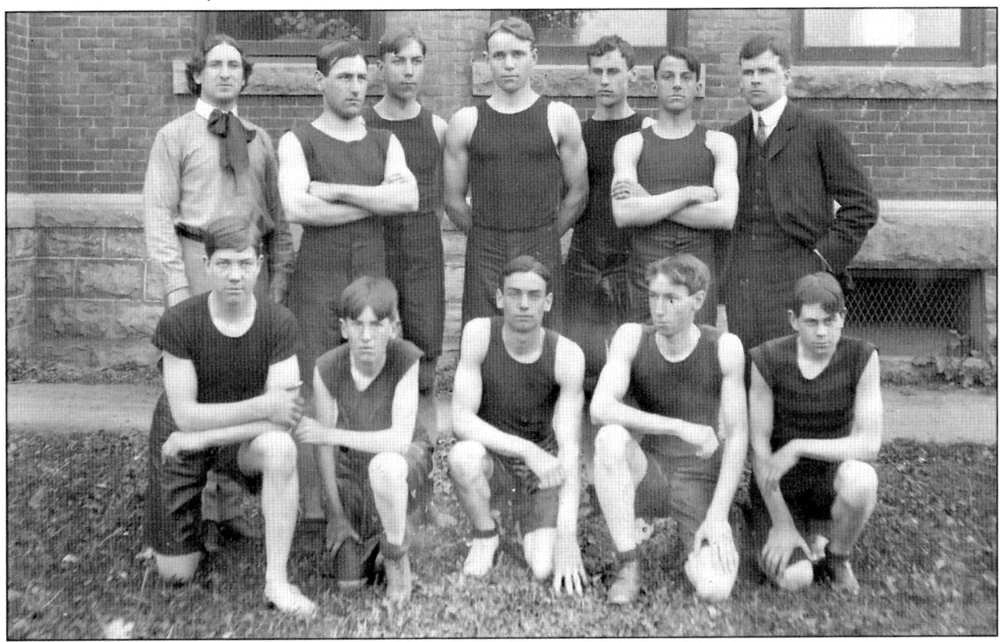

It was not too difficult to spot a Roycrofter in the community at the turn of the century. Stacy Butler, the coach of East Aurora High School's first track team in 1903, is distinguished by the unique tie he and other Roycroft men wore. Those pictured are, from left to right, (first row) Arthur Heineman, Ray Clough, Henry Adams, Andrew Kinster, and Lynn Brown; (second row) Butler, Eugene Addington, Haines Merritt, Walter Kelsey, Robert Prentice, Leonard Eldridge, and Principal George M. Wiley.

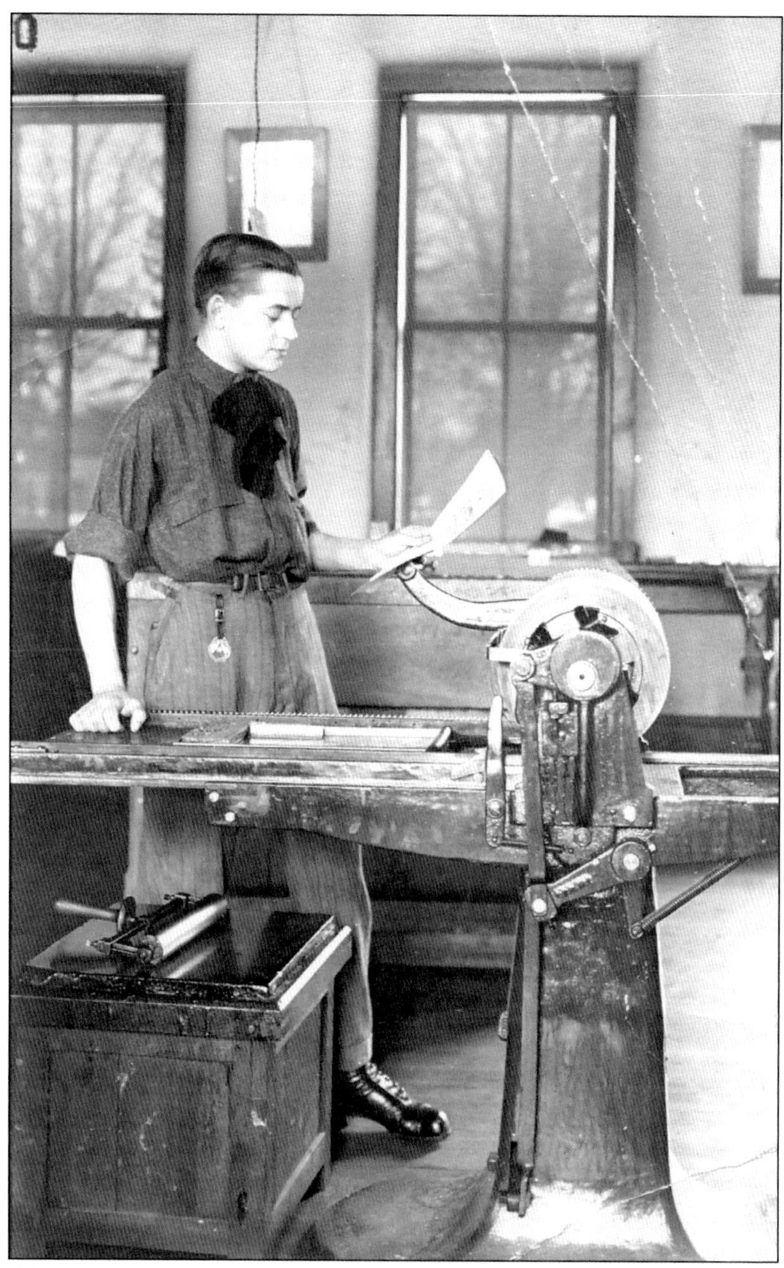

Emil G. Sahlin, shown in 1915, learned the art of typography by working on Elbert Hubbard's books and essays after following his typographer brother Axel to the Roycroft a year earlier. Emil knew little English when he came to the Roycroft from Sweden at the age of 19. About 11 years later, he left to operate another press shop. He later opened Paradise Press, which printed citations, diplomas, and special awards. In 1928, he and his brother opened their own typographic service, and he later taught the history of typography at local schools. He continued to work until his death in 1983 at the age of 88. Sahlin, whose Swedish accent followed him throughout his life, was also an accomplished drummer. He led his own dance band during the 1920s and performed at Shea's Buffalo theater during the heyday of vaudeville. To keep in top physical shape, Sahlin continued ice-skating well into his 60s.

Mary Lipsett was in charge of the subscription department at the Roycroft. After the publication of Hubbard's "A Message to Garcia" in 1899, demand for subscriptions to *The Philistine* and other Roycroft publications soared.

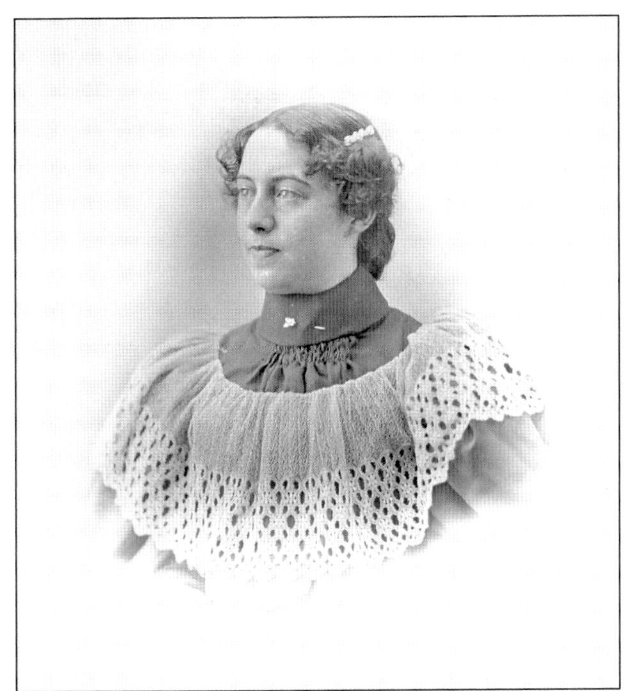

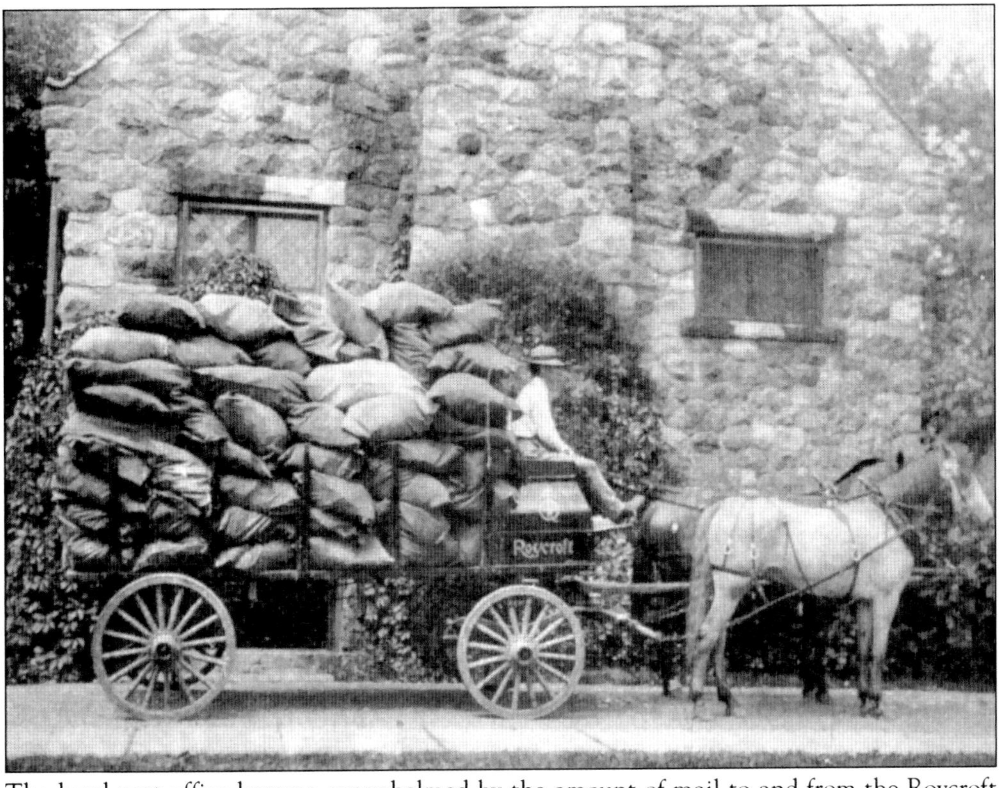

The local post office became overwhelmed by the amount of mail to and from the Roycroft Campus in the early 1900s. Phillip Dearmyer, the Roycroft mailman and driver, claimed that 70 sacks of mail were loaded onto his wagon at once for delivery to the post office.

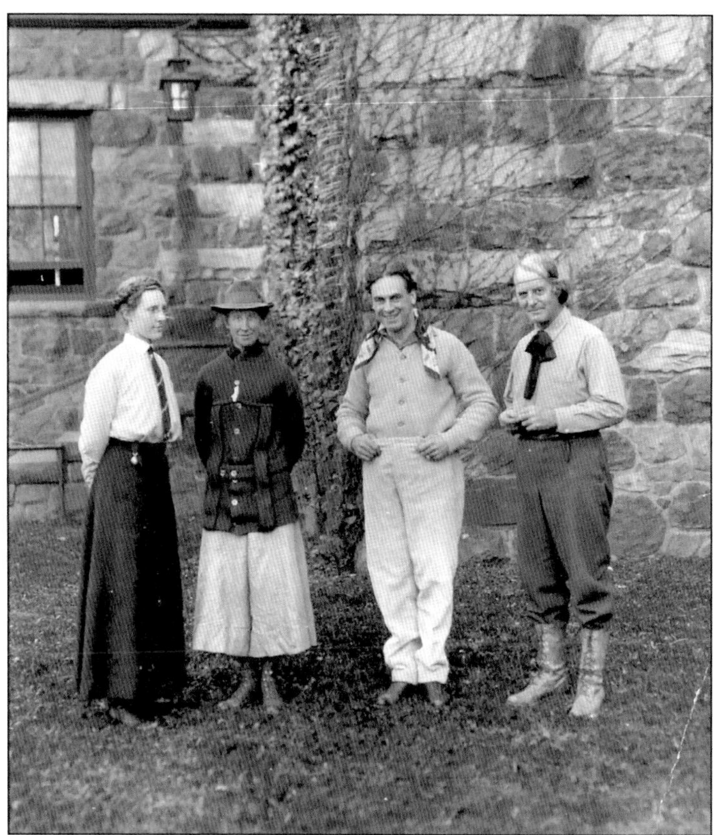

Allene Seaman, left, joins, from left to right, Alice Hubbard, an unidentified Roycroft guest, and Elbert Hubbard on the Roycroft Campus. Seaman and fellow Roycroft workers Beulah Hood and Betty Morey used the business acumen they learned at the Roycroft to venture out on their own in 1914. They purchased the variety store in the Regulator Block on Main Street, between Riley and Church Streets. Note the trademark shoestring holding Elbert Hubbard's hair back. (Courtesy of the *East Aurora Advertiser.*)

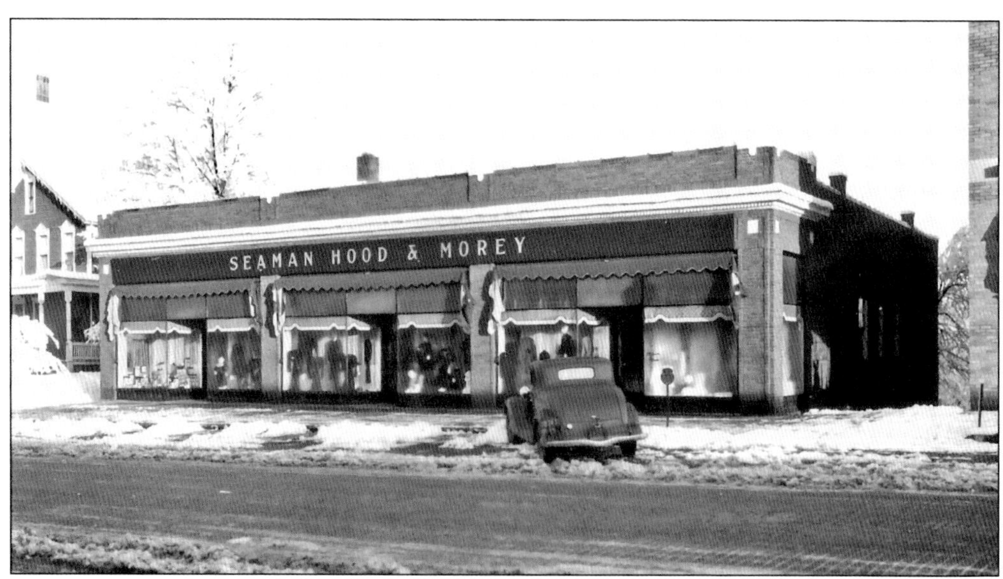

After the Regulator Block burned in 1917, the Seaman, Hood & Morey store was rebuilt. The store served the community for many decades. A Buffalo firm purchased the business in the 1950s. Though the business no longer exists, the building still stands.

Born in Minnesota on the Fourth of July in 1865, Alexis Jean Fournier was perhaps one of the most eccentric artists to come to the Roycroft. He is considered one of the most influential painters of the Roycroft Arts and Crafts era. His murals and other paintings are on public display in several community locations, and his house still stands on Walnut Street adjacent to the Roycroft Campus.

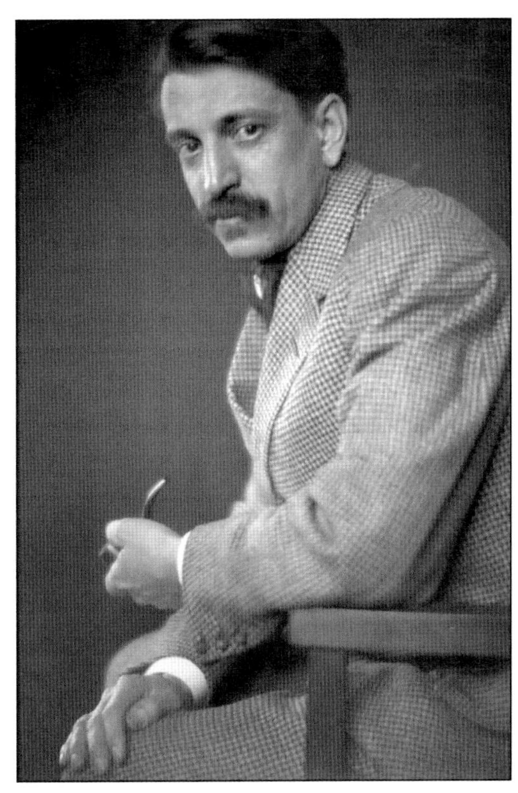

Though often at odds with local government and church leaders, Elbert Hubbard was also the community's largest employer. Taking a break from their work are Roycroft employees, from left to right, (first row) Andrew Deheck, Wallace Buffum, Frank Higgins, and Theodore Flemming; (second row) George Hochstuhl, Herbert Buffum, and Harry Buffum.

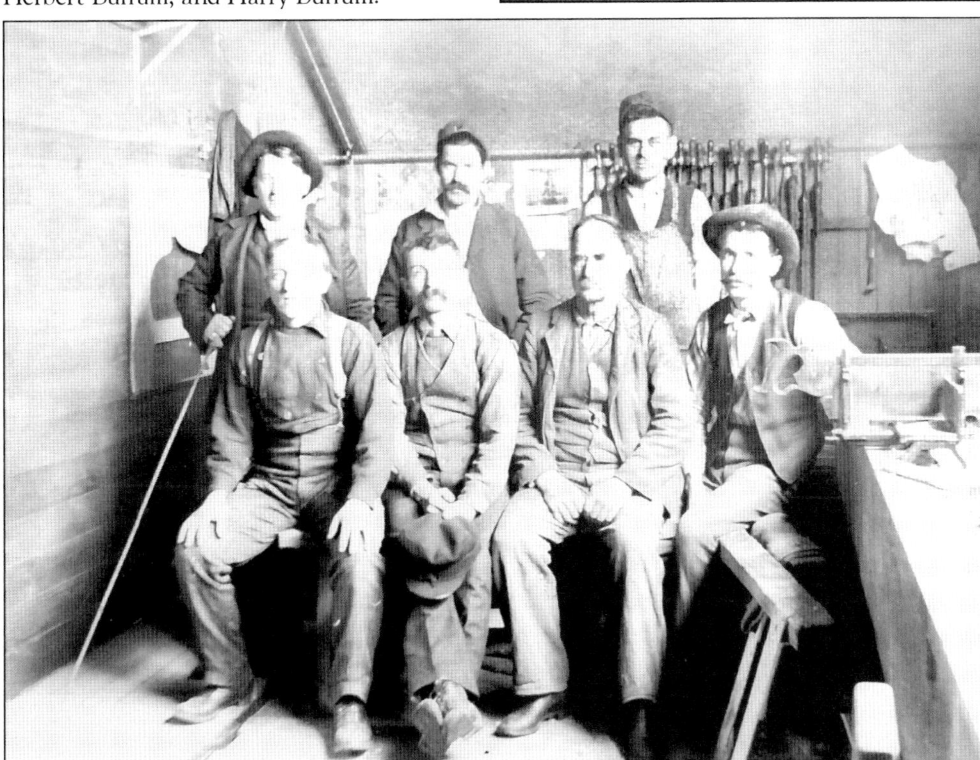

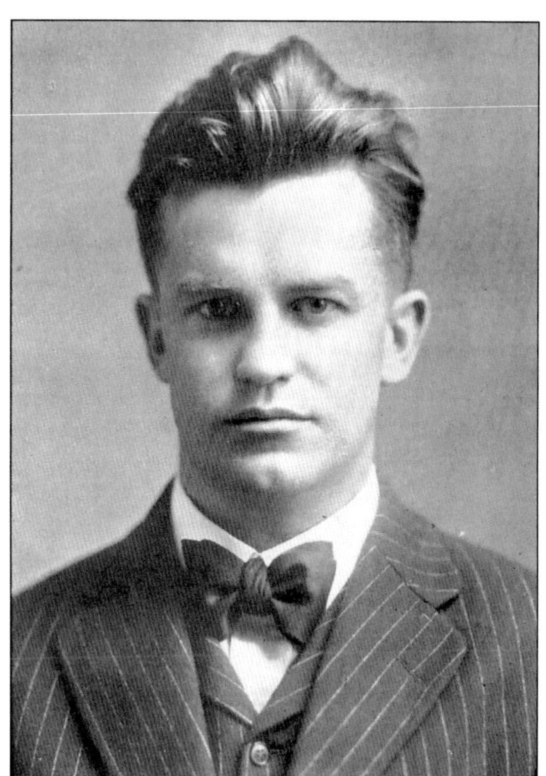

Edward Shay, known as Felix, served as general manager of the Roycroft. Before that he was the first editor of *The Fra* magazine and served as business manager for Elbert Hubbard's publications. A biography noted that he brought "sound business training to his work." In the mid-1920s, Shay published a book, *Elbert Hubbard of East Aurora*, a first-hand account of his time at the Roycroft and with Hubbard.

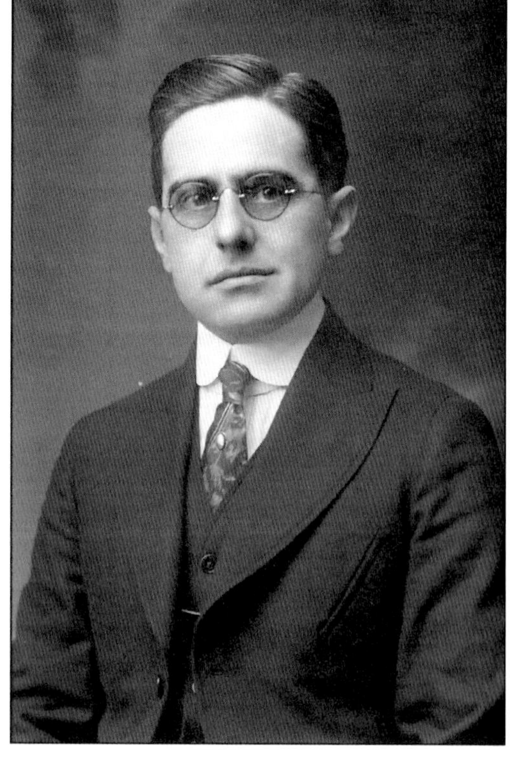

Charles W. Youngers served as secretary of the Roycroft Corporation as well as superintendent of the Roycroft Bindery. He came to the Roycroft in 1898 at the age of 16 and stayed until it went bankrupt in 1938, which was when he went to work for the Acme Book Bindery in Buffalo. He served on the Village Board from 1939 to 1955 and died on April 2, 1963, just three days shy of his 80th birthday.

Aware there was a chance that he would not return to East Aurora amid threats against the *Lusitania*, Elbert Hubbard left the Roycroft in charge of his son Elbert II, who is shown here in his younger days. "Bert" took an active role in the business end of the Roycroft Corporation and ran it successfully until the Great Depression took its toll in 1938. Bert was also active in the community, serving as village president from 1923 to 1926.

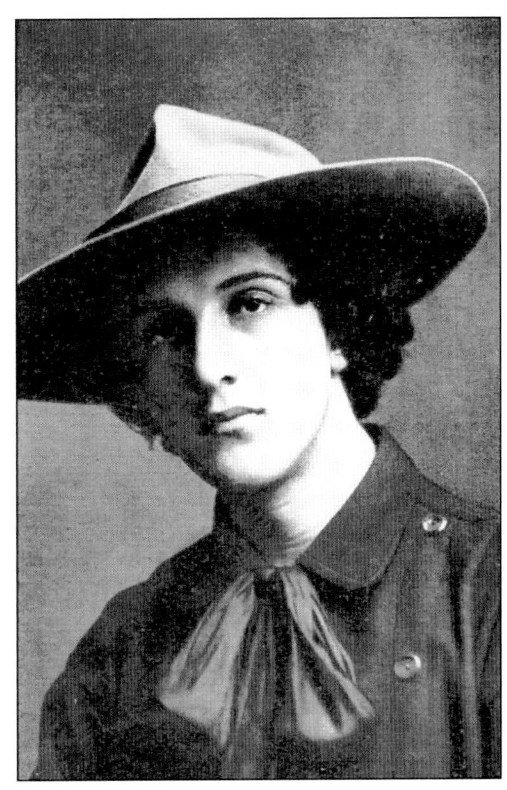

Decades after the sinking of the *Lusitania* off the coast of Ireland, veteran newspaper photographer Rile Prosser, right, captures Elbert Hubbard II displaying a scrapbook of the *New York American* headline from May 8, 1915, telling of the disaster that took 1,198 lives, including those of his father and step-mother. Early headlines incorrectly overestimated the death toll at 1,409. The German attack on the ship brought the United States into World War I.

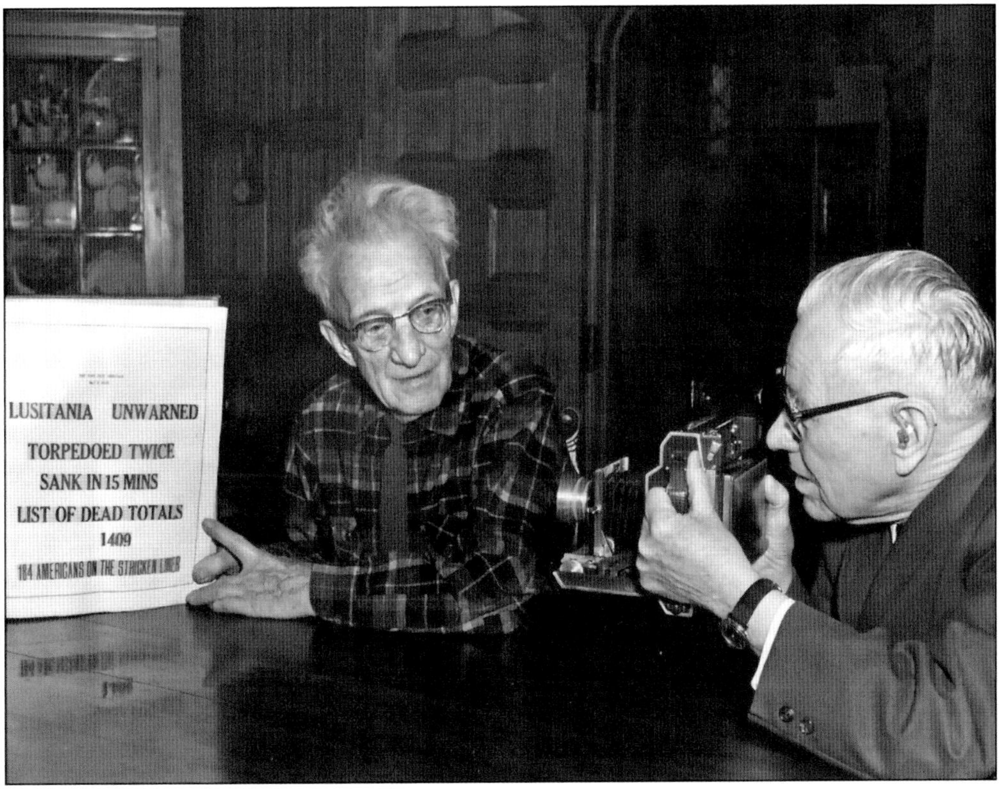

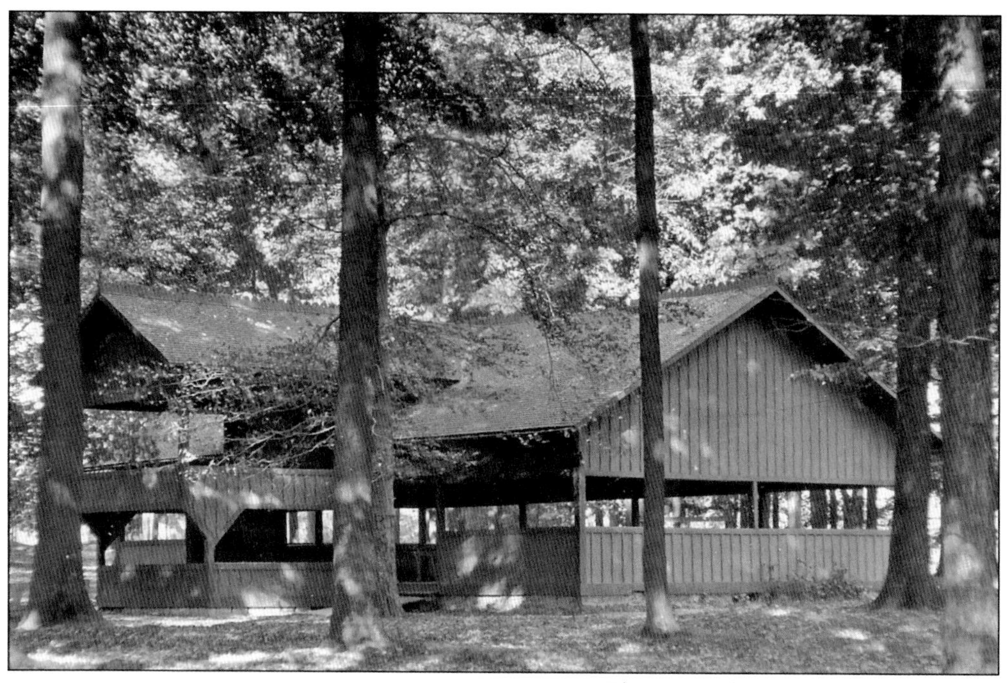

The Roycrofters constructed the open-air pavilion in Hamlin Park in the early 1900s and presented it to the village in 1903. The community gathered at the pavilion to honor Elbert and Alice Hubbard during a memorial service May 23, 1915. Aurora Players, a community theater group that enclosed the building in 1946, continues to use the pavilion. A recent addition and renovation project kept the original facade intact.

IN MEMORIAM

Commemorative
of
Elbert and Alice Hubbard
Lost with the ill-fated "Lusitania," off the
Old Head of Kinsale, Ireland,
on May 7th, 1915

A SERVICE

of appreciation and regard by the
people of the Village.
Held
at East Aurora, N. Y.
May 23d, 1915,
three o'clock.

This is the cover of the program from the memorial service for Elbert and Alice Hubbard. The service included remarks from village president Alfred Brotherhood, a French horn solo by Roycroft Band director Merritt A. Kyser, and readings from the works of Elbert and Alice Hubbard. The service concluded with the singing of "America," because of "the preference shown it by Mr. Hubbard as the closing feature of Roycroft entertainment."

Bert Havens, Wells W. Parker, and James Castle are shown in this undated photograph. When he died in 1965 at the age of 91, Parker had been a lawyer in East Aurora for 67 years and was the oldest member of the Erie County Bar Association. Born in Wales Hollow, he walked seven miles each day to attend classes in East Aurora. He graduated in 1892, the only boy in a class of 13.

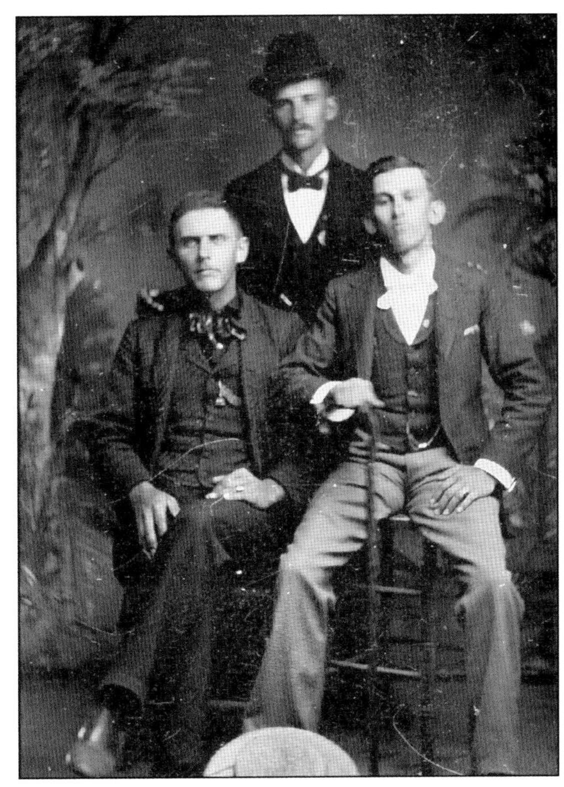

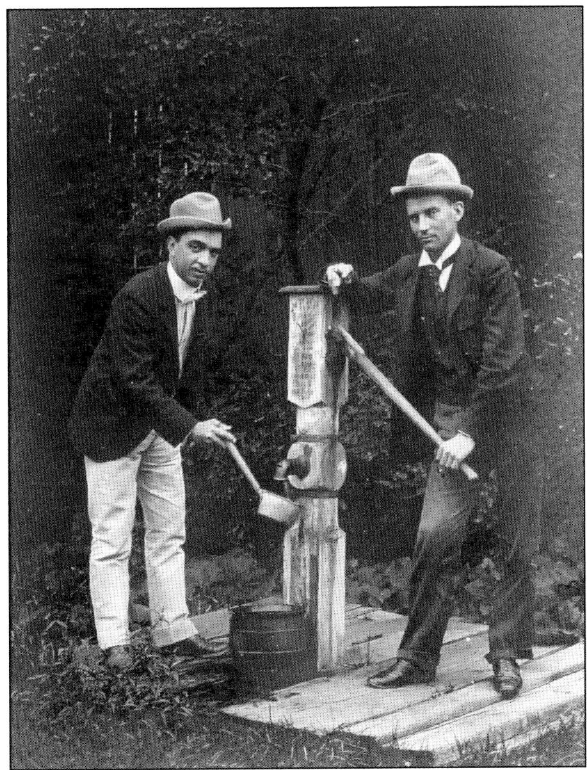

What does a man need to do to get a drink of water? Harry Whitney and Wells W. Parker pump water from an outdoor well. Water mains were installed in the village in the 1890s, but it would take several more decades for municipal water to make its way to more rural areas of the town.

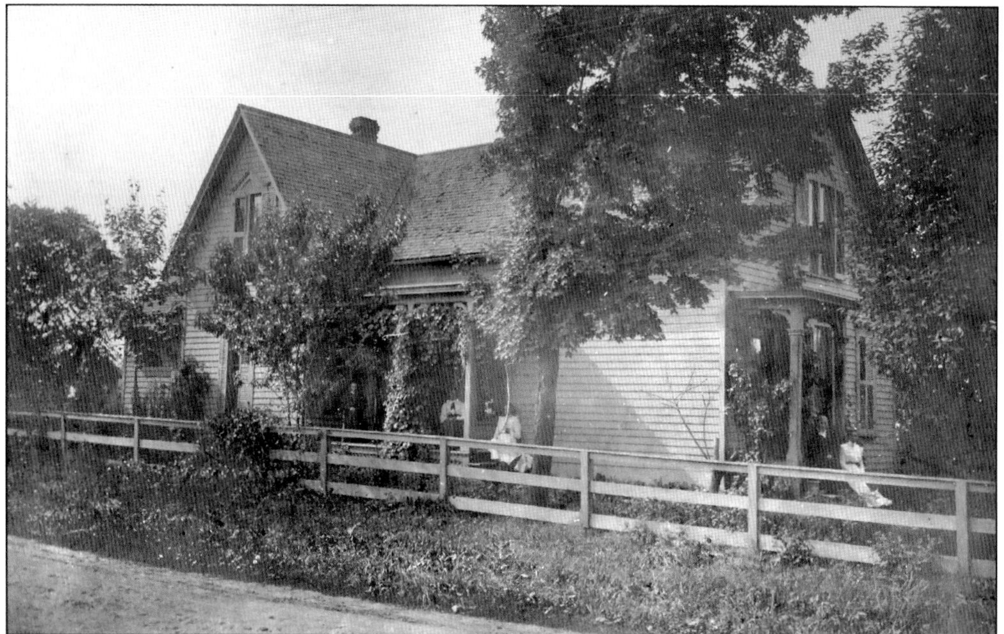

The Townley residence, located on the northwest corner of Walnut Street and Prospect Avenue, is shown in 1902. The house still exists with very few exterior modifications. Following the success of the Roycroft just a few blocks away, the number of houses constructed in the neighborhood surrounding this home skyrocketed through the 1920s.

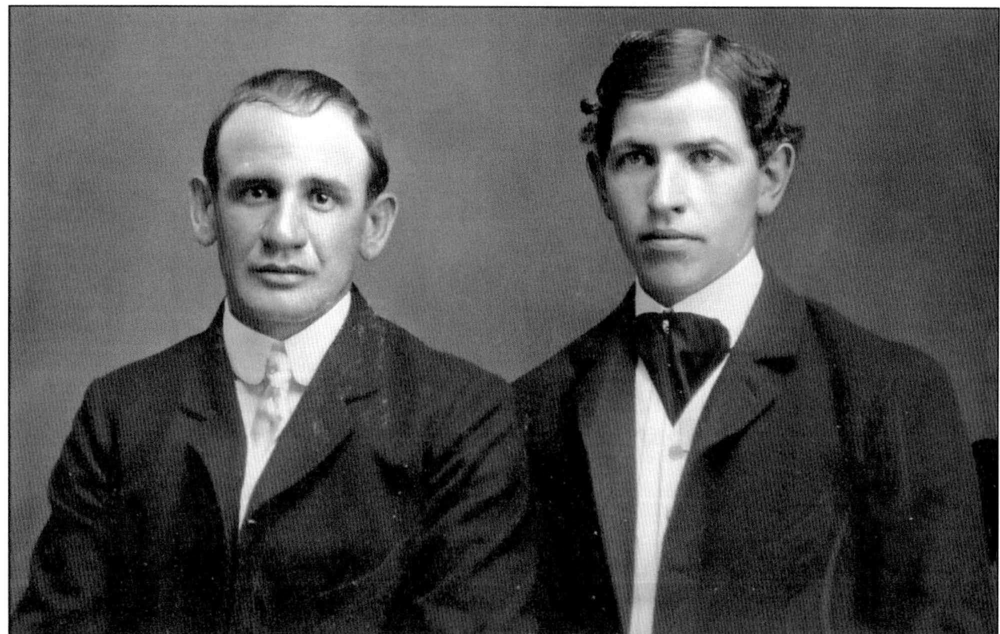

Information on the back of this photograph identifies the young men as Joe Sorge and Thomas Rogers Jr. Thomas was the son of a wagon maker on East Main Street. At the age of 27, three years after he married Lulu Wilson in a ceremony at her parents' house south of the village, Rogers became unexpectedly ill while attending a manufacturers' convention in Buffalo, where he had moved to take a job. He fell unconscious and never recovered.

Five

A Town in Transition 1916–1929

The deaths of Elbert and Alice Hubbard aboard the *Lusitania* sent the Roycroft into a new era. The sinking of the *Lusitania* also sent the United States into World War I. More than 200 Aurorans served in military and auxiliary capacities, and some did not return home.

Back in Aurora, the community built a new high school at the corner of Main and North Grove Streets in 1916 to replace the old Aurora Academy building and subsequent addition. Over 11 years later, the school's west wing was built to accommodate the need for even more space. Just six years after that, in 1933, another addition with a gymnasium was added on to the west wing to accommodate the additional students traveling to East Aurora from more rural areas of the town.

The 1920s also saw the construction of new entertainment venues. In 1923, the hamlet of South Wales built its own community hall, which still stands, and the Aurora Theater, which remains a Main Street landmark, opened in 1925 to replace the old Millard Fillmore Theater at about the same location.

This period in Aurora's history also saw the birth of several civic efforts, including the establishment of the East Aurora Free Library in one room of the old Board of Trade Building on the southeast corner of Main and Paine Streets.

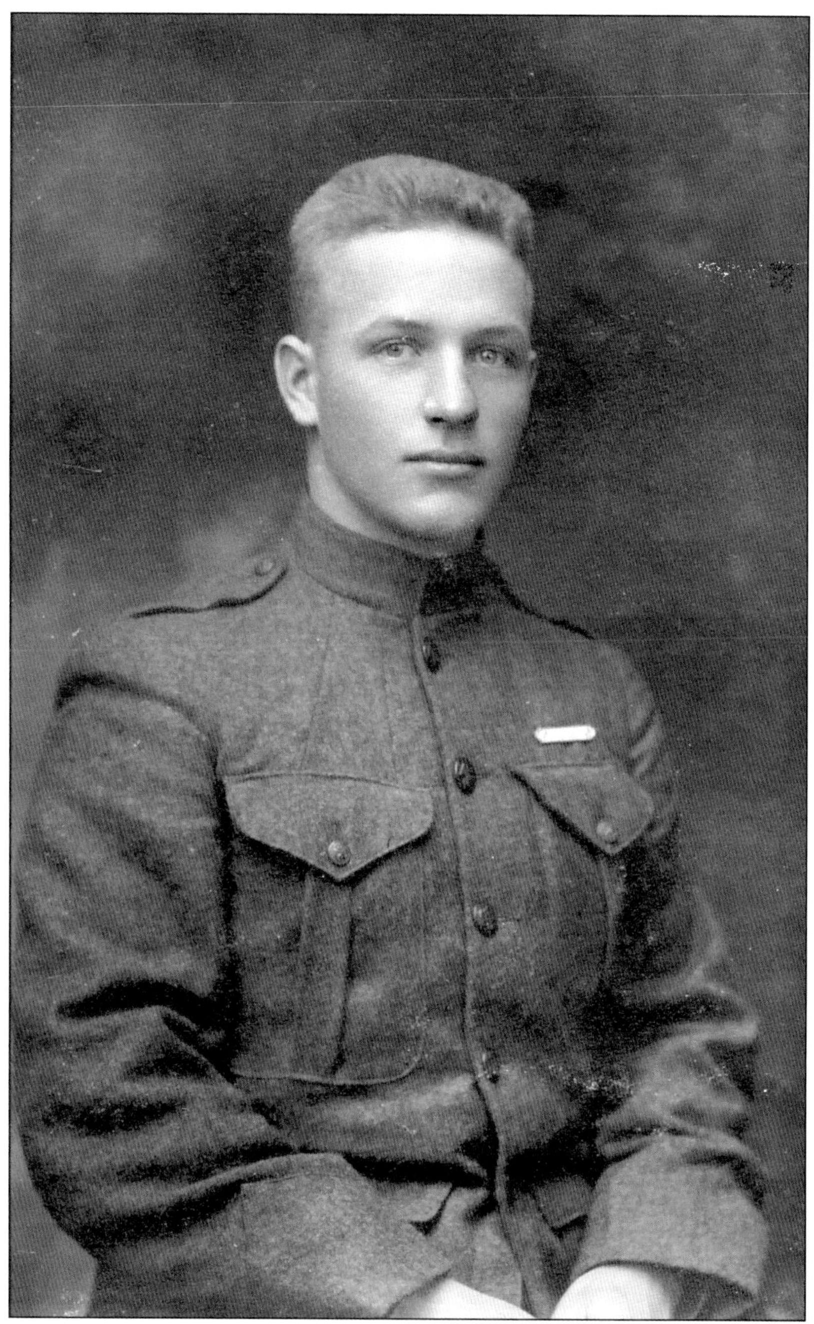

Lawrence F. Ernst was the first young man from East Aurora to make the ultimate sacrifice in World War I. The oldest of 11 children, he joined the Marine Corps and was killed in action June 14, 1918. In his memory, the village named the short street at the circle Ernst Place. The street is located in front of the present site of McDonald's restaurant. The honor given to Ernst is often overlooked because of the street's location on the circle. Due to travel limitations, the bodies of many soldiers were not brought home until after the war, forcing families to hold off memorial services. In some cases, families had to wait several years. After his remains were returned home, Ernst was buried in the Catholic cemetery on Bowen Road.

With just 11 days of World War I remaining, Cpl. Charles L. Clough was killed in action in the Argonne region of France on October 31, 1918. He lost his life while leading a squad of automatic riflemen. He had just returned to his unit, the 74th Company of the 6th Regiment of the US Marine Corp, after recovering in five different hospitals from previous gassing, burns, and wounds. He was 24 years old.

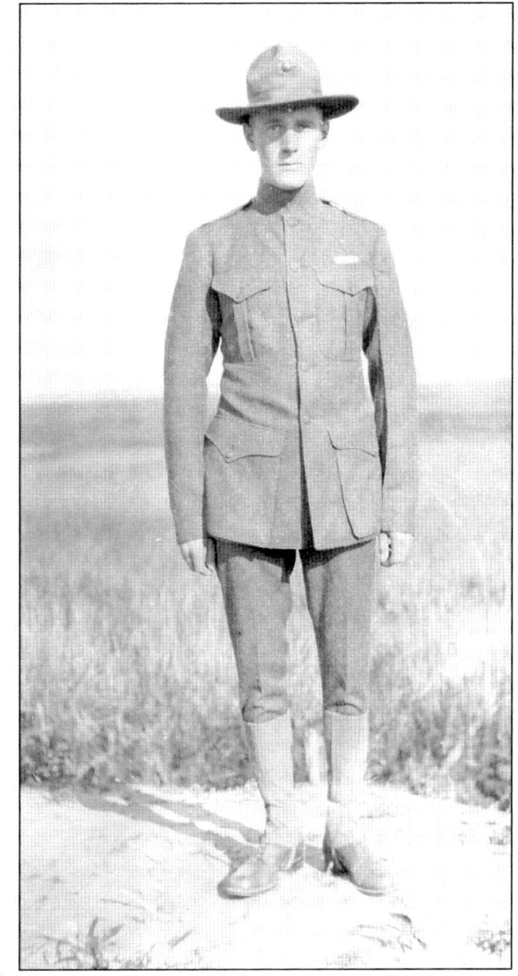

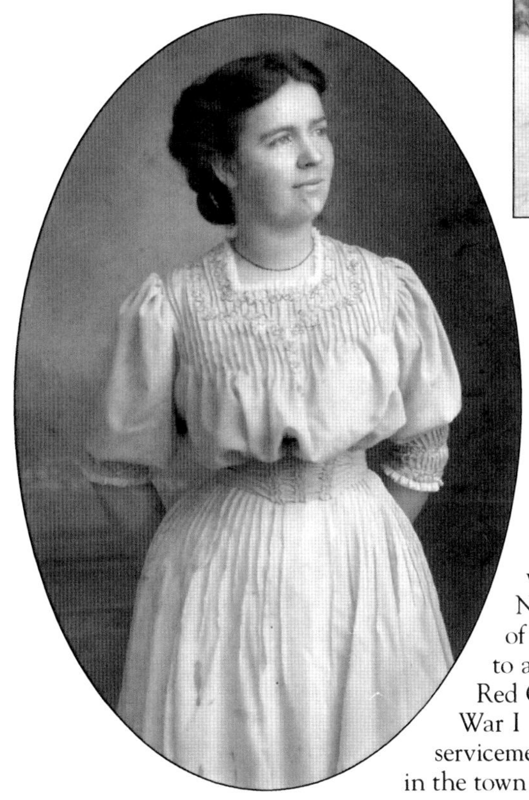

Frances A. Little was an American Red Cross worker in East Aurora during World War I. Never married, she died from complications of the flu in 1918. In addition to sending letters to and aiding soldiers, members of the American Red Cross kept detailed records of Aurora's World War I servicemen. Two scrapbooks, which contain servicemen's photographs and letters home, are preserved in the town historian's office.

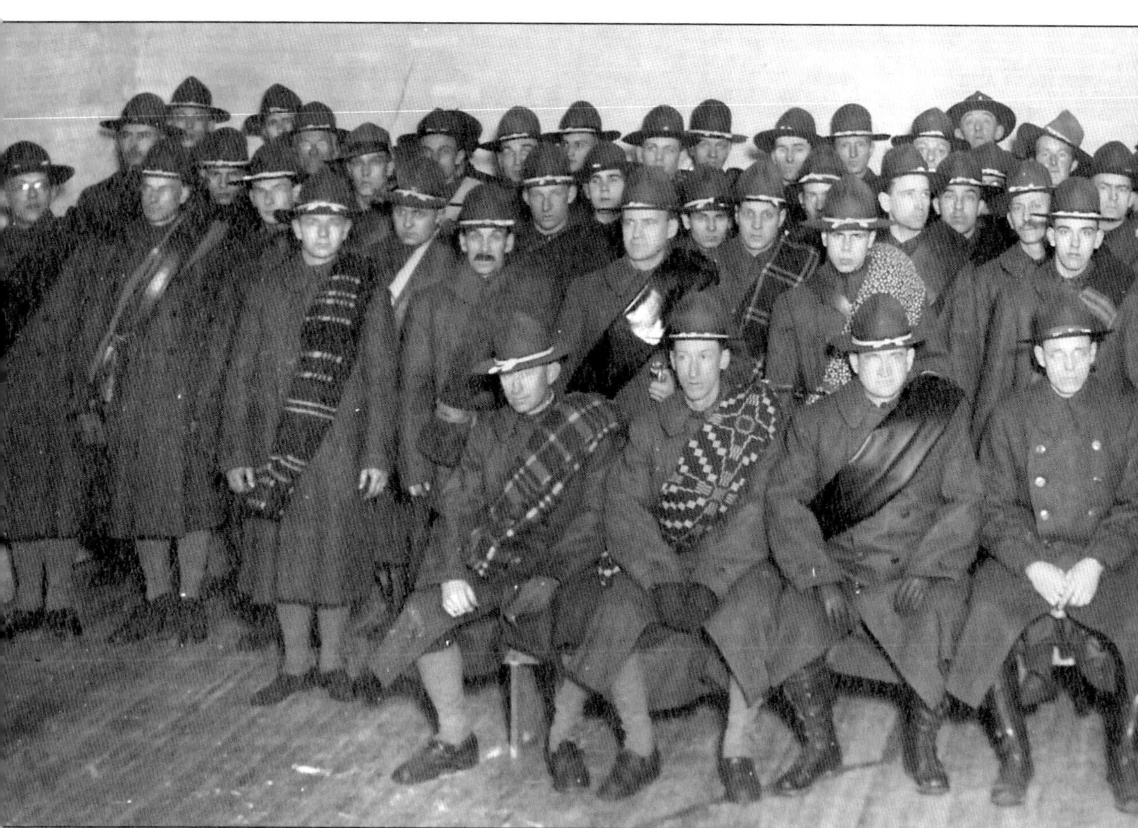

Members of Company M of the 65th Infantry of the Home Guard in World War I were housed in Emerson Hall, a Roycroft building on Prospect Avenue, between South Grove and Walnut Streets. One of the soldiers, Charles E. Simmons, had a dog, named Rex, who was born on the front lines.

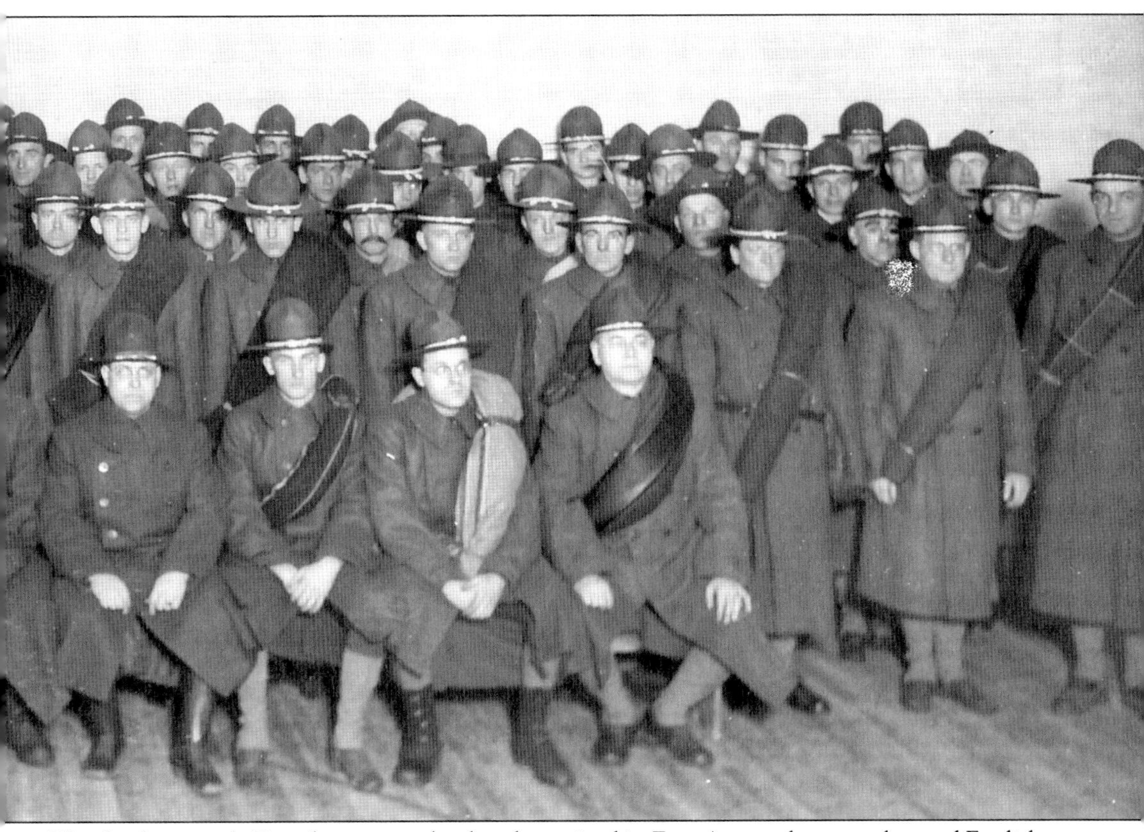

The dog knew only French commands when he arrived in East Aurora, but soon learned English ones as well. He became a mascot of the infantry, spending his days with the men before staying overnight with a local family. Emerson Hall was later converted into an apartment building.

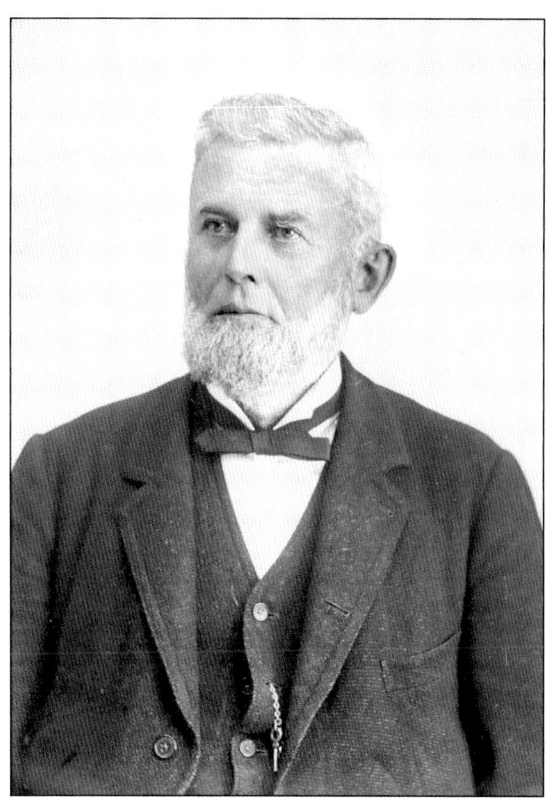

Josiah Emery II and his family owned the land in South Wales that became Emery Park. His father moved to Aurora on a four-horse sleigh in 1811 and served as a colonel in the state militia during the War of 1812. Josiah II, described as a man of intellectual power, had six children. Among them were two State Supreme Court justices, Edward Kellogg Emery and Asher Bates Emery, who also served as town supervisor.

Members of the Erie County Board of Supervisors and Park Commission meet outside the Emery Inn at Emery Park in the late 1920s to officially reopen the building after an extensive remodeling project. Erie County purchased 175 acres in 1925 from Helen B. Emery. The inn, once part of the Emery pioneer homestead, was later used as a museum and restaurant. Emery Park has since grown to 489 acres.

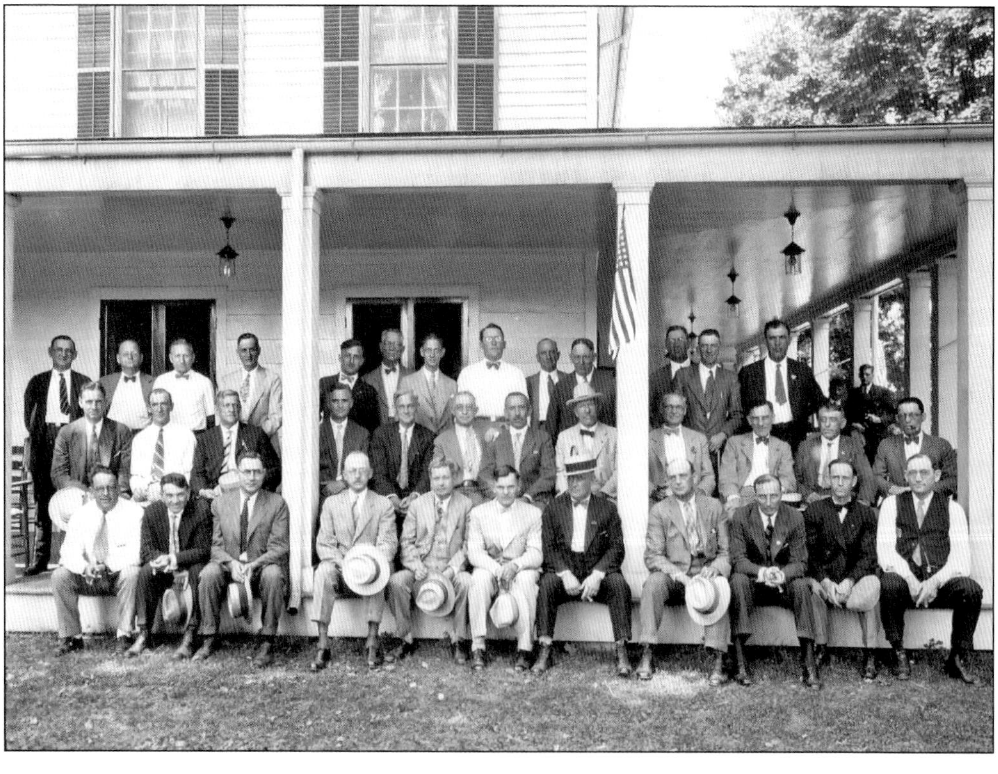

The Blazing Star Lodge Masonic Temple, located on the south side of Main Street between Elm Street and Temple Place, was built in 1906. At the time this photograph was taken, about 9:00 p.m., February 5, 1921, a ceremony to burn the mortgage was being held inside. The Blazing Star Lodge traces its roots in the community back to 1817.

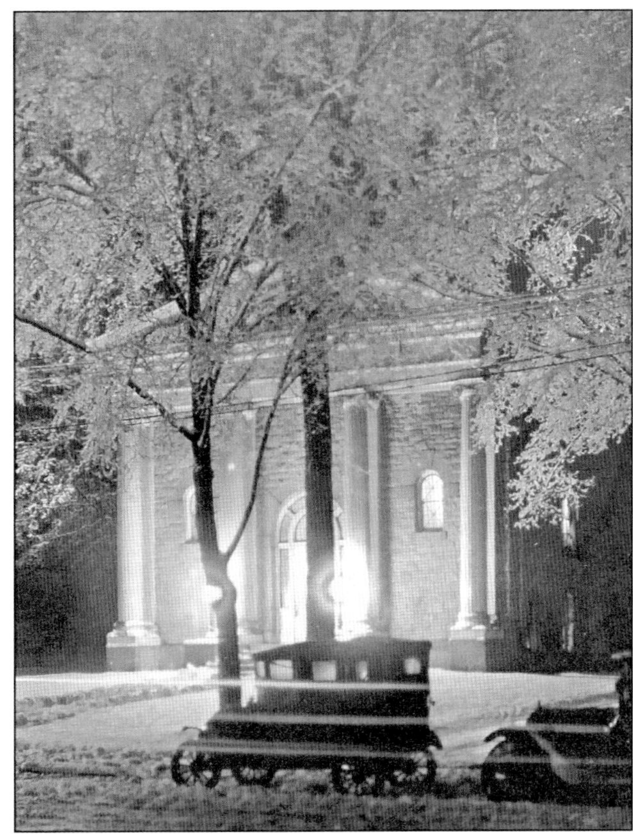

The Rebeccas are shown here in an undated photograph. Bertha Persons, wife of Frank O. Persons, is at the far left of the first row. The other women are not identified. The Rebeccas and the affiliated Independent Order of Odd Fellows for many years in the early 1900s sponsored East Aurora's Independence Day celebration that included a grand parade that went up and down Main Street twice before ending at Hamlin Park.

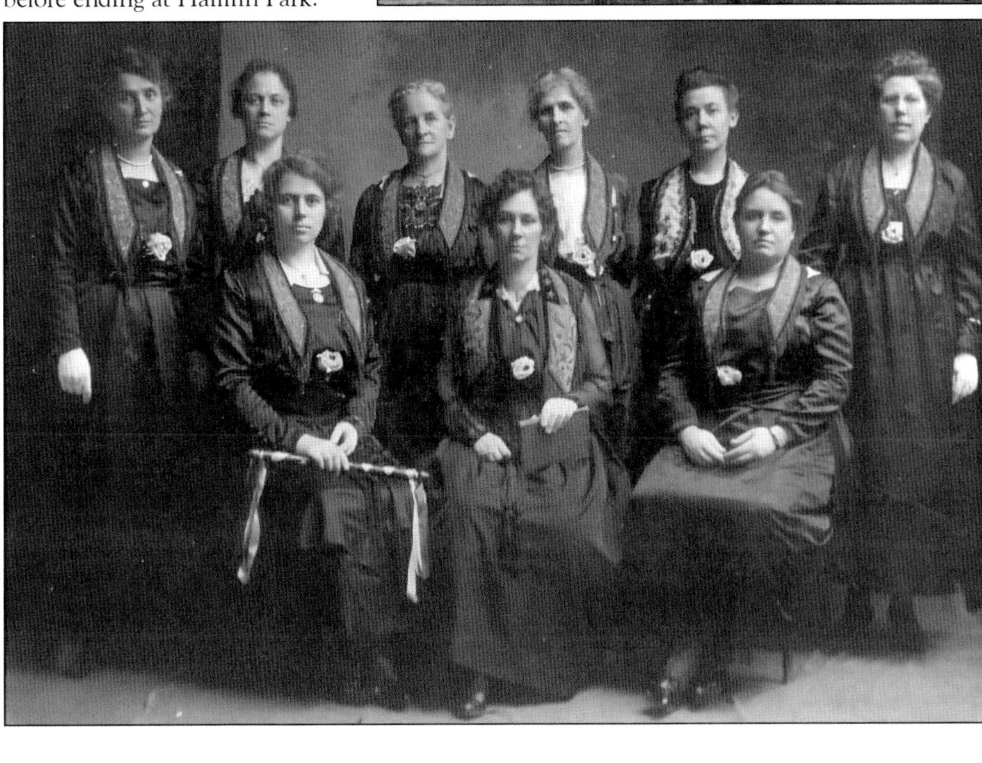

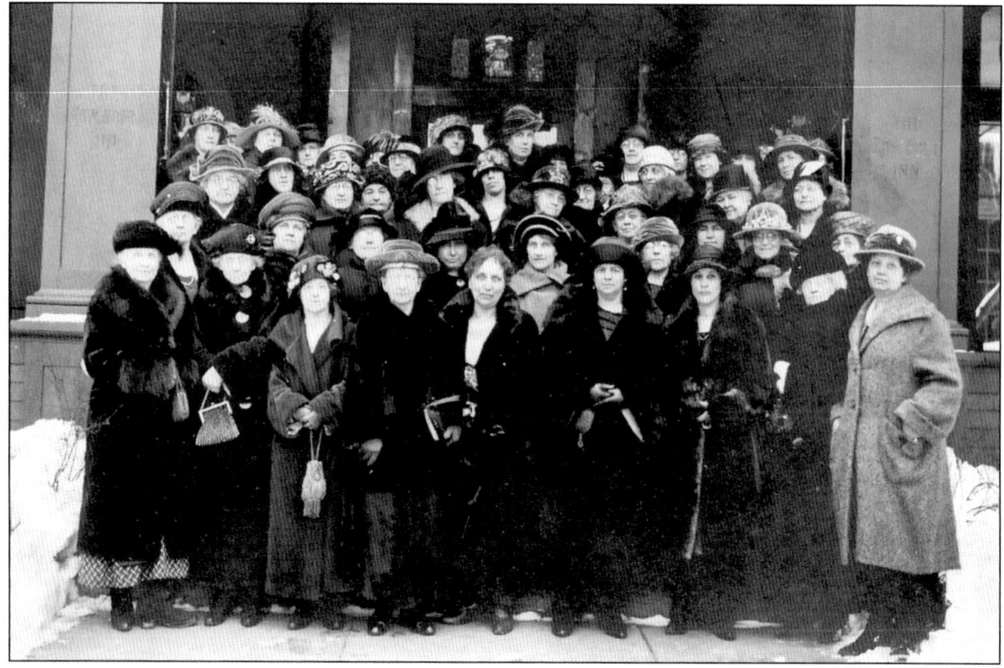

The Aurora Women's Club, originally organized as the Mother's Club in March 1894, celebrates its 30th anniversary with a luncheon at the Roycroft Inn on February 25, 1924. The club is still an active part of the community more than eight decades later.

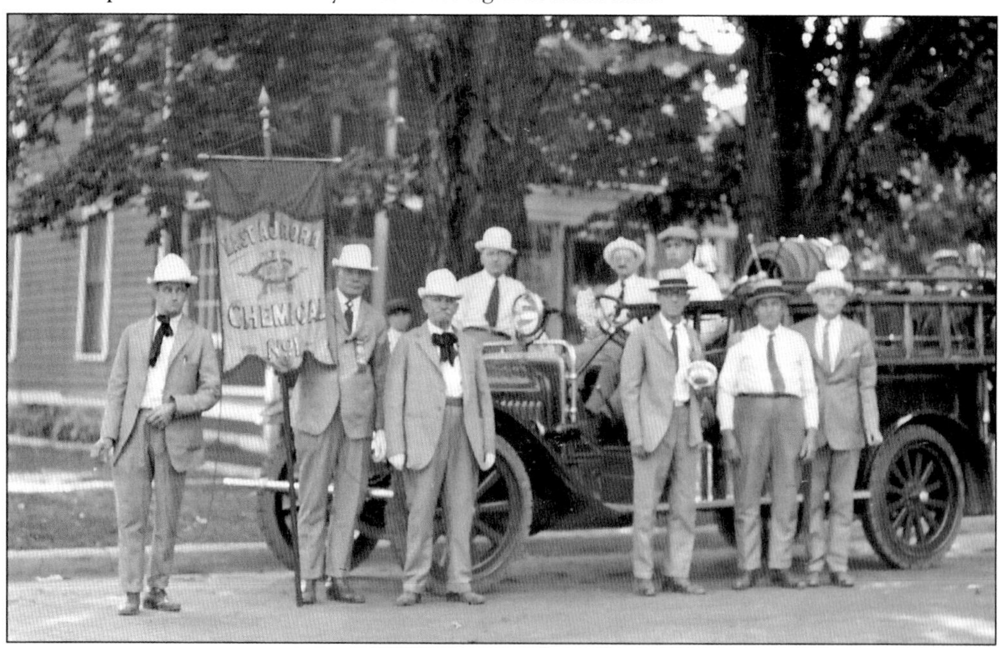

East Aurora Chemical Engine Company No. 1 prepares for a parade in 1924. The company was organized in 1885 by the Lutheran Singing Society and built its own fire hall on Oakwood Avenue in 1887. A new fire hall was built at Oakwood Avenue and Elm Street around 1905. The company later moved with three other fire companies into a central fire hall at Oakwood Avenue and Paine Street.

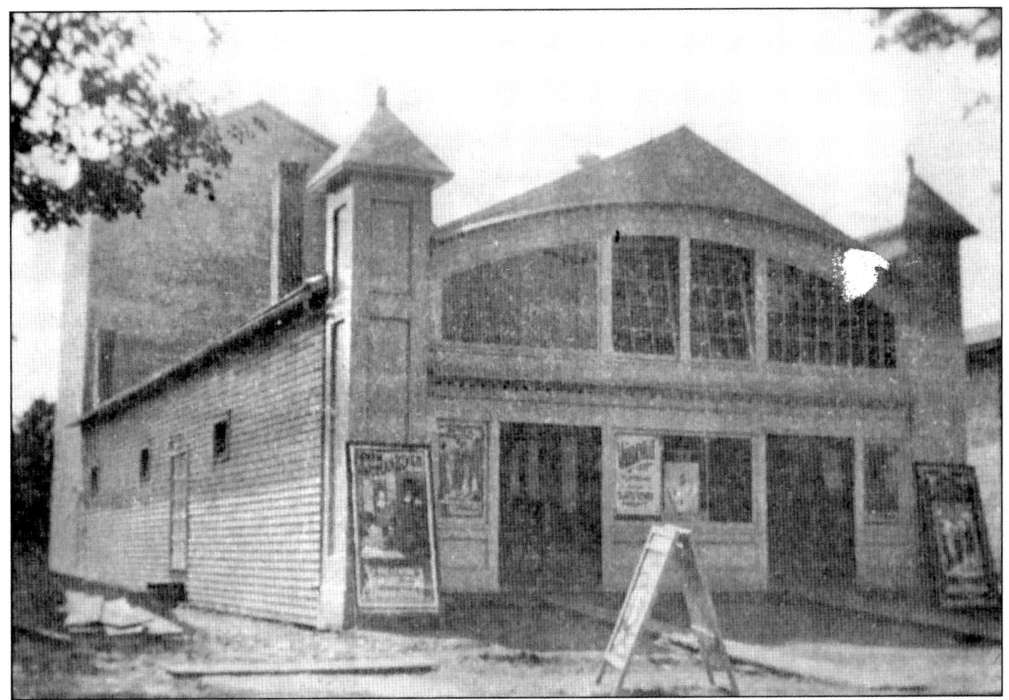

The Millard Fillmore Theater was located just east of the present Aurora Theater. Silent films were accompanied by piano. Vaudeville was offered on Tuesday and Saturday. Tickets during World War I cost between 11¢ and 20¢; seats in the first six rows were extra. The theater was torn down in the early 1920s. This was not the only venue for silent films, however. Tents were also erected in the village for moving pictures.

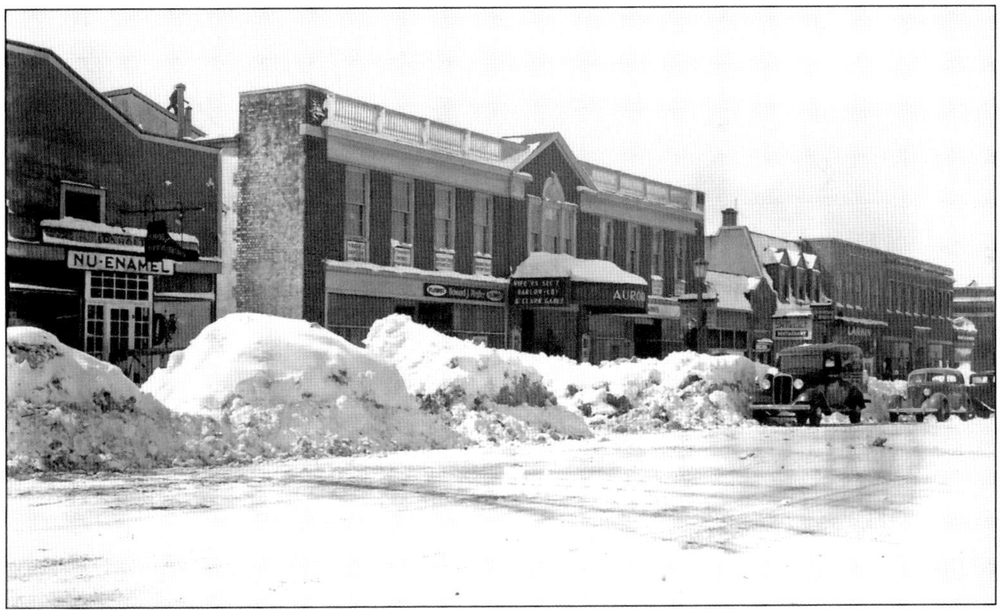

The old marquee of the Aurora Theater is shown following a snowstorm on March 22, 1936. The growing popularity of motion pictures led a committee, headed by Irving L. Price, to erect the theater in 1925. A new neon marquee later replaced the one that is pictured.

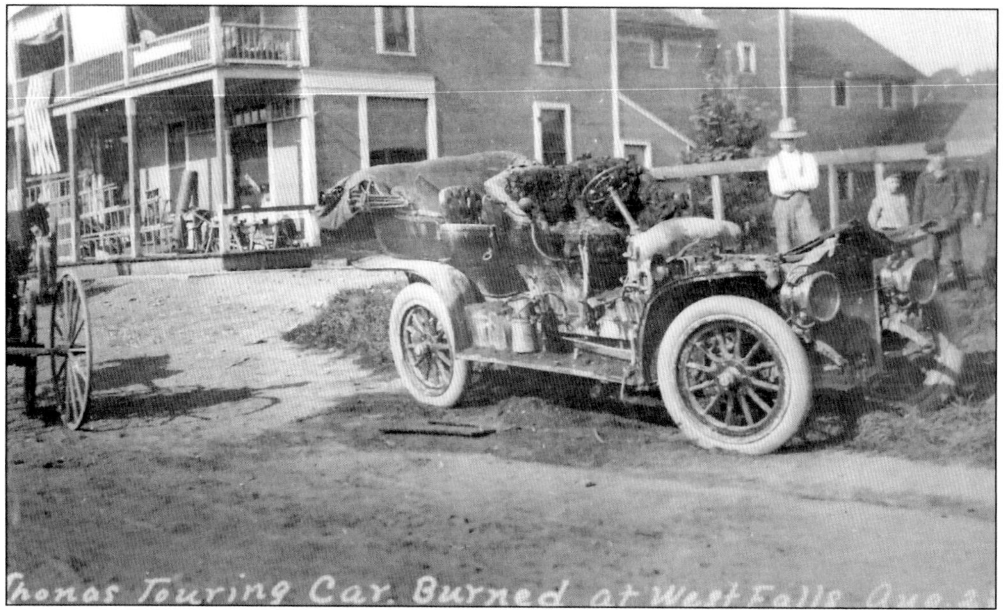

Mechanical problems caught the driver of this Thomas Touring Car off guard. The vehicle caught fire while passing through the hamlet in August 1923. The W.A. Paul Store can be seen in the background.

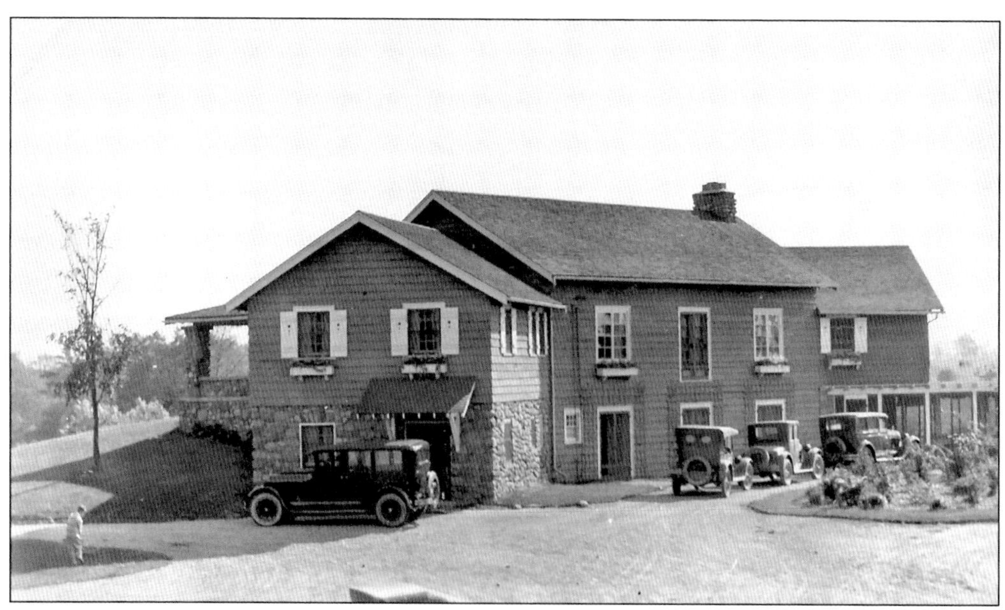

The East Aurora Country Club is shown in the late 1920s. The club was established during World War I with the purchase of land off Girdle Road for $12,000. An 18-hole course was laid out in 1916, but only the first nine holes were built right away. The second nine were constructed in 1963. The club annually hosts the International Junior Masters.

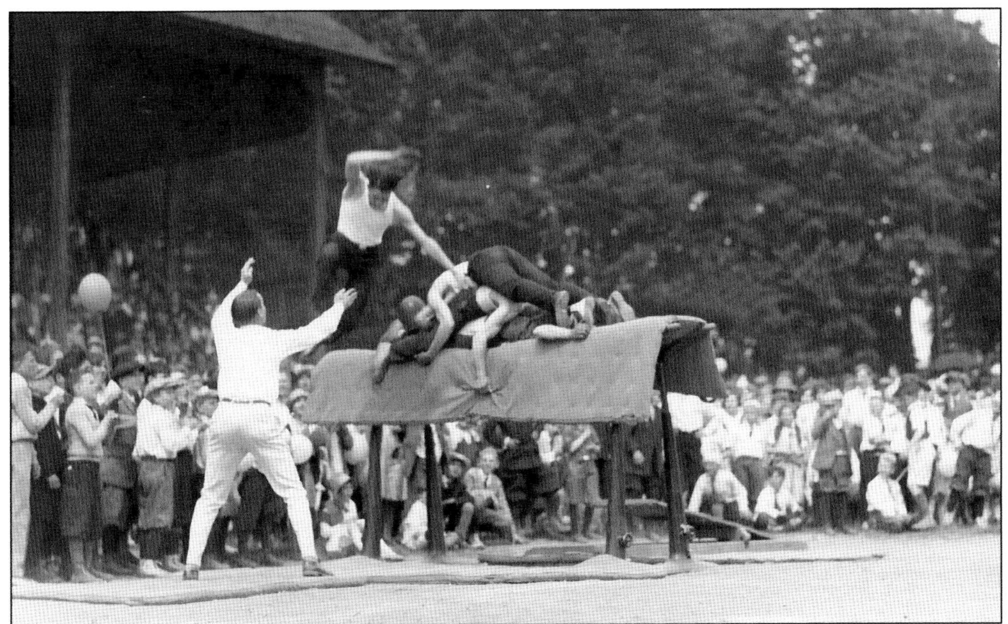

For more than a century, Hamlin Park, located in the middle of the village, has been popular place for school field days. These boys, under the watchful eye of an instructor, wrestle in one of the contests at the 1925 event, which attracted hundreds of students from schools in Aurora and surrounding towns.

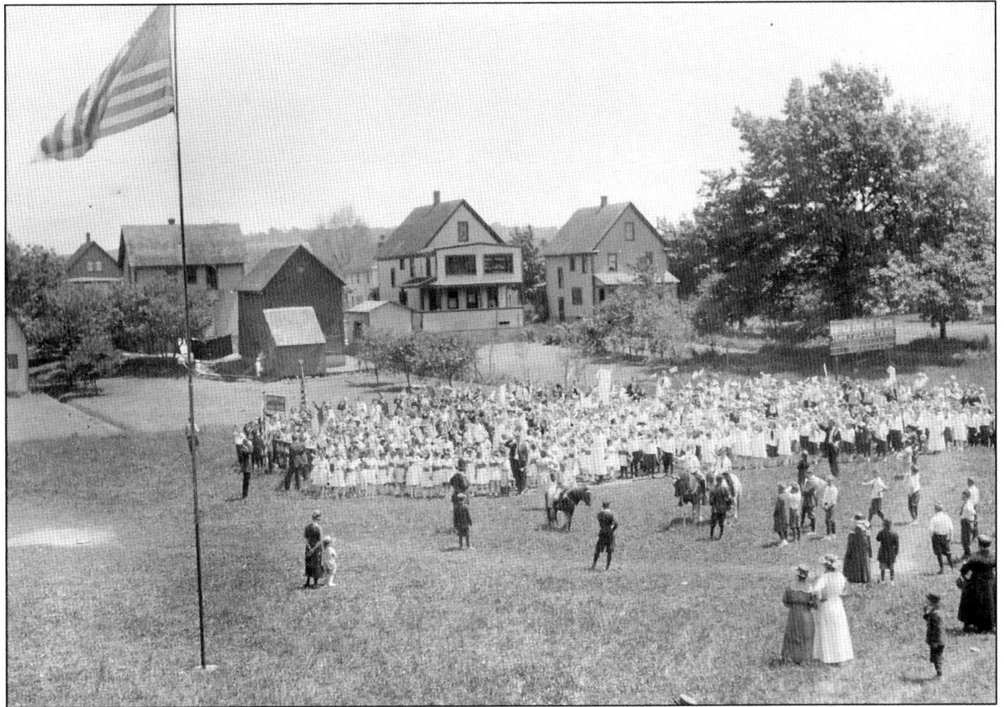

The backyards of Sycamore Street homes can be seen, as students gather around the flagpole on the baseball diamond to begin one of their field days in the late 1920s. The *Buffalo Evening News* baseball scoreboard is in the outfield on the right.

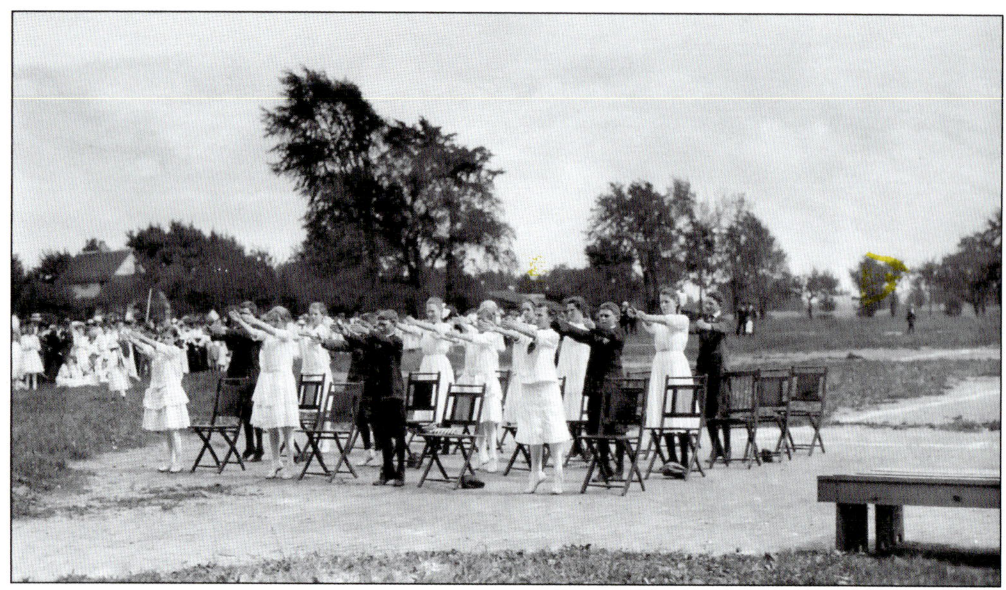

Boys and girls demonstrate their stretching exercises during a field day. Their clothing hardly seems appropriate for a recreational day out in the sun. Field day was a highly anticipated event in East Aurora and included a large parade of area schoolchildren down South Grove Street in addition to numerous athletic and academic contests.

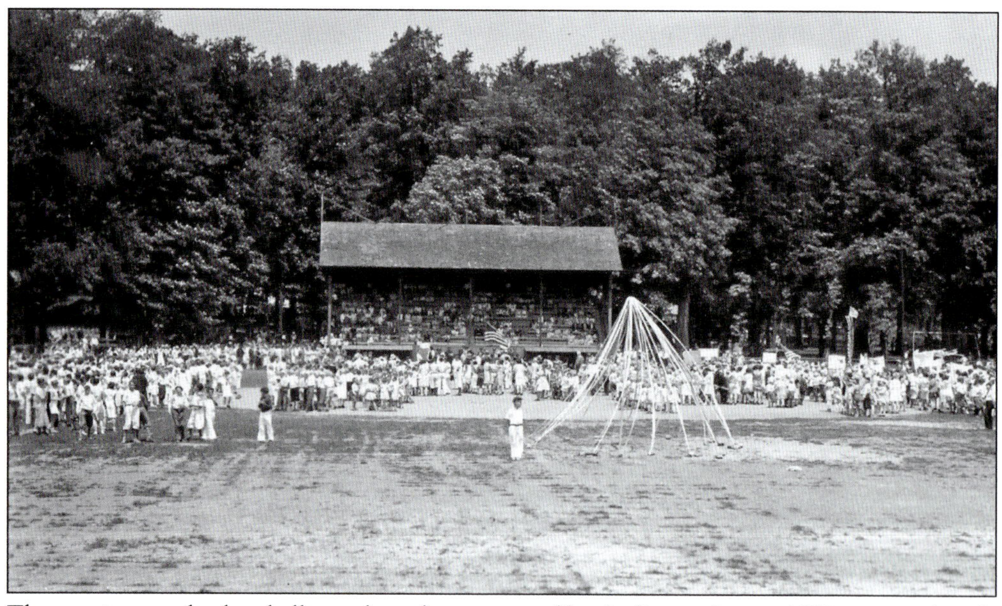

The massive wooden baseball grandstand, constructed by the Roycrofters in 1902, came in handy for spectators during field days at Hamlin Park. Horse farm owner Cicero Hamlin donated the grove of trees behind it to the village in 1901. Eyed for a short time by housing developers, the land was named in Hamlin's honor after he ensured through deed restrictions that the property would forever be a village park.

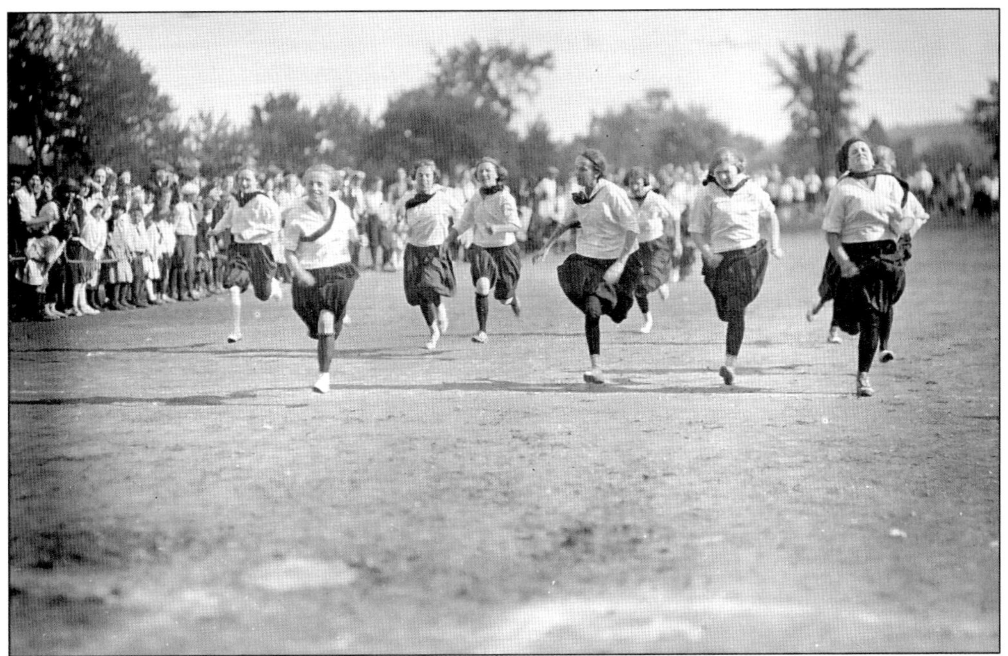

Giving it their all, these girls race to the finish line during a field day at Hamlin Park. The athletic and academic competitions drew large participation, and the winners were congratulated with great fanfare in the local newspaper, the *East Aurora Advertiser*.

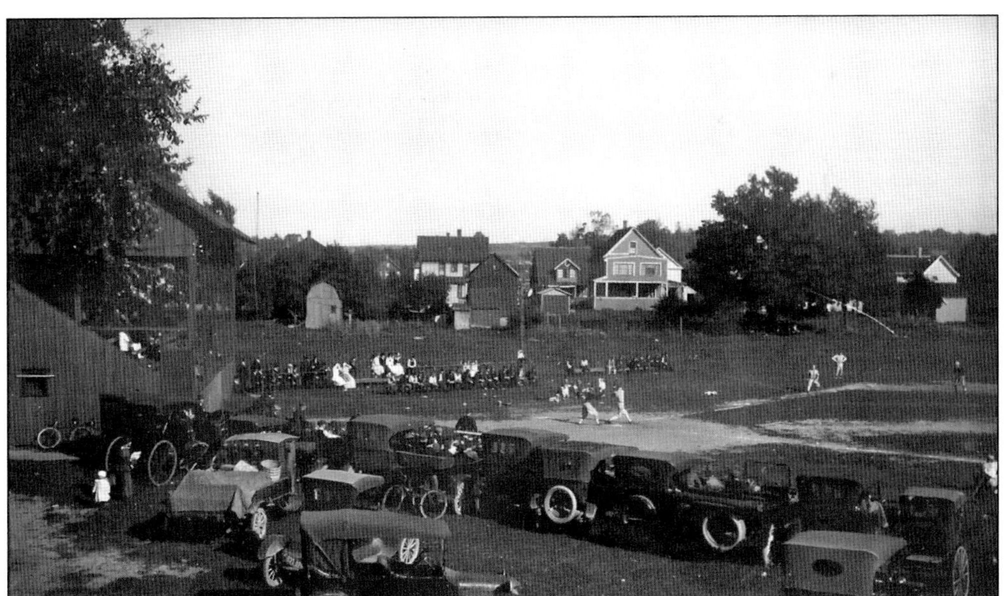

Before television, there was nothing like an afternoon baseball game! The diamond in Hamlin Park has drawn spectators for more than a century. It is one of the oldest continuously used baseball diamonds in Western New York. East Aurora school and town teams still play on this diamond.

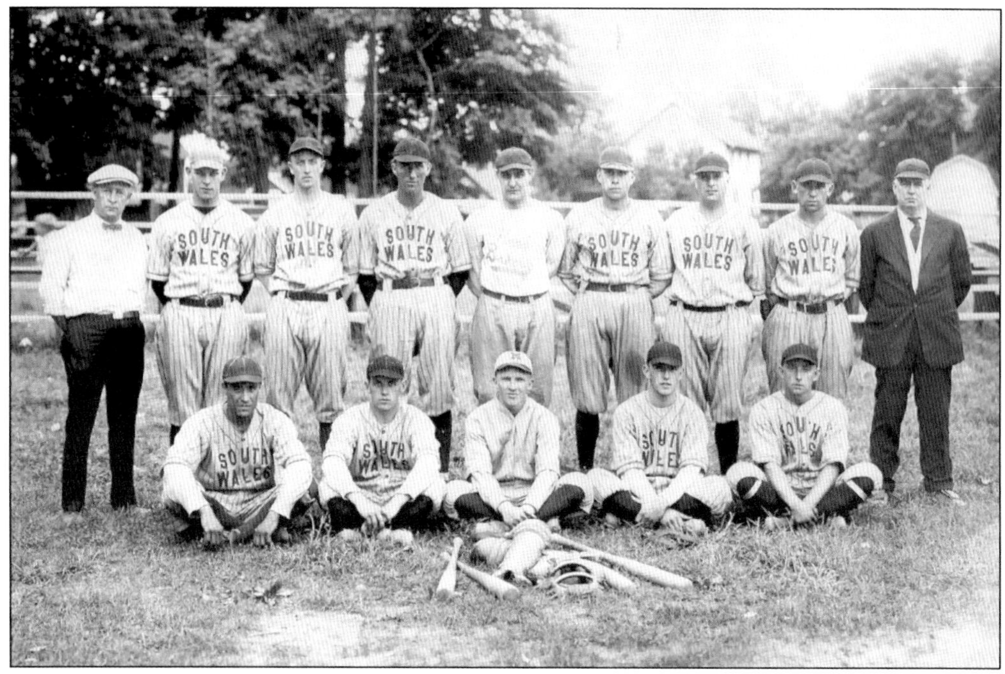

South Wales baseball players pose for a team picture before a game in 1927. Baseball teams became a source of community pride in the hamlets and villages of Aurora and surrounding towns. Results of weekend games were front-page news in the *East Aurora Advertiser* in the 1920s.

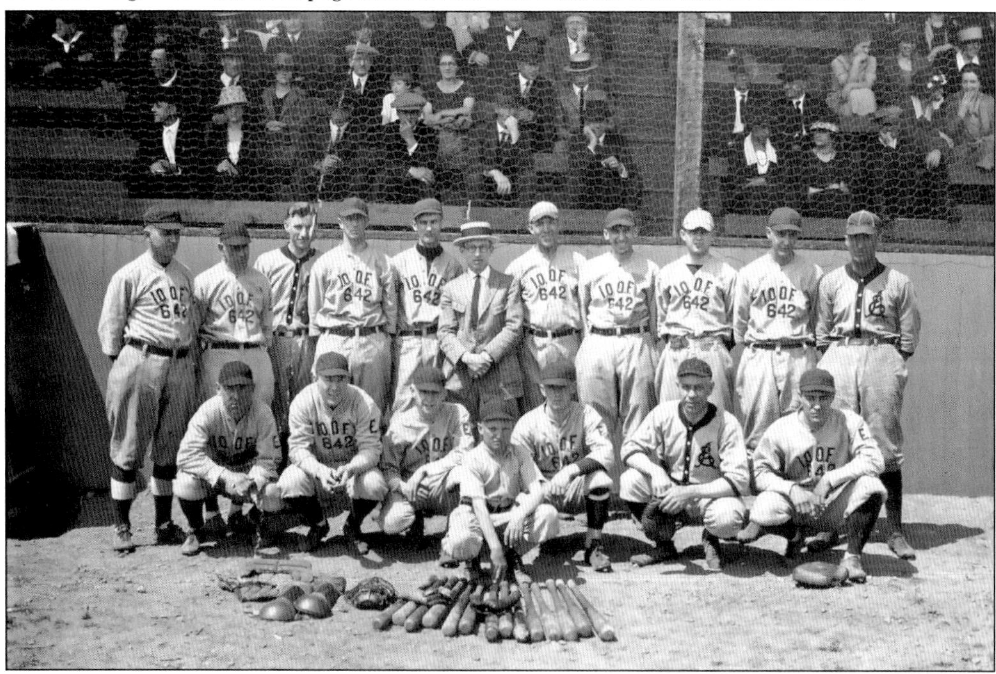

The Independent Order of Odd Fellows team poses in front of the old, wooden grandstand in 1923. Many local organizations, including the Roycrofters, fielded their own baseball teams. Wire fencing over the front of the grandstand prevented injuries from foul balls. The massive structure, later torn down, could seat several hundred people.

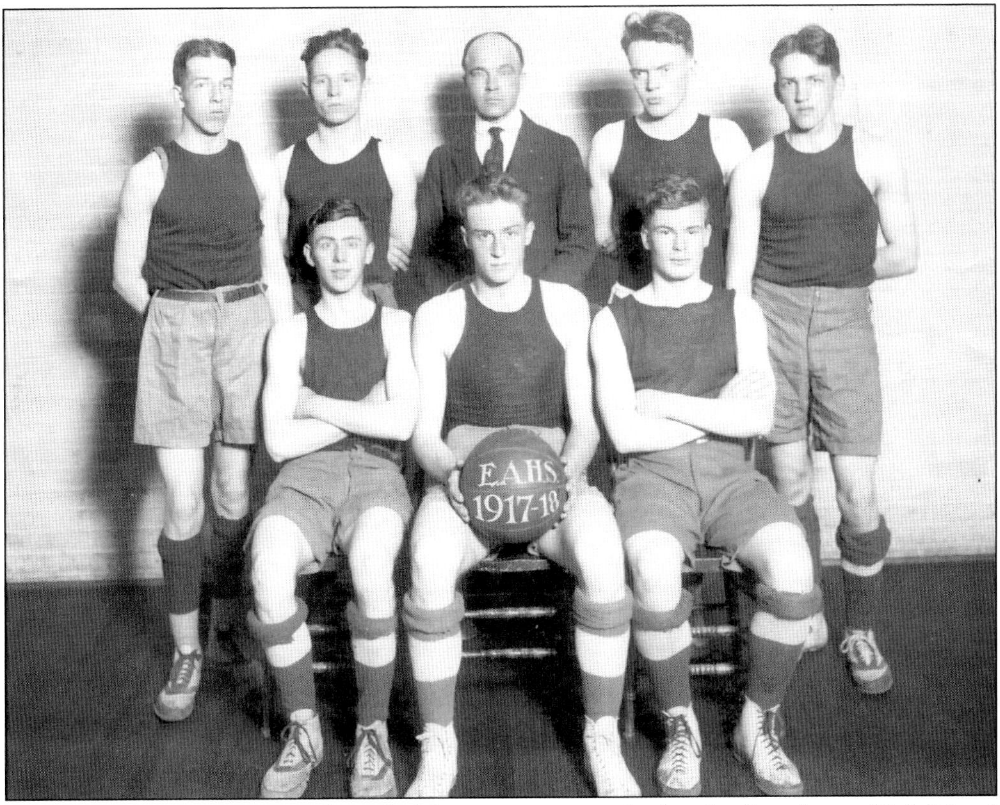

Long before Title IX guaranteed equal athletic opportunities for females, East Aurora High School had basketball teams for both boys and girls. The boys' team in 1917–1918 included Clark H. Daggett, who is second from the left in the second row. The other players are unidentified. The girls' team in 1923–1924 included, from left to right, (sitting) Mildred Schopper, Lenore Daggett, Bertha Smith, Adelaide Smith, and Ella Reuss; (standing) coach Olga Christenson, Grace Lathrop, Ida Long, Dorothy King, Carol Slosson, Myra Thur, and manager Elberta Hubbard. Other area high schools, including neighboring Orchard Park, also had girls' basketball teams, and reports of their games were prominently displayed in the local newspaper.

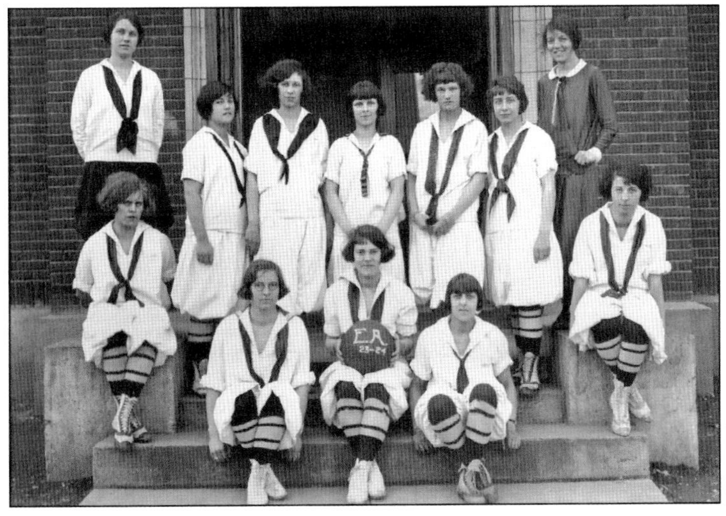

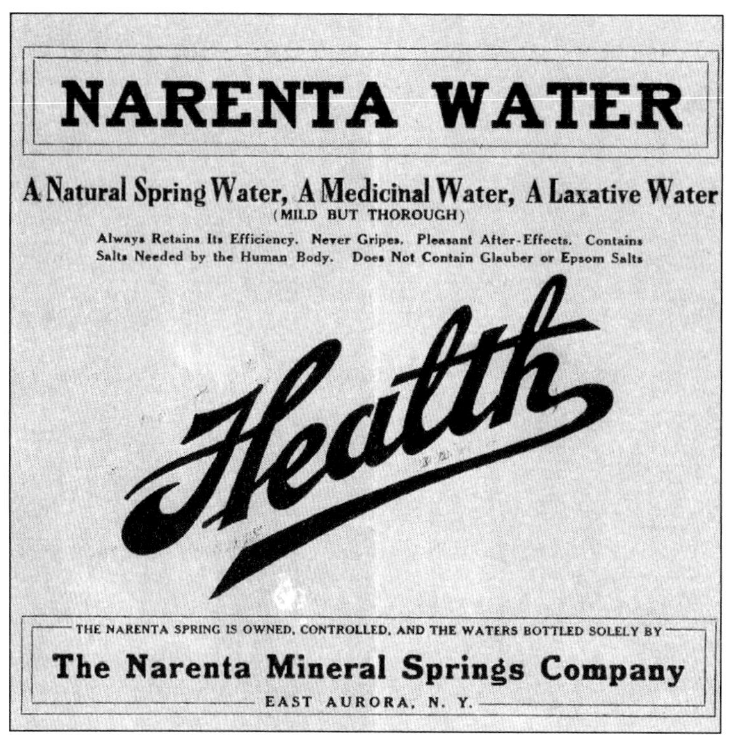

Henry Jewett, who constructed the covered, mile-long racetrack off Grover Road, later claimed that water from wells drilled on his property had medicinal qualities. He sold the water, advertising it in this booklet as "mild but thorough." Many illnesses "that had resisted treatment of various kinds received great benefit from only a brief trial of this mineral water," the advertisement claimed. Jewett also planned a resort hotel, the Narenta Springs, but it never materialized.

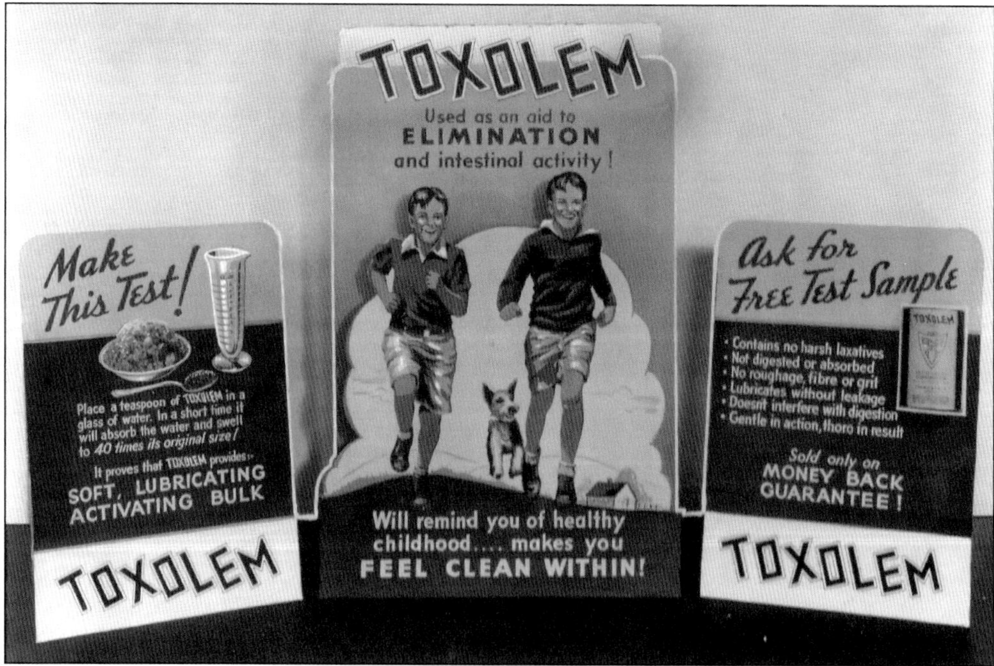

East Aurora's focus on health remedies continued into the 1940s, when Toxolem was marketed from a facility on the Roycroft Campus to help with digestive problems. A broad marketing campaign, including advertisements in national health magazines, was launched.

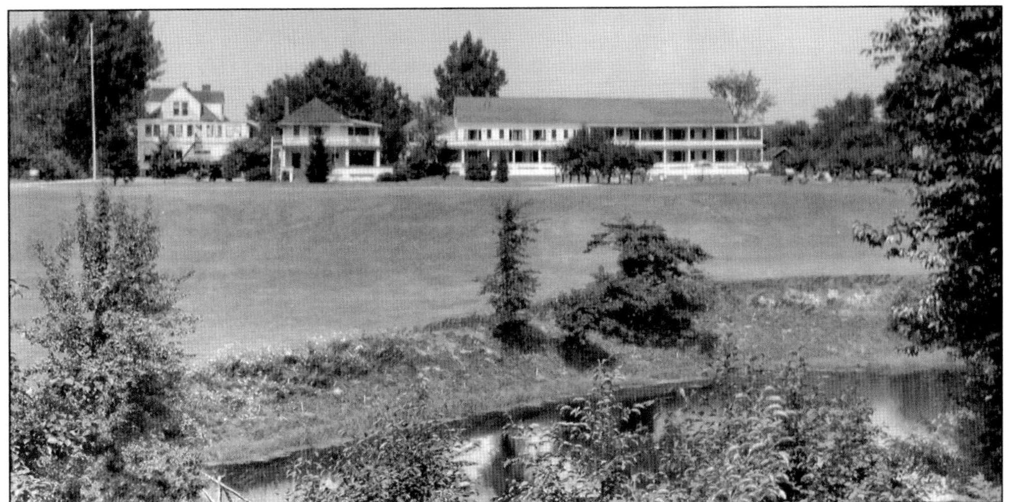

Following his return from World War I, Dr. John J. Hanavan developed the idea of starting a health facility on the banks of the creek along Cazenovia Street. The Sun-Diet Sanitorium attracted patients from all over the United States for treatments ranging from arthritis to skin conditions. After the 80-room facility, which included an outdoor swimming pool, closed in the early 1940s, the buildings were converted into an apartment complex.

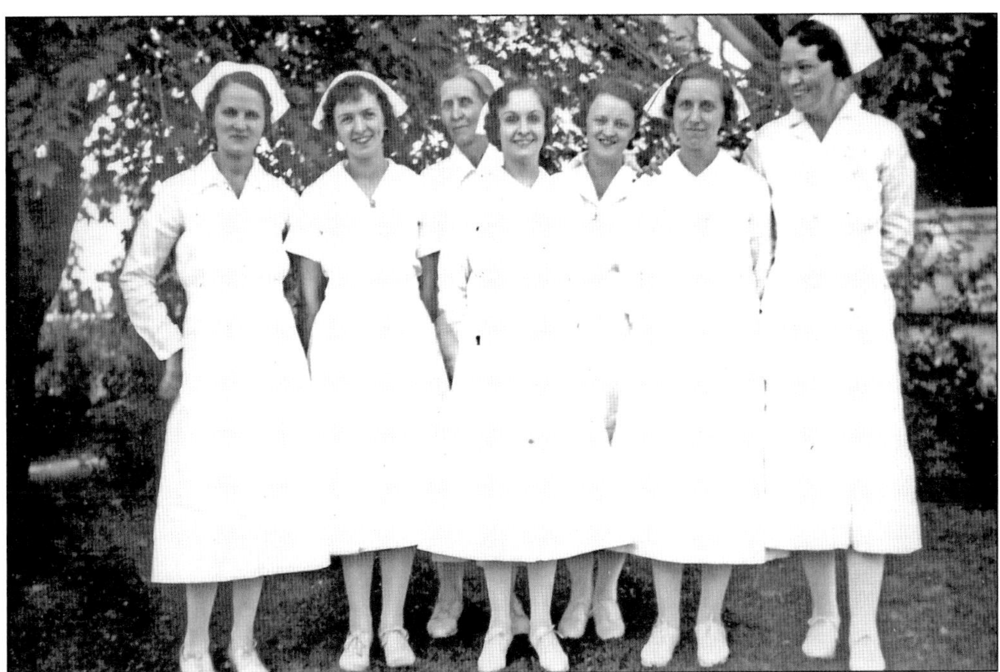

Ahead of its time, the Sun-Diet Sanatorium raised eyebrows among some traditional doctors, who frowned upon the new form of medical treatments for ailments. Shown in this 1932 photograph are members of the nursing staff, from left to right, Mary Scanlon, Mary Judge, Mrs. Stiker, Agnes Diamond, Aldea West, Pearl Besecker, and Ruth Baker.

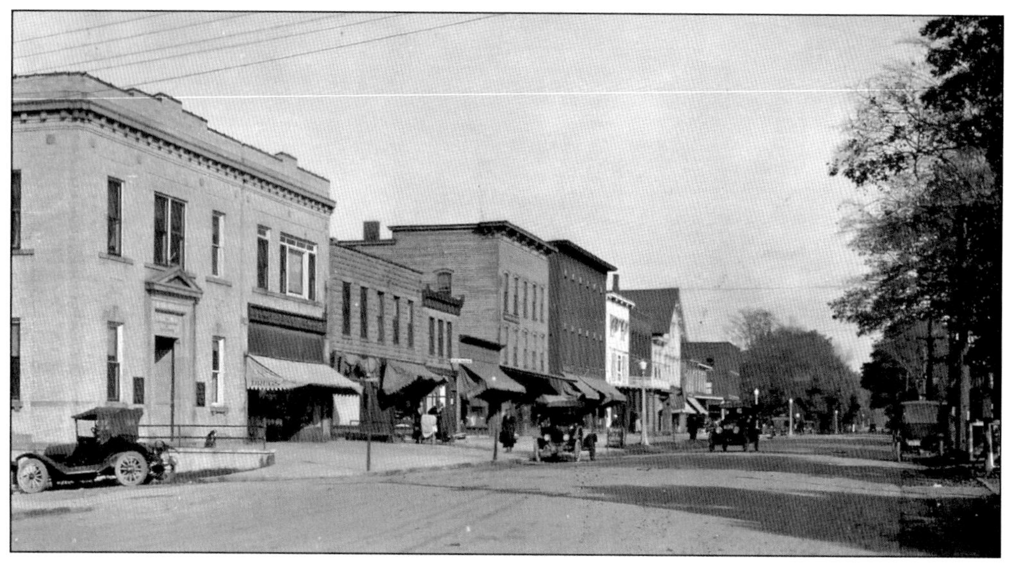

These two photographs offer a unique glimpse into the changes along Main Street, between Church and Pine Streets, in just a few years around the 1910s and 1920s. New signs were erected outside the Erie County Trust Company bank and E.M. Cummings's Rexall drugstore. The Erie County Trust Company took over the building at the corner of Church Street in 1916 after the reorganization of the short-lived First National Bank of East Aurora. A closer look above the center window in the photograph below shows that a burglar alarm was also added above the bank entrance. The increase in the popularity and affordability of cars is evident from the change in parking style, from parallel to angled, which provided more spaces. (Below, courtesy of the *East Aurora Advertiser.*)

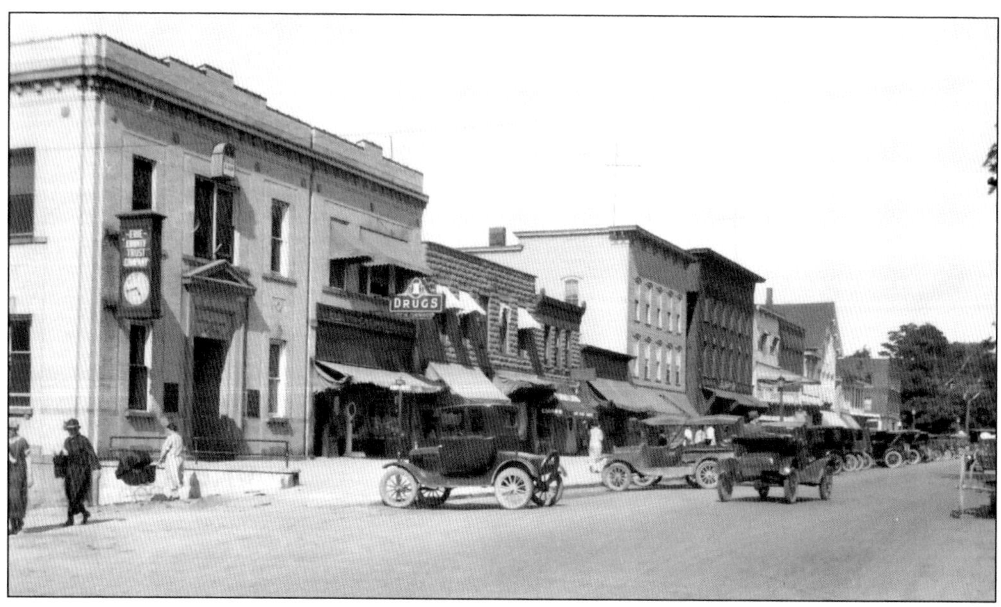

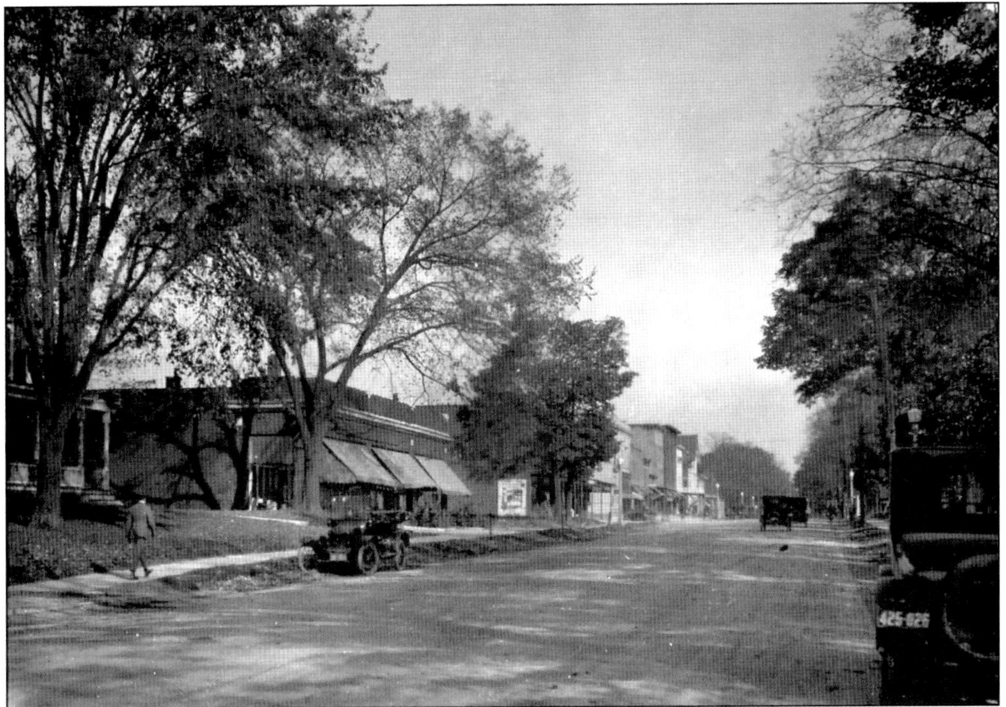

The Seaman, Hood & Morey Building, constructed in 1917, is on the left side of this view looking east on Main Street shortly after World War I. Dutch elm disease later wiped out many of the beautiful trees along Main Street and other roads in the village. The house to the left was later removed for an expansion to the Griggs & Ball Building.

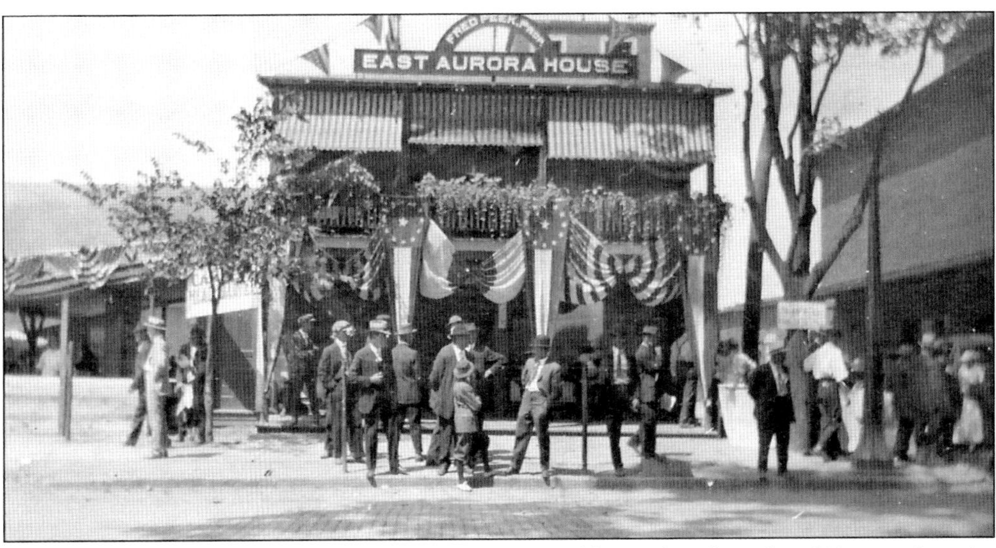

The East Aurora House, a hotel and restaurant operated by Fred Peek in the 1910s, stood on the northwest corner of Main and Riley Streets. It is shown in this view during the summer of 1916, just before a parade passed by. The old Griggs & Ball Building, which burned and was replaced by a new structure in 1917, can be seen on the right.

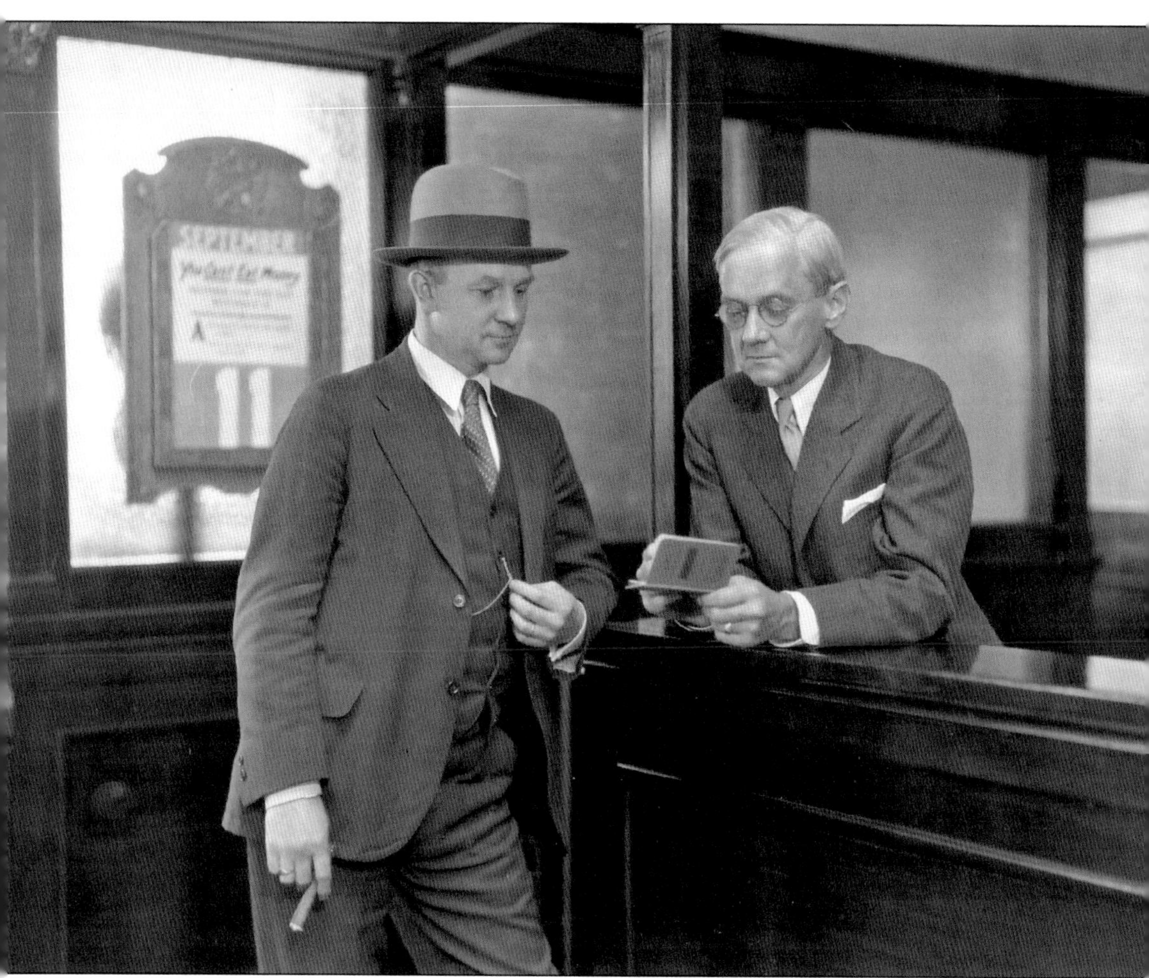

Myron L. Harlow, left, and Richard Persons look over a bank book in an obviously posed photograph in the Bank of East Aurora Building, located east of the Masonic Temple, sometime between 1925 and 1930. Persons was the president of the bank for many years and also served as town supervisor, chairman of the Erie County Board of Supervisors, town historian, Erie County comptroller, and chairman of the Erie County Parks Commission. His grandfather Henry Z. Persons, and father, Henry H. Persons, founded the Bank of East Aurora, the village's first financial institution, in 1882. The bank previously was located in the brick building at 706 Main Street from 1890 until the 1920s. It merged with the Marine Trust Company in the 1930s.

Six

Aurora and the Great Depression 1930–1940

While most of the country was suffering from the Great Depression, Aurora was actually experiencing commercial growth. Two of the town's most well-known businesses, Fisher-Price Toys and Vidler's 5&10, were founded less than a year after the stock market crash.

Robert S. Vidler opened The Fair on Main Street in June 1930. His sons and grandchildren still operate the nostalgic five-and-dime store in the same location.

The 1930s also saw the birth of the Boys Club (which later changed its mission to include girls) and Aurora Players, one of the nation's oldest community theater groups.

The Great Depression did take its toll on one local enterprise, however. The Roycroft, a bastion of original craftsmanship, went bankrupt in large part due to the tough economic climate and the popularity of mass production. The buildings were sold off to various new owners. Following the successful quest to have the Roycroft Campus named a National Historic Landmark in the 1980s, the Roycroft Inn reopened in 1995, following an $8-million restoration.

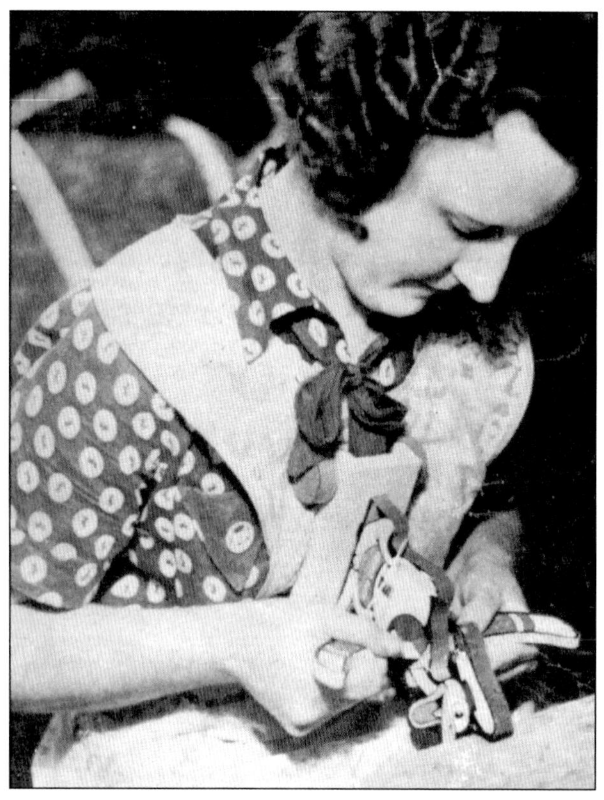

Donald Duck makes his way through the production process during the early years of Fisher-Price Toys. With an initial investment of $100,000, Herman Fisher, Irving Price, and Helen Schelle launched the company in a little house on Church Street in 1930. The company later built a much-larger production facility on Girard Avenue. Now under the umbrella of Mattell, Fisher-Price no longer makes toys in East Aurora but maintains its world headquarters and some product testing operations on Girard Avenue. From 1986 through the mid-2000s, East Aurora celebrated its toy-making heritage with an annual festival, ToyFest, which drew thousands to the community during the last weekend of August. (Courtesy of the *East Aurora Advertiser.*)

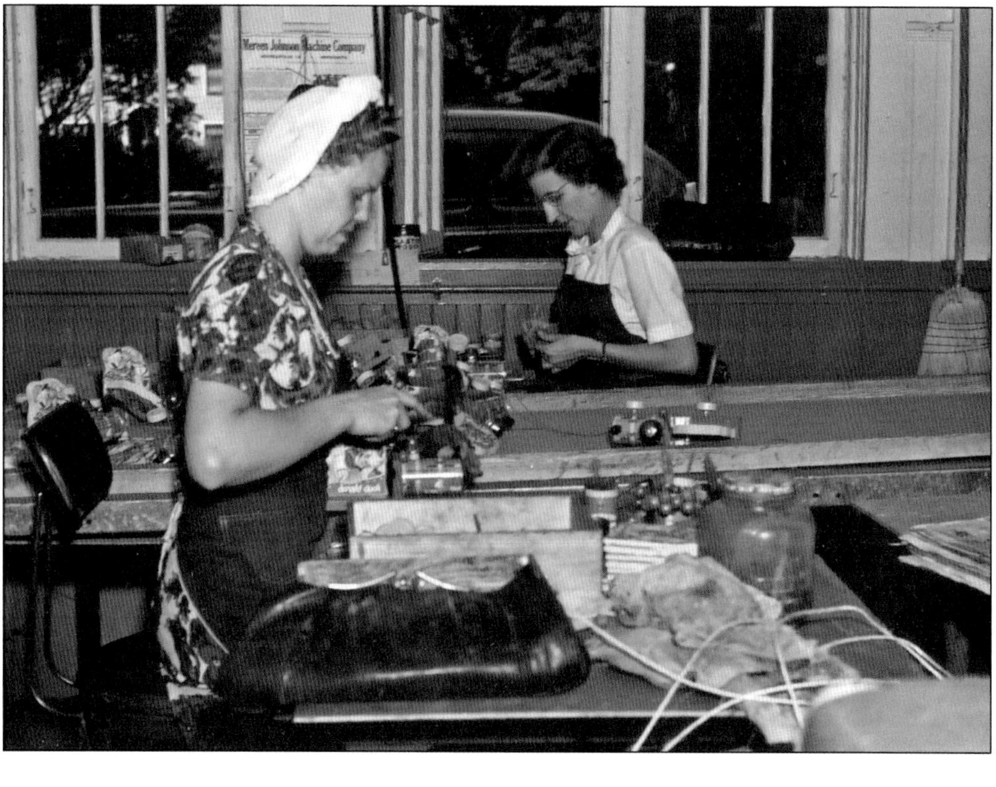

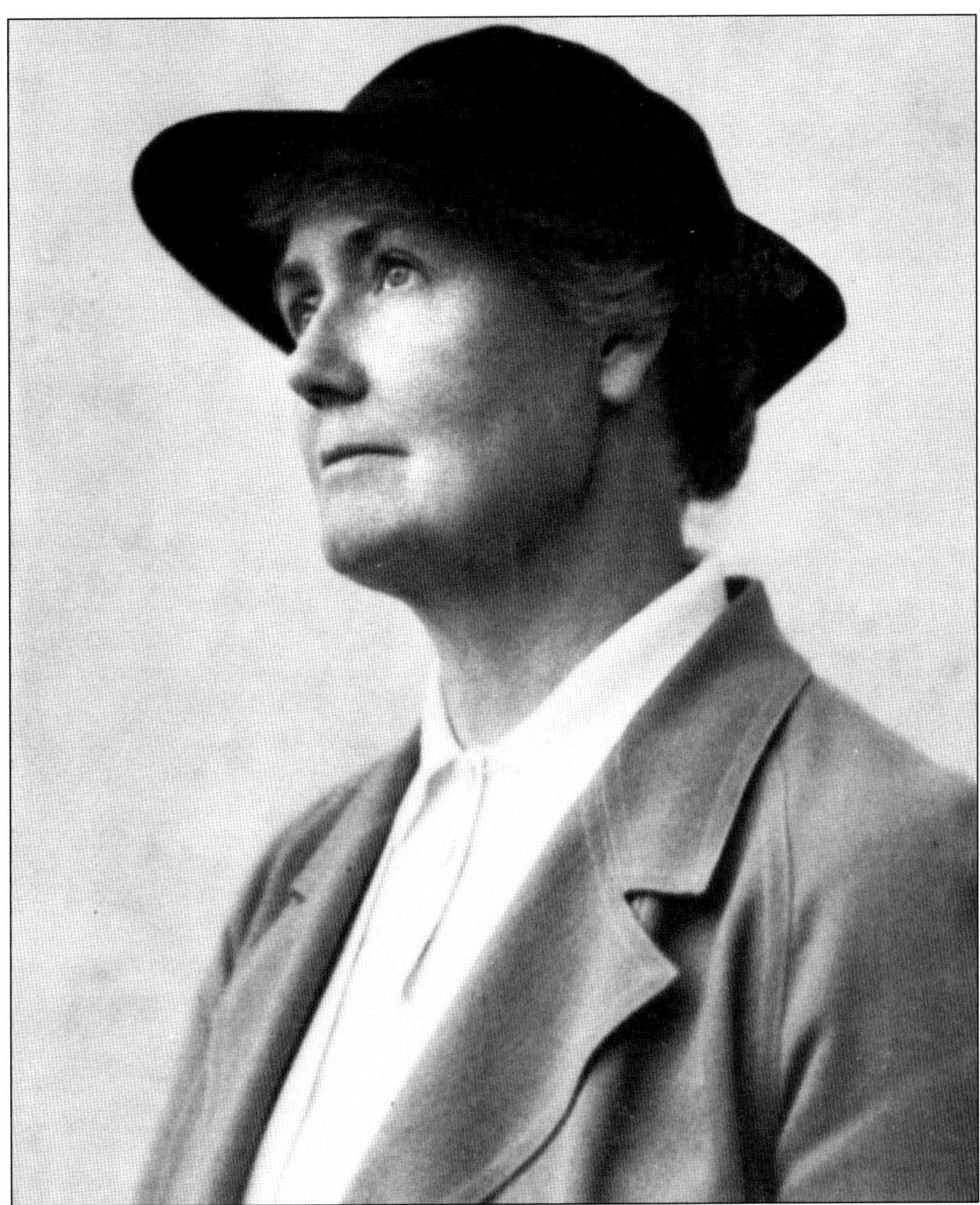

Margaret Evans Price, wife of Fisher-Price founder and one-time East Aurora mayor Irving Price, was a well-known artist in East Aurora. She specialized in illustrating children's books but also illustrated adult novels. She focused on painting oil portraits of children. The New York Historical Society acquired her series of paintings of historic New York City churches. Back home in East Aurora, the Chicago native designed toys for Fisher-Price and was credited with saving Pres. Millard Fillmore's house, which she converted into her studio. Margaret Price moved the president's house from behind the Aurora Theater to its present location on Shearer Avenue in the fall of 1930. When the Aurora Theater opened in 1925, she painted murals for the walls. After an absence of several years, the murals were returned to the lobby following an expansion and remodeling project in the early 2000s. Margaret Price died in 1973. A short time later, the Aurora Historical Society purchased the Millard Fillmore House and opened it as a museum.

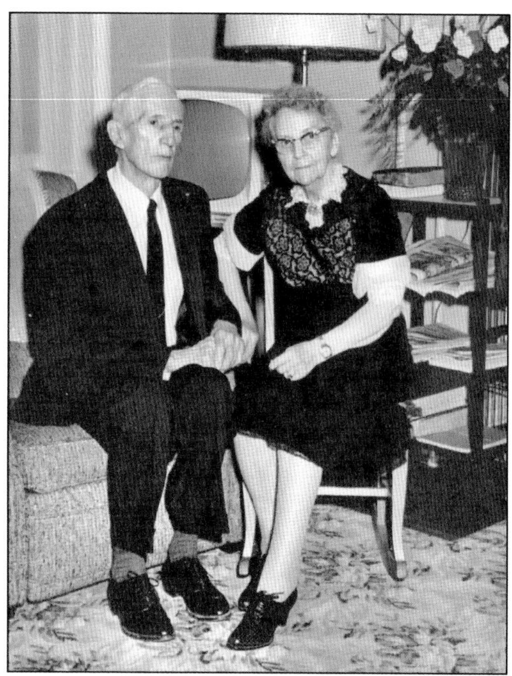

Drs. Stephen J. and Margaret Penfold Gilmore, married in 1914, practiced osteopathy together in Missouri and Iowa before moving to East Aurora with their two children, Frances Ann and Samuel Jordan, in 1930. Dr. Stephen Gilmore was also an accomplished pianist and gardener. The couple belonged to the East Aurora Christian Church and the Aurora Senior Citizens.

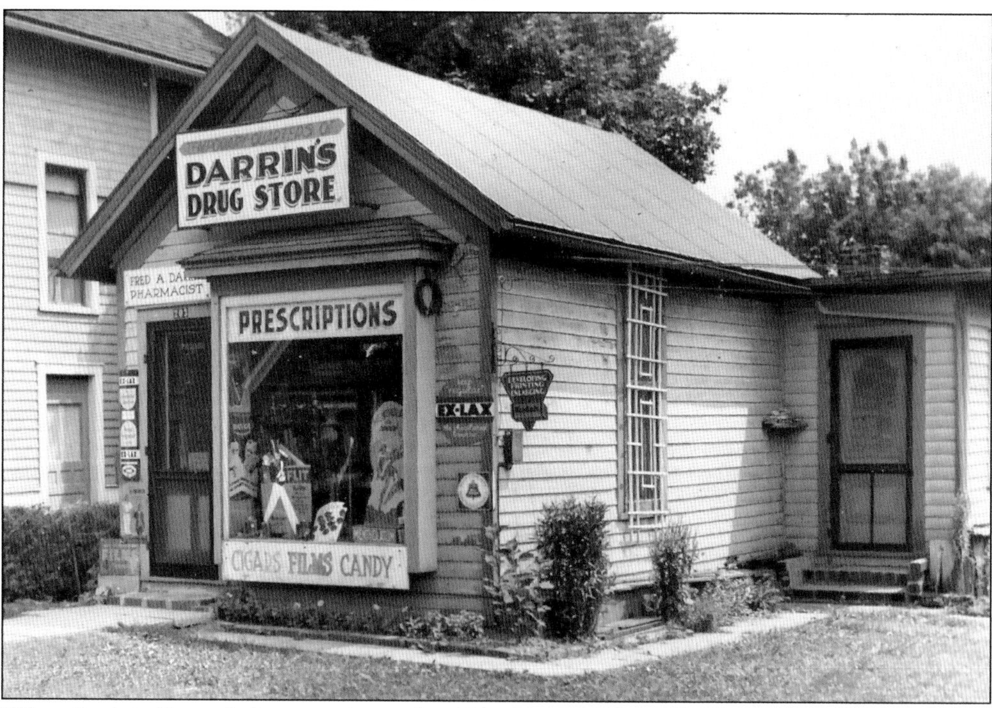

When Fred A. Darrin's drugstore burned in February 1933, he opened temporary quarters in an 18-by-22-foot room across Main Street, between the circle and South Willow Street. Darrin and his wife lived in the back. "A soda fountain and lunch counter is about the only feature lacking in the modern store," a newspaper account noted. The building now houses a locksmith. Before coming to East Aurora, Darrin supplied some of the medicines for William McKinley after the president was shot at the Pan-American Exposition in 1901.

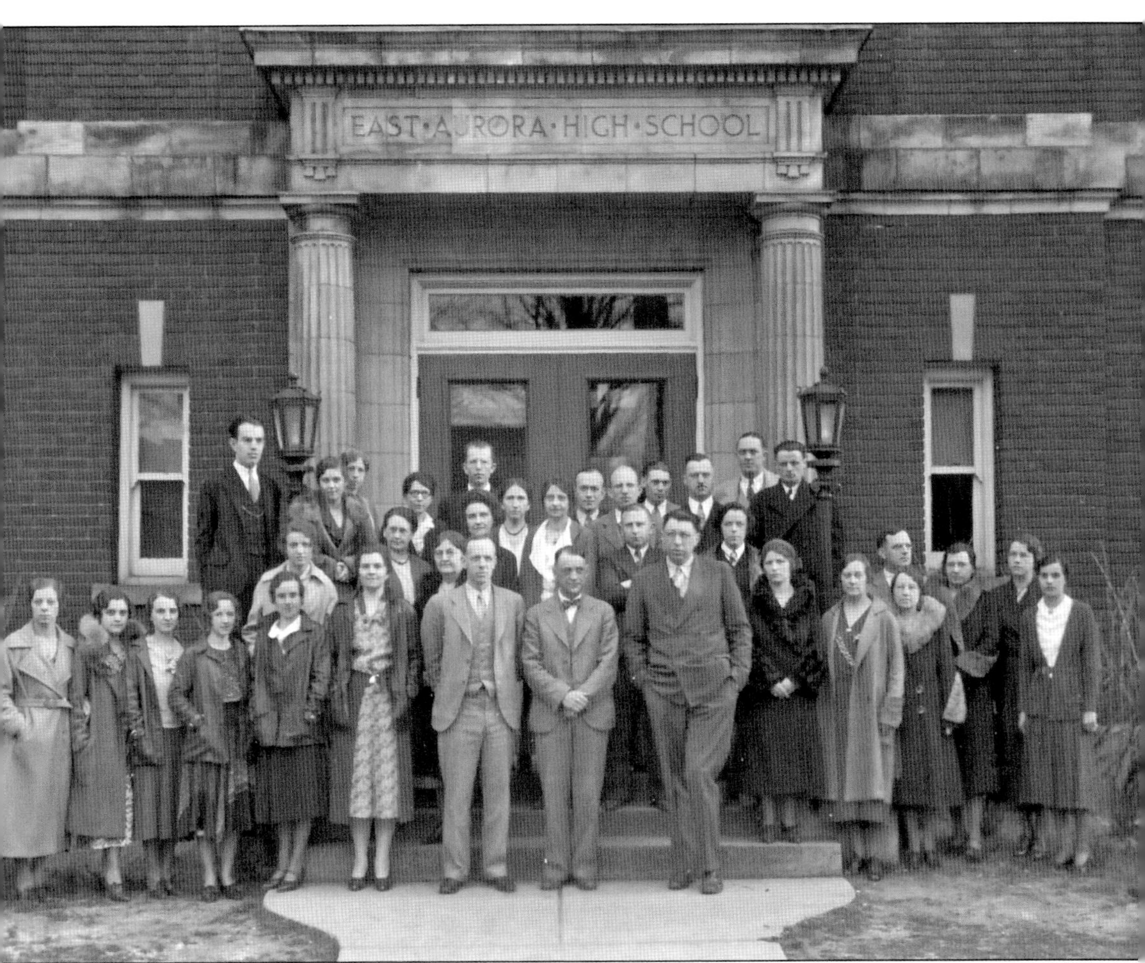

The East Aurora High School faculty poses in front of the main entrance at Main and North Grove Streets around 1932. Those pictured are, from left to right, (first row) M. Windnagle (Cowell), Olive Stonier Whiting, Marie Taylor, C. Bowers, Margaret Aronson, Beth Rundell, Walter Bumgardner, Harry W. Mead, Joseph Barber, Marion Peek, Jessie Schneckenberger, William Kendall, Harriet Hyde, Evangeline Rosen Barber, Olga Stoddard, and Marie West (Keller); (second row) T. Leland Burdick, Ruth Frei (Childs), Elizabeth Smith, Mary Smith, Margaret Davis, F. Lawrence, Katherine Chapin, Genevieve Pratt, Donald Childs, Nellie Krehbiel, Frances Byran, Judson Hulbert, Wilber Getz, George Stoddard, Raymond Lindley, Cecil Fattey, Harriet Stanbro, Earl Wadsworth, and John MacDonald. Though the building has not been used as a high school since 1970, the stone facade above the main door facing Main Street still has the old name, a relic of the bygone era when the high school was located in the center of the village.

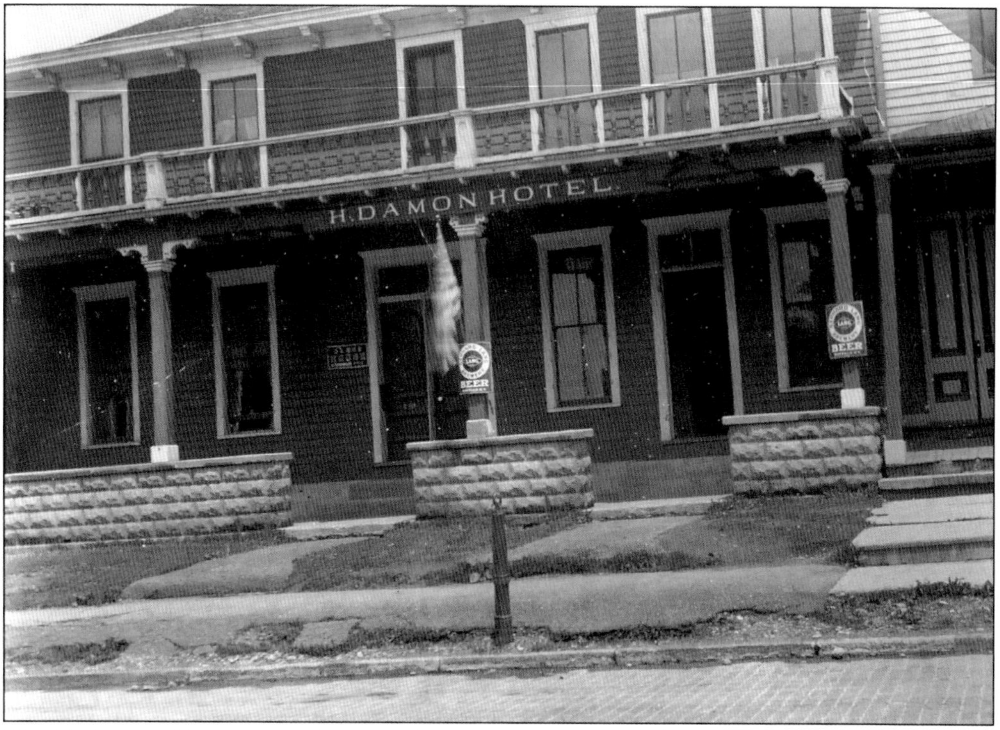

The H. Damon Hotel, known by several previous names, including C.H. Smith's Hotel and the Blakely House, burned to the ground on February 26, 1932, after it had become Lange's Village Inn. The large hotel was located on the north side of Main Street, west of Hamlin Avenue. Arthur Lange extensively remodeled it just a few years earlier. The property became the site of Tops Friendly Market and later Rite Aid pharmacy. The building immediately to the right of the burned structure in the photograph below still stands and now houses a flower shop. In the photograph above, signs on the posts remind passersby that the hotel served beer from the Gerhard Lang Brewery in Buffalo. Also note the hitching post for horses in front of the hotel. The original bricks on Main Street can also be seen.

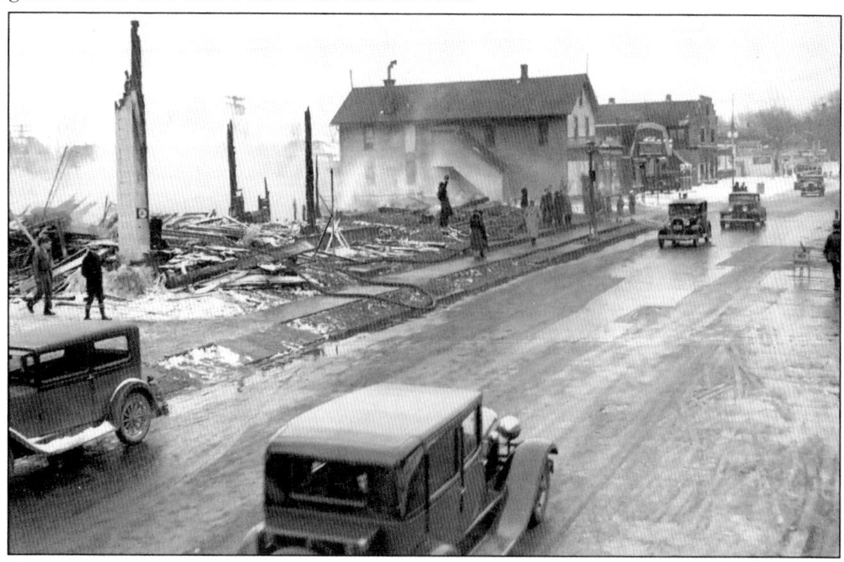

Frederic C. Lewis operated the Oakwood Garage behind a house at the corner of Oakwood Avenue and Sycamore Street in the 1940s. The building has since been converted into an apartment house.

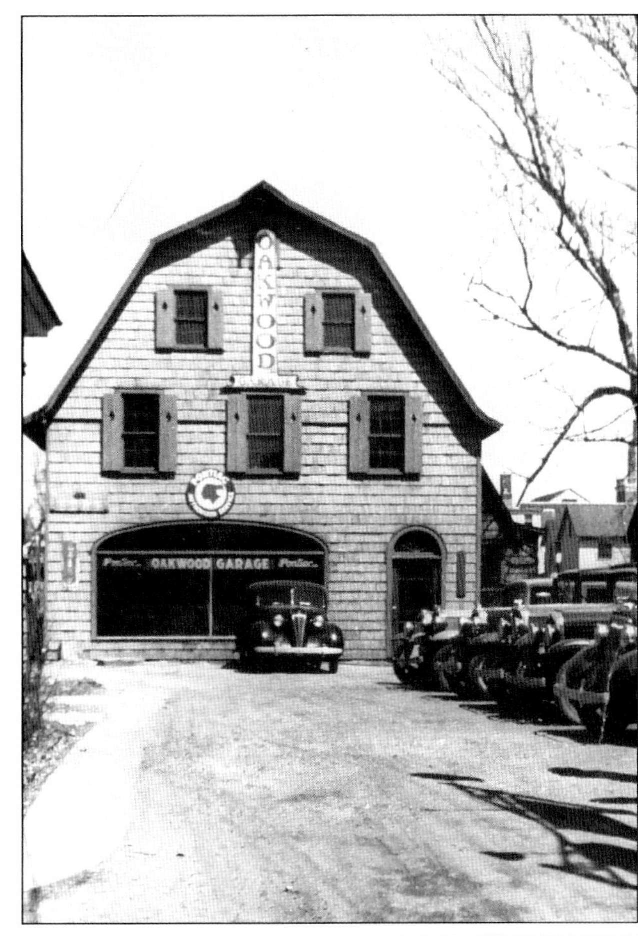

Curbside gasoline service was available in front of the East Aurora Hardware Company on the south side of Main Street, just west of the Aurora Theater. The building, which still stands, housed three offices upstairs at the time of this photograph, and they belonged to chiropractor O.E. Wright, dentist T.G. Martin, and Marie's Beauty Parlor. Note the night deposit box outside Shirton's laundry next door.

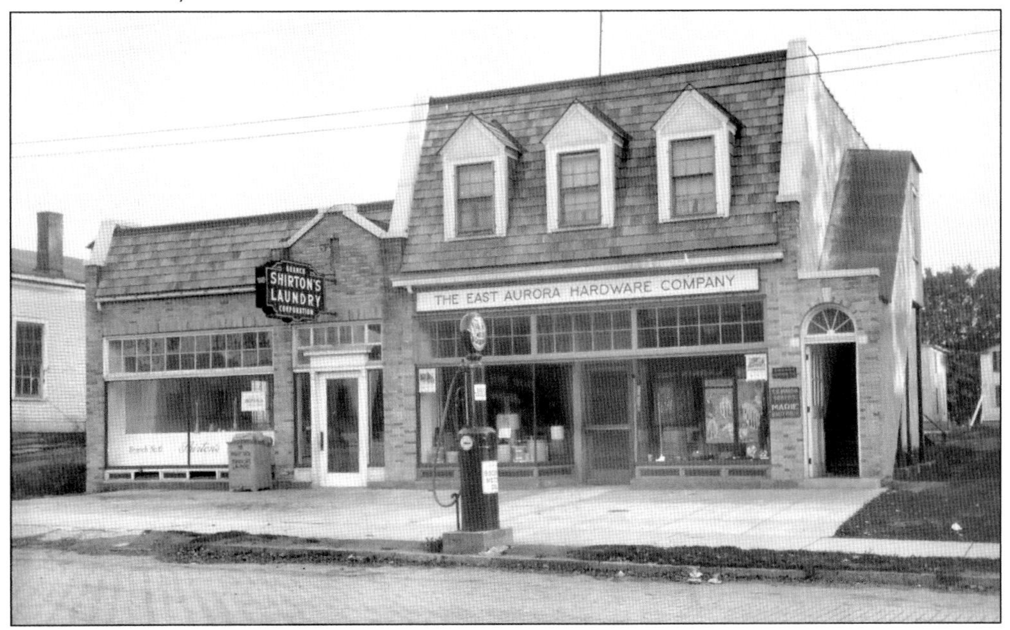

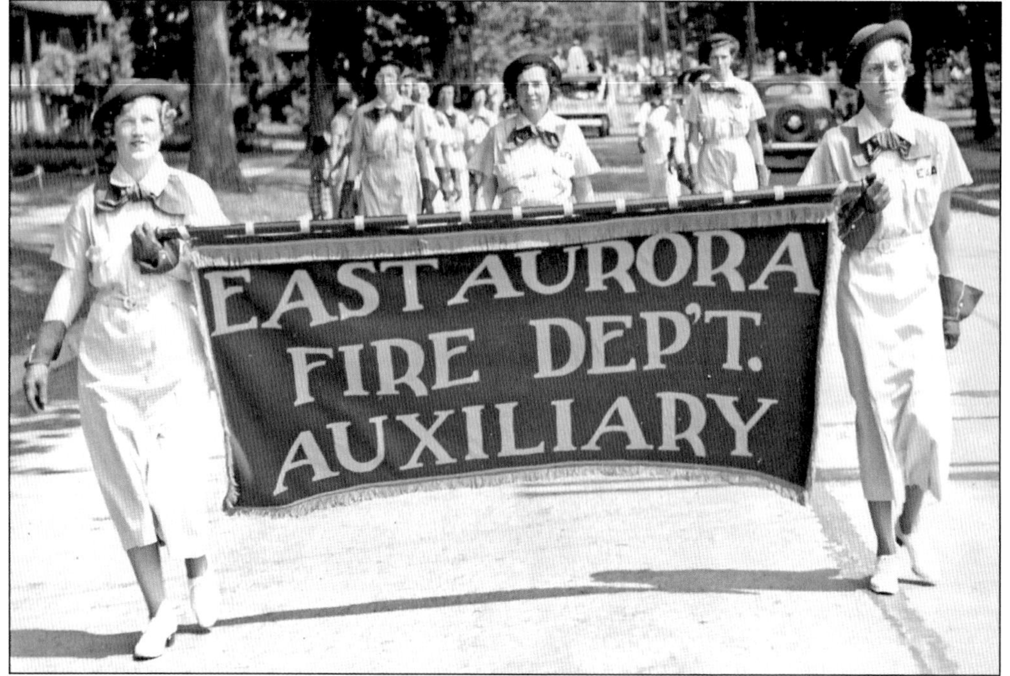

The East Aurora Fire Department Auxiliary marches in a parade in August 1936. Though women had played an auxiliary role in local fire companies for decades, the Women's Auxiliary was not officially formed as a group until February 1935.

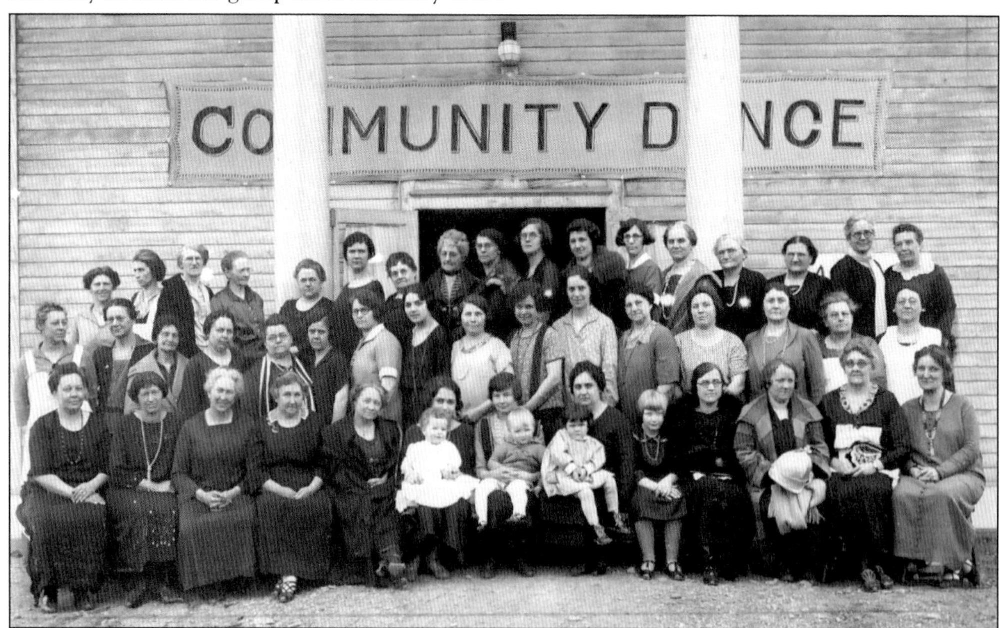

Members of the South Wales Home Bureau, stalwarts of the early community fairs, pose in front of the South Wales Community Hall on Olean Road, which was completed in time for the 1923 fair. The South Wales Community Fair began in 1916. A lack of funds threatened the Community Hall in both 1966 and 1975, but the building remains open. The annual fair continued until the late 1960s. (Courtesy of the *East Aurora Advertiser*.)

Sherman Bunnell, pictured about 1935, owned and operated Bunnell's Dining Car Restaurant on Main Street. The business, located on the southeastern corner of Main and Elm Streets, was later known as the Village Kitchen, and in 1964, the structure was moved to the parking lot behind the Griggs & Ball Building across the street, where it still operates today.

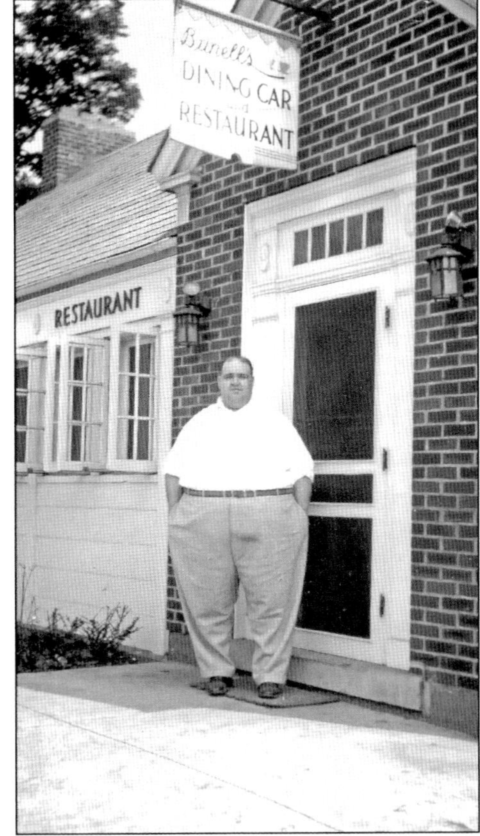

The Spring Brook Fire Company makes its way under the railroad overpass on Main Street near Riley Street during the late 1930s or early 1940s. The railroad tracks were raised above village streets in 1934. Notice how Main Street is decked for the patriotic holiday, most likely the Fourth of July. The Griggs & Ball Building is in the background. (Courtesy of the *East Aurora Advertiser.*)

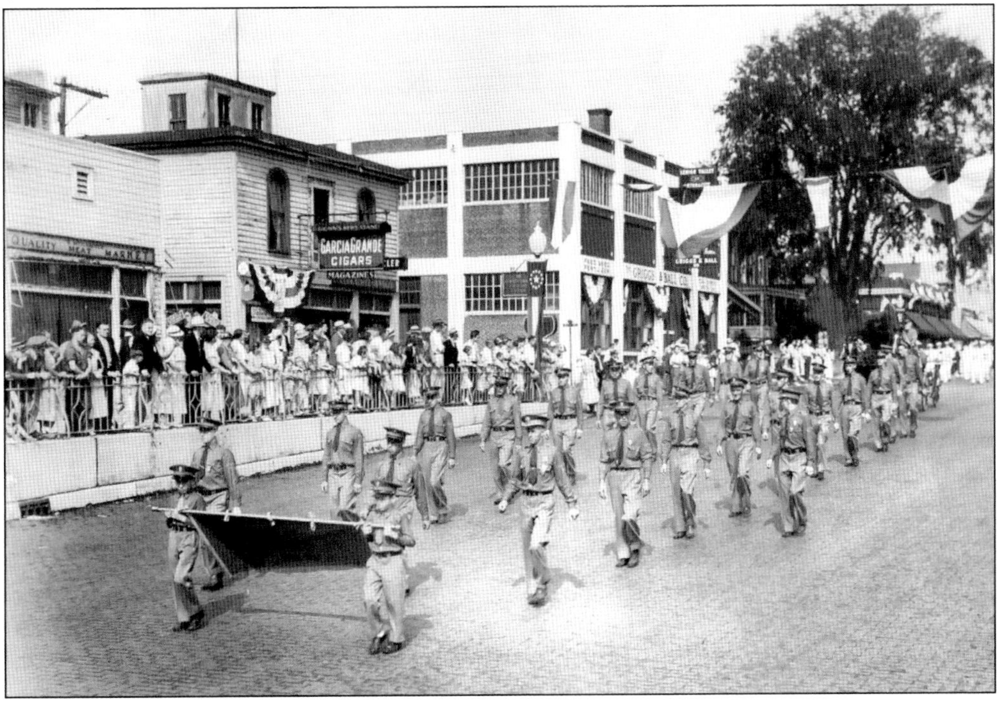

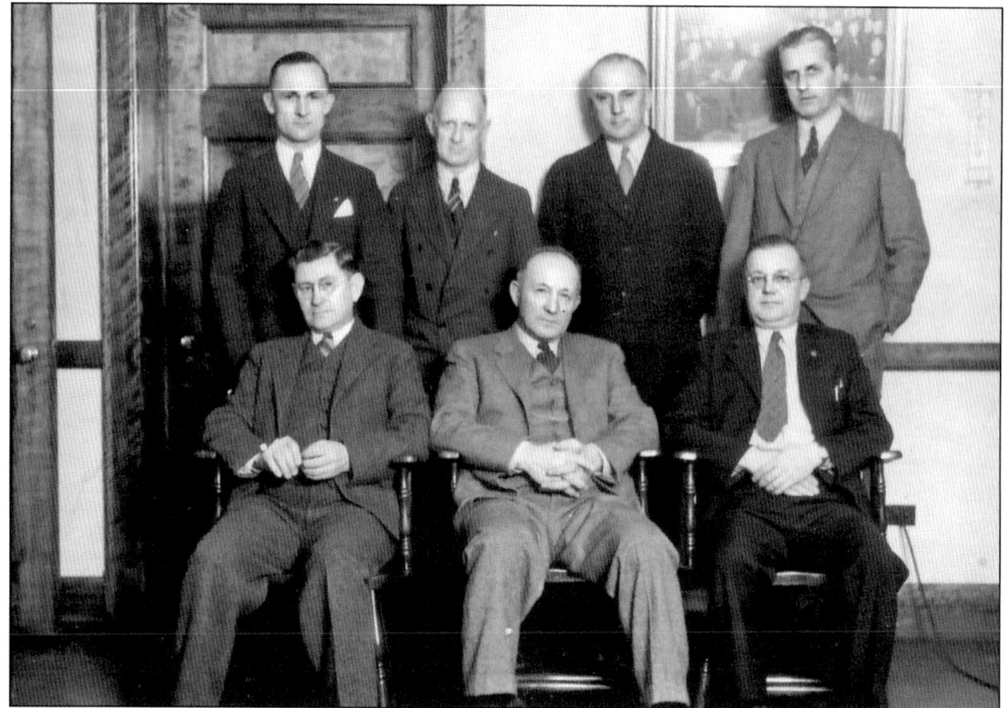

The East Aurora Village Board in 1937 included, from left to right, (first row) Fred Marshall, Mayor Al Frantz, and Louie Fuchs; (second row) Fred Morgan, Bill Blake, Bill Lydle, and Paul V. Ingalls. Though women have since been elected to the Village Board, as of 2011 no woman has been elected mayor. The first female Aurora town supervisor, Jolene Jeffe, took office in 2010.

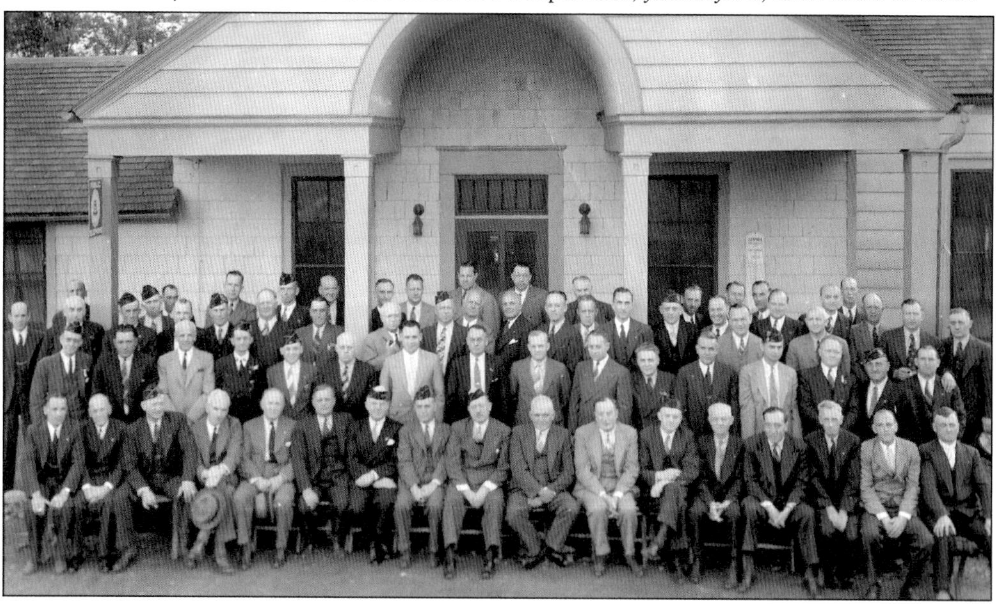

In 1939, the members of the Last Man's Club, World War I veterans associated with American Legion Post 362, gathered for their first Memorial Day eve dinner. A bottle of sherry and box of hardtack were placed in the vault to be given to the last surviving member. On the eve of Veteran's Day in 1978, the six remaining members convened for the last time formally and shared the wine and hardtack.

Seven

A More Modern Aurora 1941–1970

The town of Aurora had grown significantly by the time the United States entered World War II. The second Great War had a much further reach in Aurora than the first. More than 750 answered the call to service. The end of the war was greeted with church bells and car horns on the streets of Aurora, and the postwar years were marked by additional growth, especially as the baby boomers reached school age. The school district opened neighborhood elementary schools, including West Falls, South Side, and Parkdale, in the 1950s and 1960s.

In 1951, inventor William Moog started an aircraft and missile flight control systems company in East Aurora that evolved into a worldwide corporation.

The 1960s brought limited suburbanization to Aurora. While small mom-and-pop stores continued to grace Main Street and farmers continued to operate in more rural areas of the town, the community entered a new commercial age with the opening of the Village Shopping Center plaza on Grey Street in 1960.

The growth of the community was also evidenced in the need for a more modern public library. The former Whaley House at the northwest corner of Main Street and Whaley Avenue, which housed the library for several years, was demolished to make room for the new structure.

A community effort also led to one of the most important community legacies. A fundraising drive led to the construction of the Aurora Community Pool on South Street in 1966. The pool continues to be a popular summer destination for local families.

As the 1960s came to a close, a new era dawned in Aurora. A new, more modern high school was constructed on farmland at Center and Sweet Roads, and the journey to and from Buffalo via car became quicker than ever with the construction of the Route 400 highway at the eastern edge of the town.

While more modern infrastructure made its way into Aurora, the community has gone to great lengths to retain Aurora's unique historic heritage and character.

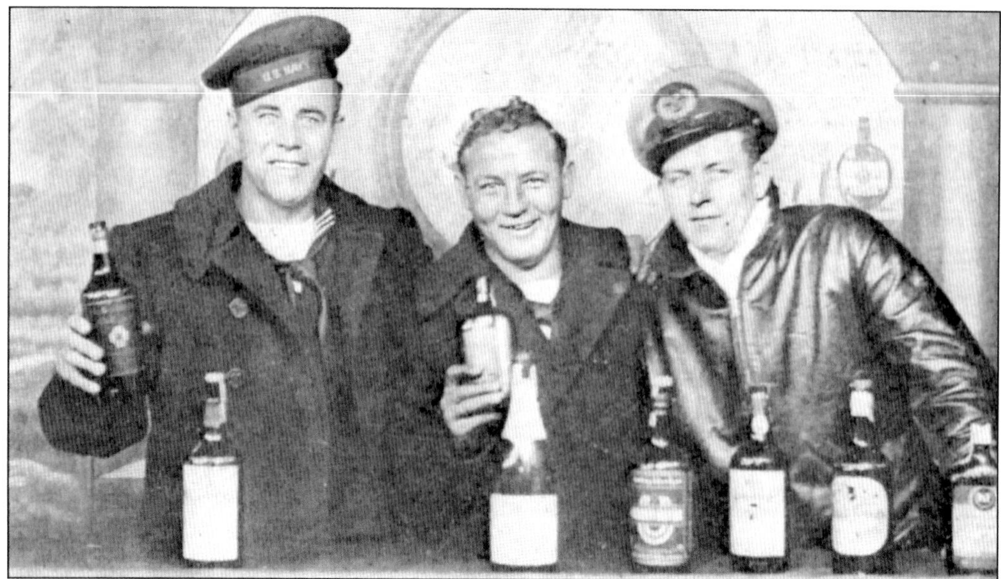

Clarence Shopper of the Navy and Bob Ernst and Lester Doty of the Merchant Marines celebrate in New York's Times Square shortly after returning to the United States in 1944 following their World War II service. Their trip home from France took longer than expected. Their ship developed turban trouble and had to stop for repairs at a shipyard in Belfast, Ireland.

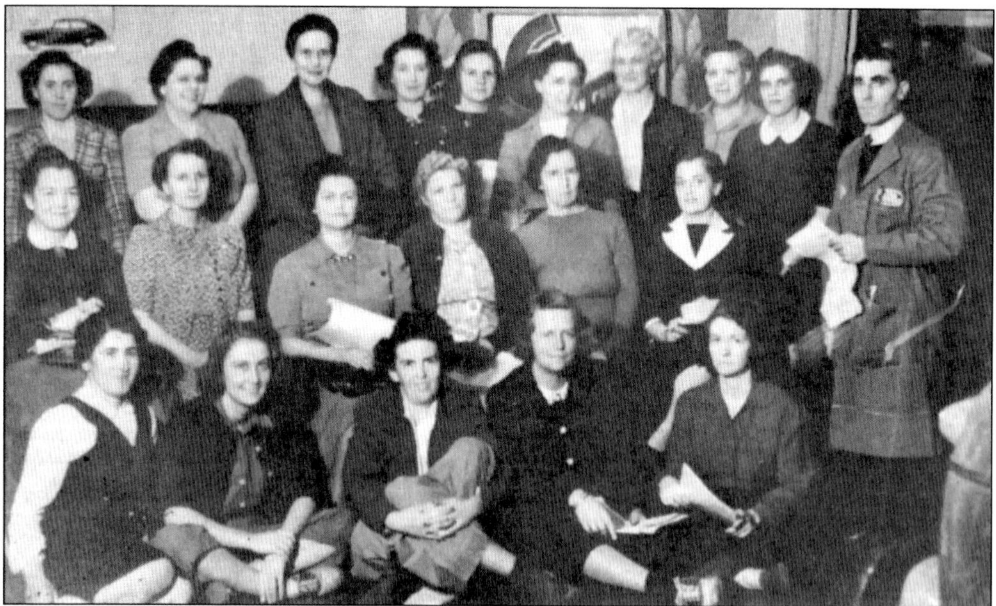

Aurora stepped up at home and abroad during World War II. With many men serving, these women joined the East Aurora branch of the American Red Cross Motor Pool Division and learned how to keep a car running. The 1942 class included, from left to right, (first row) Anne Mack, Mary Lou Merritt, Ruth Roes, Sis Gowans, and Kath Zapf; (second row) Nancy Hubbard, Dorothy Smith, Gert Blake, Anna Lippert, Vera Smith, and Glad Hackwell; (third row, one name is missing from original list) Katherine London, Ann Day, Peg Wheeler, Louise Urban, Florence May Sly, Marj Lanz, Edna Buehl, Helen Koenig, and their teacher Fred Meatyard. (Courtesy of the *East Aurora Advertiser.*)

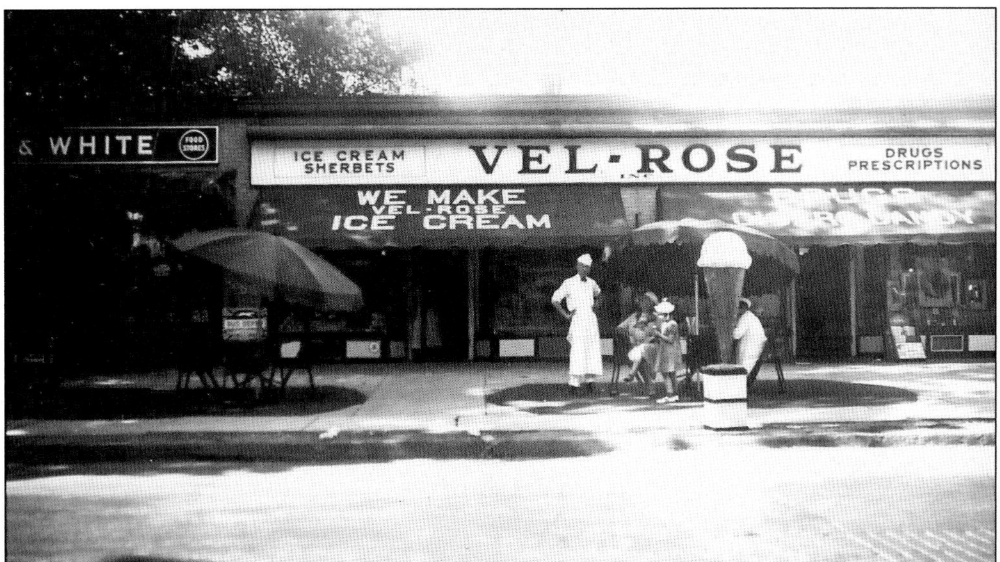

The ice cream and candy counter at Vel-Rose Pharmacy was a popular destination for children and adults alike in the 1940s and 1950s. Above, owner Stanley Rosenberg meets with customers in front of the store at 396 Main Street, which is at the intersection of Walnut Street. In 1948, the shop was moved to 703 Main Street, where these women, below, prepared pies and other desserts in the kitchen a few years later. Note the saddle shoes being worn by the woman on the right. The front part of the building at 703 Main Street was later destroyed by fire.

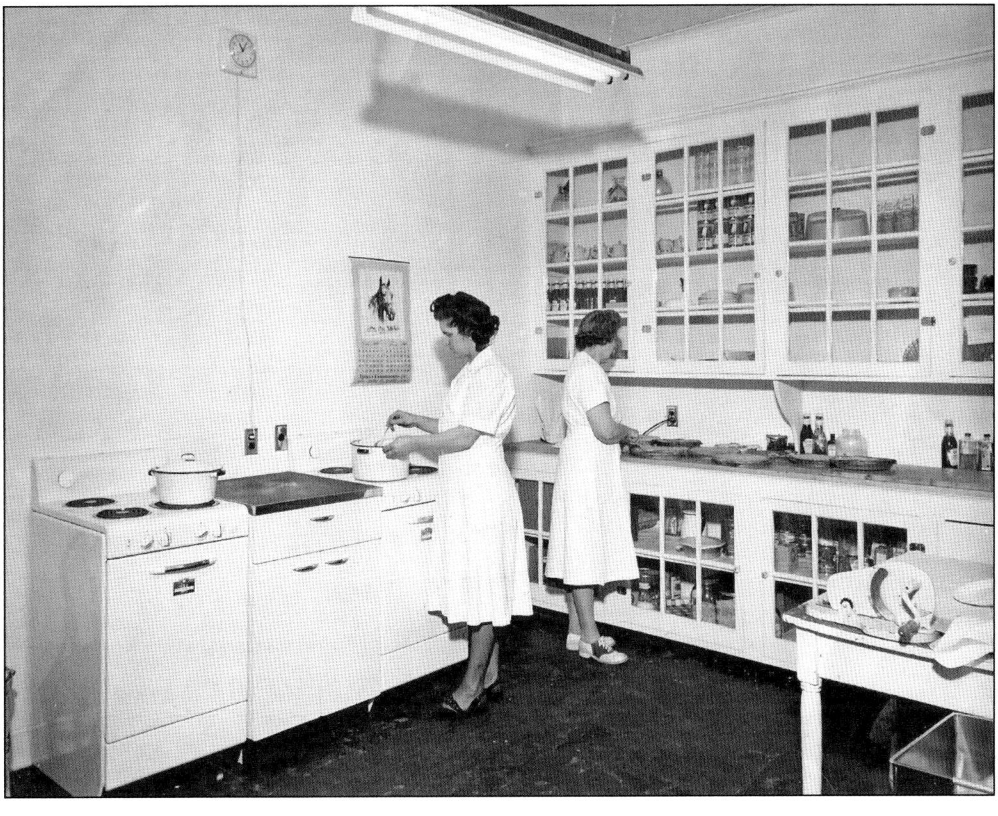

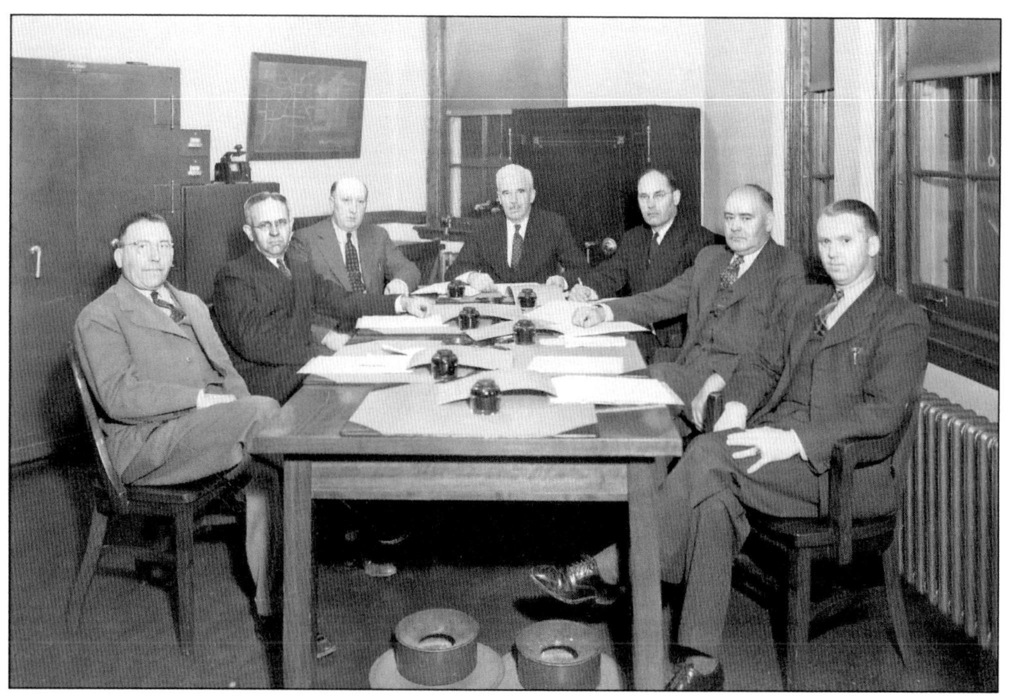

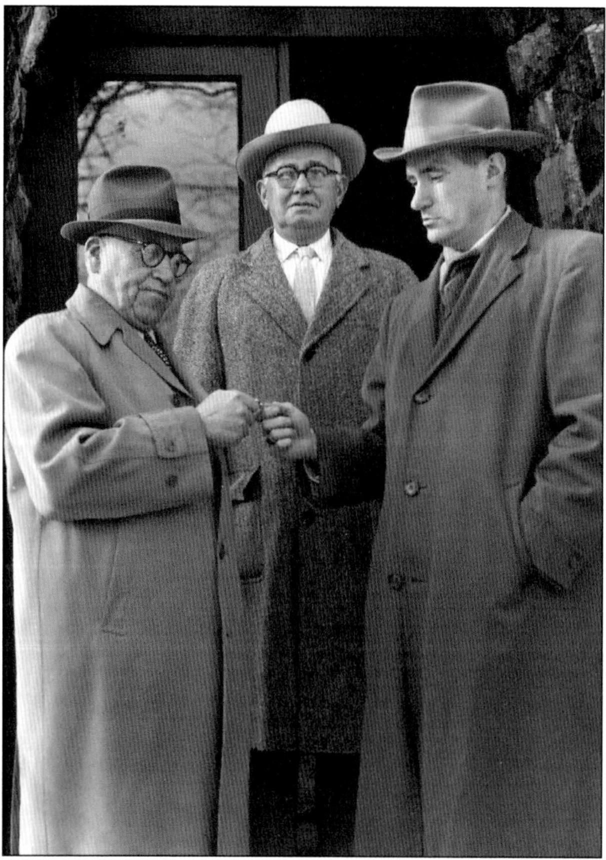

Leslie F. Robinson, center, town supervisor from November 1932 through 1943, presides over a town board meeting. Before there was a town hall, meetings were held in the village hall at Main and Paine Streets. Seated around the table are, from left to right, Dr. Lyle J. Tillou; G. Norman Reading; highway superintendent Howard Lippert; Robinson; Hugh C. Williamson; Reuben Morse; and town clerk Harry R. Hennessey. The town moved into its first town hall in 1958. Shown at left, Tillou, left, who became town supervisor in 1944, accepts the key to the Roycroft Chapel from the Reverend Robert Edmunds, the pastor of the Baptist church, as George Herold, center, looks on. The town purchased the Roycroft Chapel from the Baptist church for $35,000. The Baptists, who had bought the building in the early 1940s after the Roycroft went bankrupt, moved to a new church on Porterville Road.

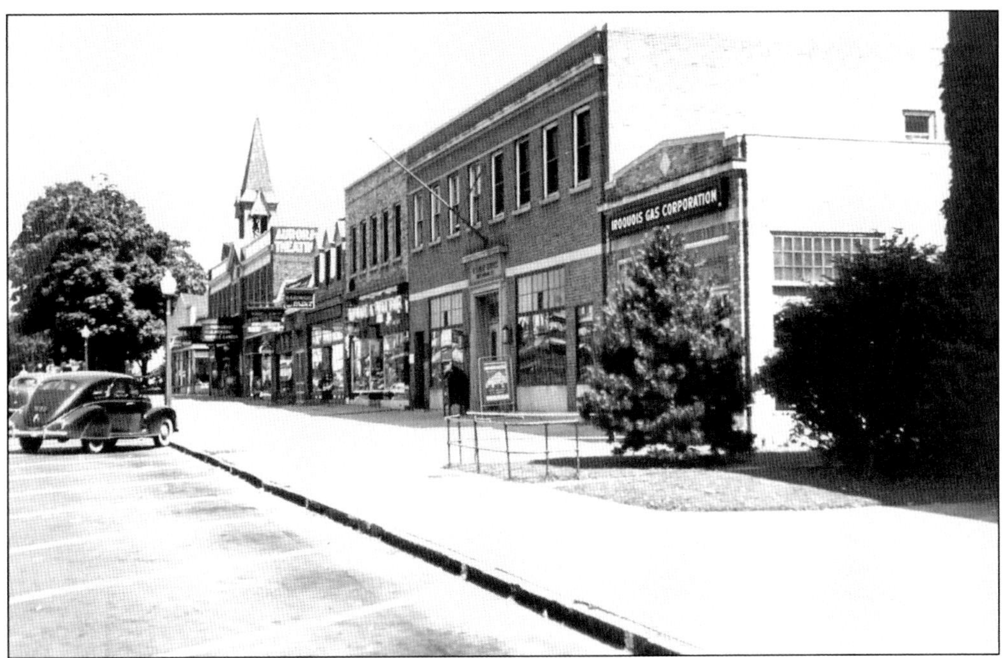

The south side of Main Street looking east toward the Aurora Theater is shown in the early 1940s. The steeple of the First Baptist Church, which was demolished a short time later, is visible in the background. The East Aurora Post Office was located to the left of the Iroquois Gas Corporation. Note that angled parking was still the norm on Main Street.

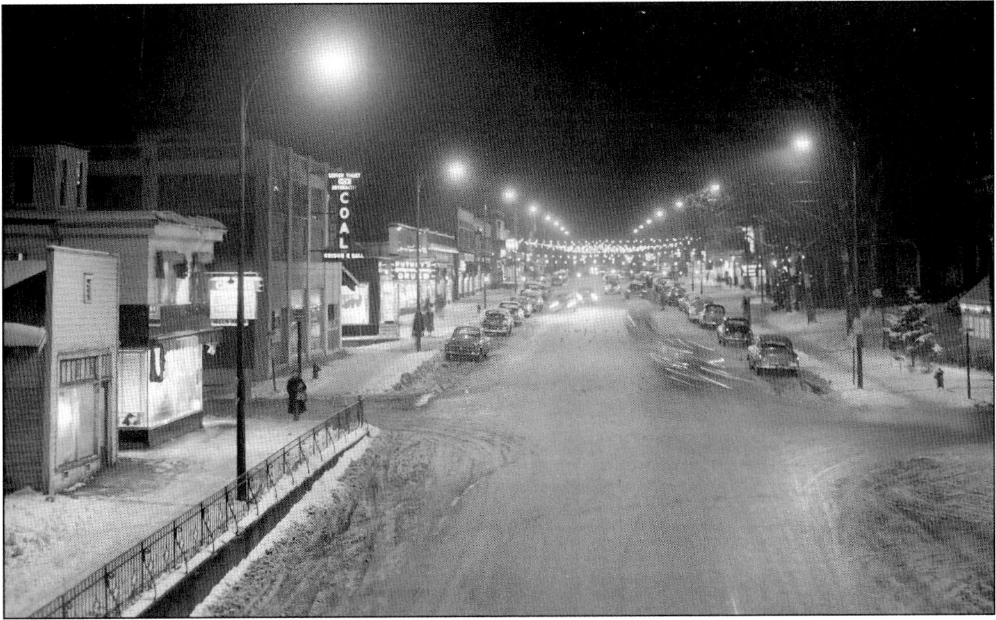

Strings of Christmas lights cross above Main Street in this nighttime view looking east from the railroad overpass sometime during the 1950s. The Village Kitchen diner can be seen at the far right. The sign for Hill's newsstand advertises its ice cream and cigars on the left side of the street. The building was demolished in 1970. The photograph also shows the growing popularity of neon signs. (Courtesy of the *East Aurora Advertiser*.)

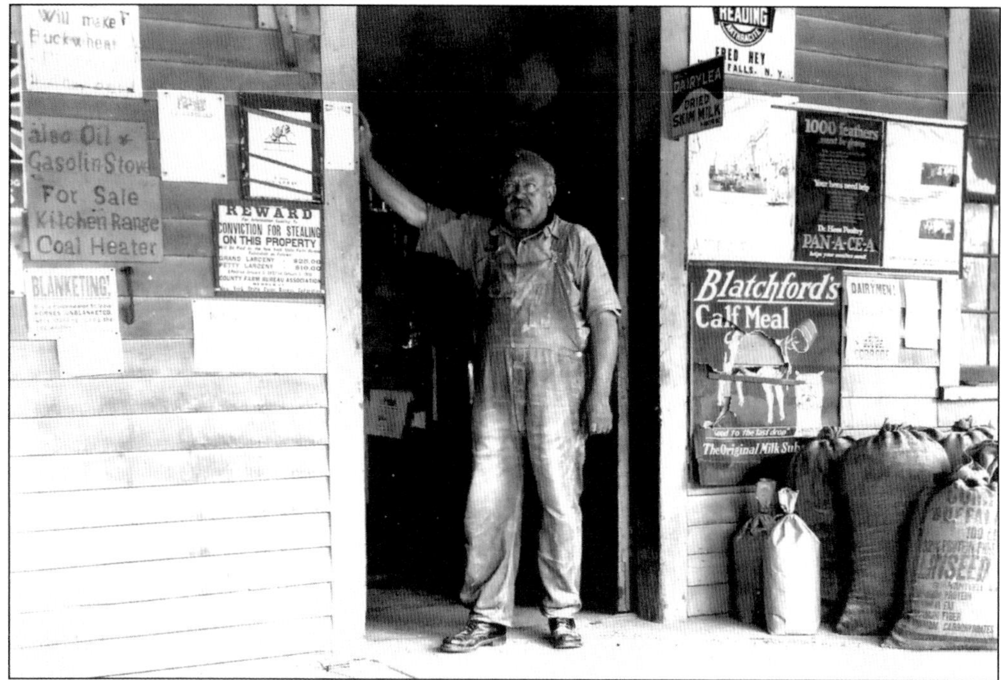

Fred Hey operated a gristmill and store in West Falls for more than 25 years. Note the bags waiting for pickup on the porch. The sign on the left states that buckwheat flour was only available on Fridays, and the sign immediately to the left of the door offers a reward for information leading to the conviction of anyone stealing from the store.

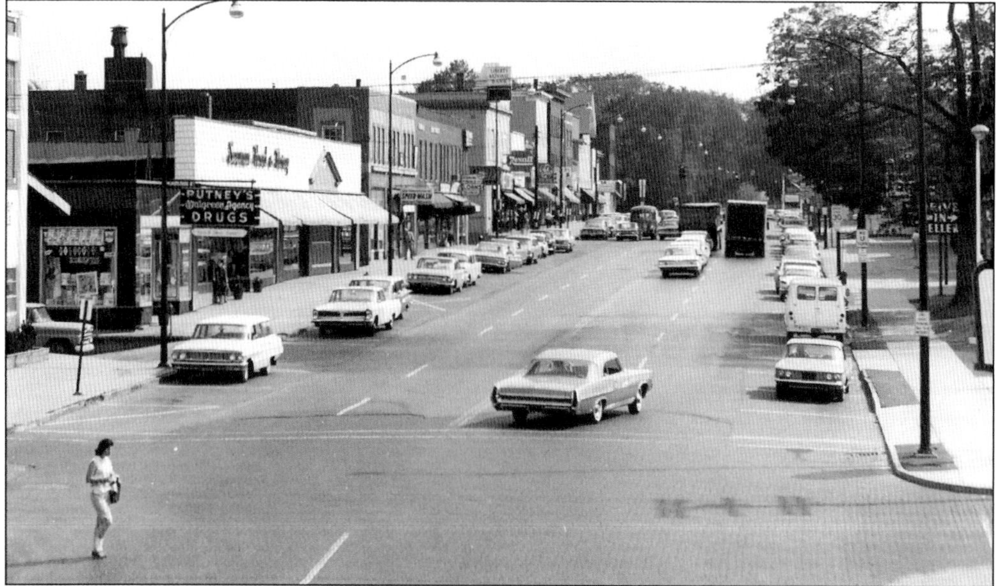

This is a 1960s view of Main Street looking east from the railroad overpass. To allow tall trucks clearance under the overpass, the bricks under the viaduct were left exposed until they were removed as part of the state's reconstruction of Main Street in 2008 and 2009. Seaman, Hood & Morey is shown in the same location it was built in 1917. A Buffalo firm bought the store in 1952. (Courtesy of the *East Aurora Advertiser*.)

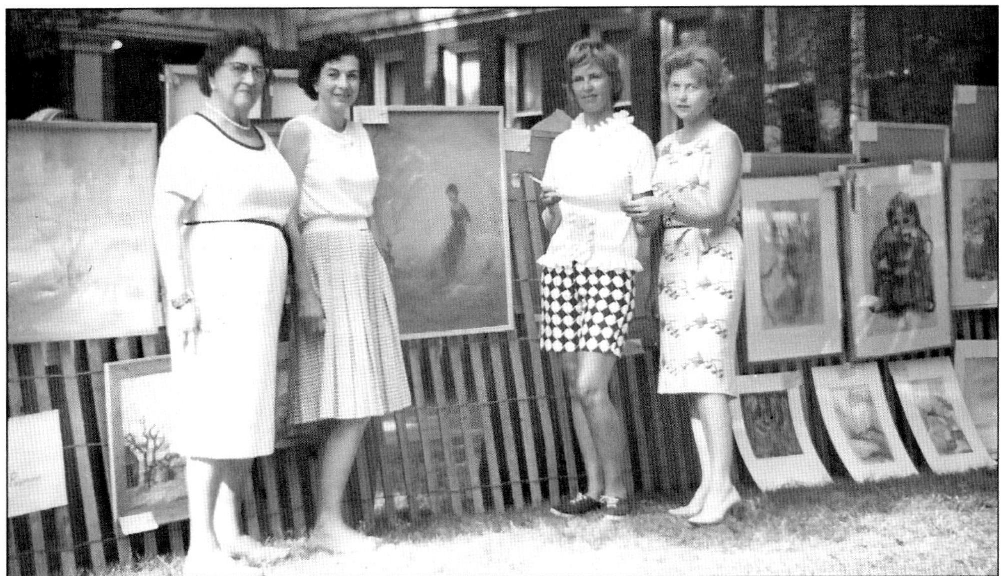

The East Aurora Art Society began holding its annual art show in 1953, and it has become a popular annual tradition the last weekend of June. Shown at the 11th annual outdoor show in 1963 are, from left to right, show chairwoman Laura Hudson; Nen Rexford, winner of the Larwood Award for most popular piece of artwork; and Larwood Award chairwomen Louise Orzell and Peg Mooney. (Courtesy of the *East Aurora Advertiser.*)

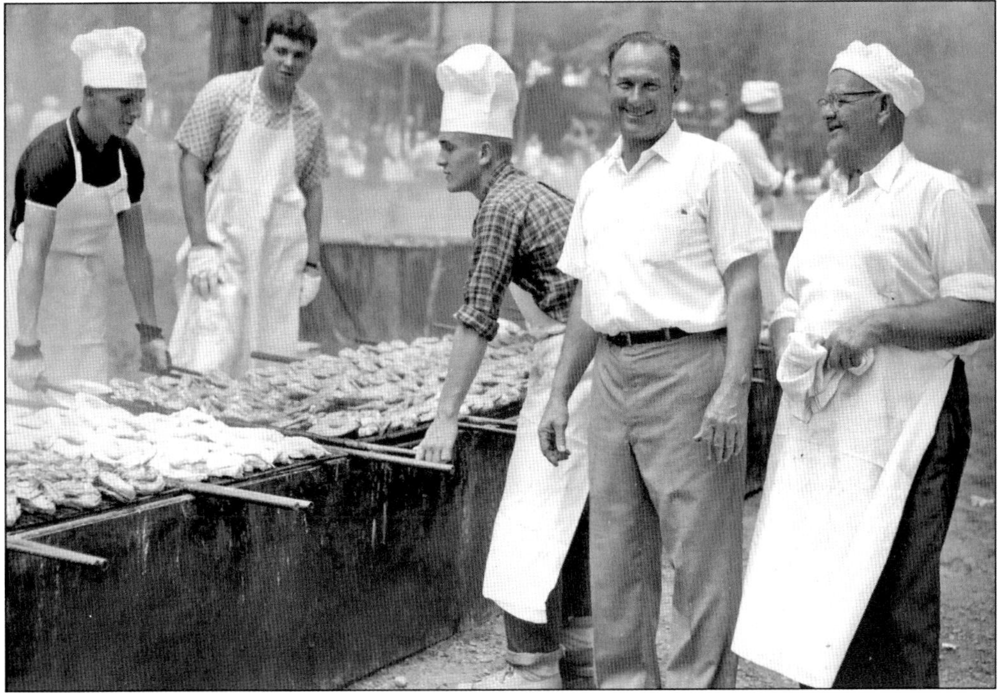

Another popular annual tradition is the Kiwanis Club's chicken barbecue in Hamlin Park. At the seventh annual barbecue in June 1963, more than 4,200 dinners were served. Shown cooking the chicken in the park are, from left to right, Joseph Steinwachs, Jack Persons, Tom Maxwell, Durward Keller, and Dr. Francis Reed. (Courtesy of the *East Aurora Advertiser.*)

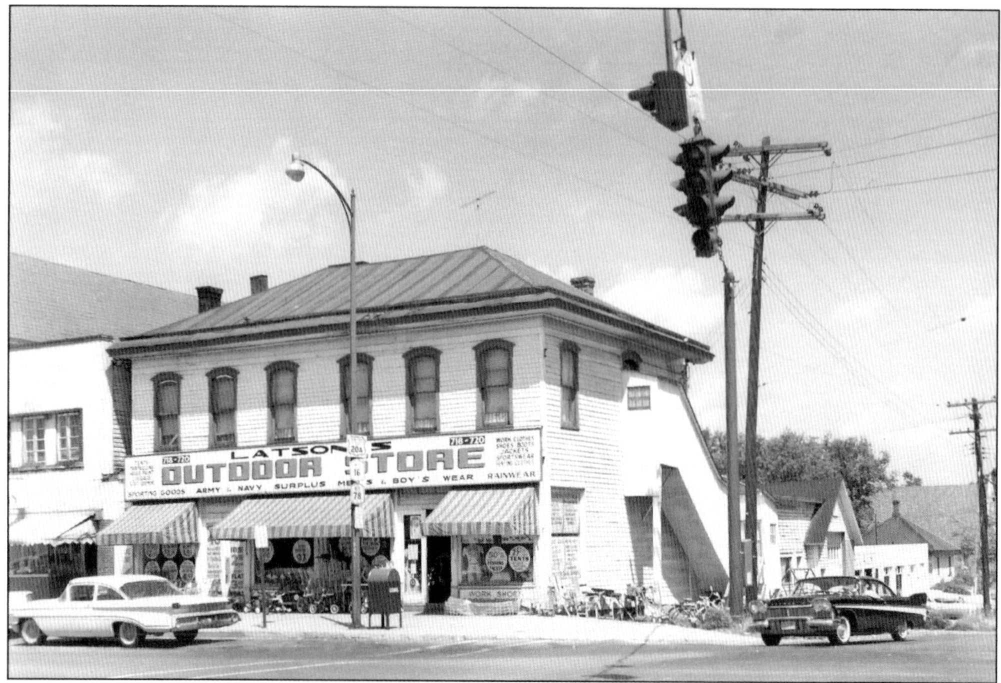

Latson's Outdoor Store occupied the former E.E. Henshaw Block for several years until it closed in 1983. The store specialized in sporting goods and men's clothing. The building on the northwestern corner of Main and Pine Streets has housed two smaller stores in recent years. The stairway on the side of the building has been removed.

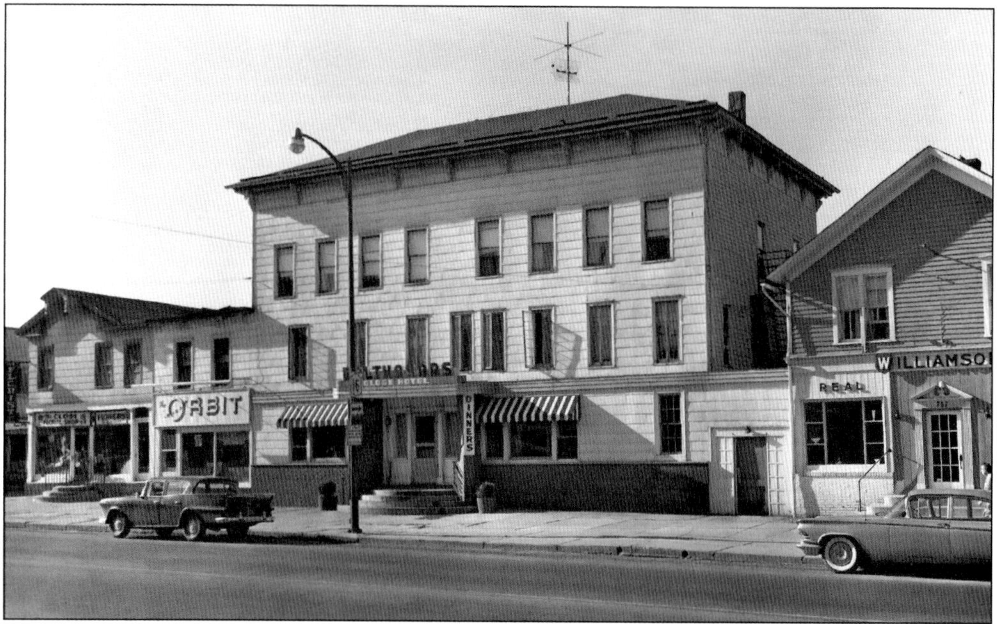

The Globe Hotel, the oldest business in the town of Aurora, is shown in 1963. Victor Balthasar operated the business at this time. To the left is the office of the *Orbit*, a short-lived weekly newspaper that published from 1959 to 1963. The Closs Flower Shop is at the far left. Note a sign of the times—the large antennae on top of the hotel.

The editor of the *East Aurora Advertiser* between 1948 and 1964 and a correspondent for several other newspapers, Rile Prosser is perhaps better remembered for his work as a photographer. He captured images of countless local events and people in the 1950s and 1960s before failing eyesight forced him to give up his life's passion in the 1970s. He died on October 17, 1979, at the age of 94.

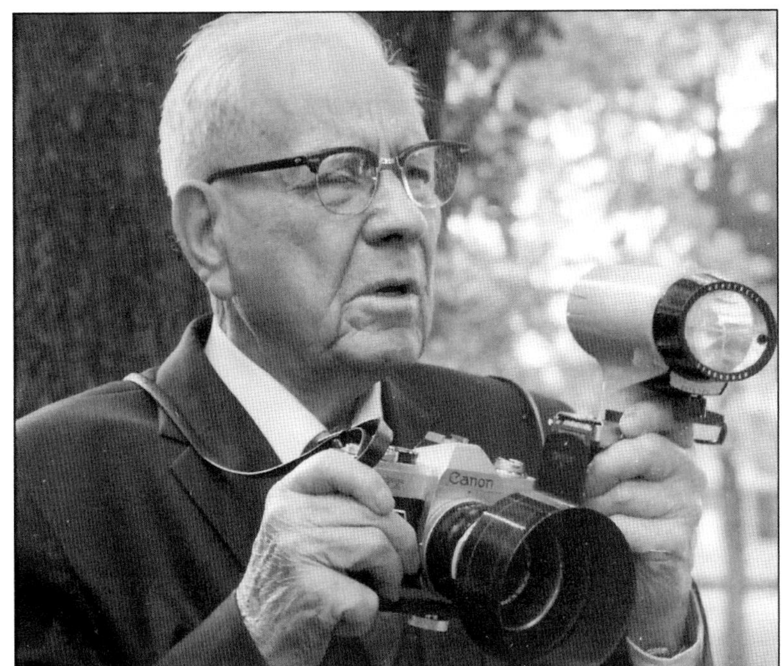

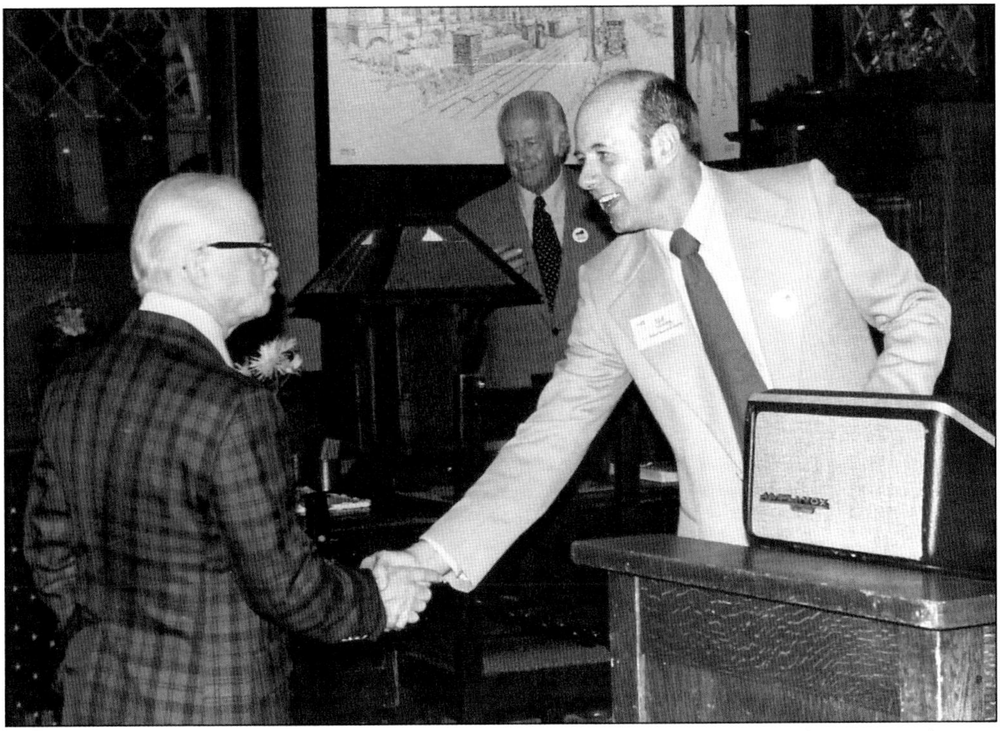

The following three men were among several people who, in the 1960s and 1970s, took steps to preserve Aurora's history: artist Rixford Jennings, left; Aurora Historical Society president William Young; and Edward Godfrey, in the background, who was a descendent of Aurora's earliest settlers. The murals in the Aurora Town Museum, which highlight nearly two centuries of the community's history, are among Jennings's most appreciated contributions.

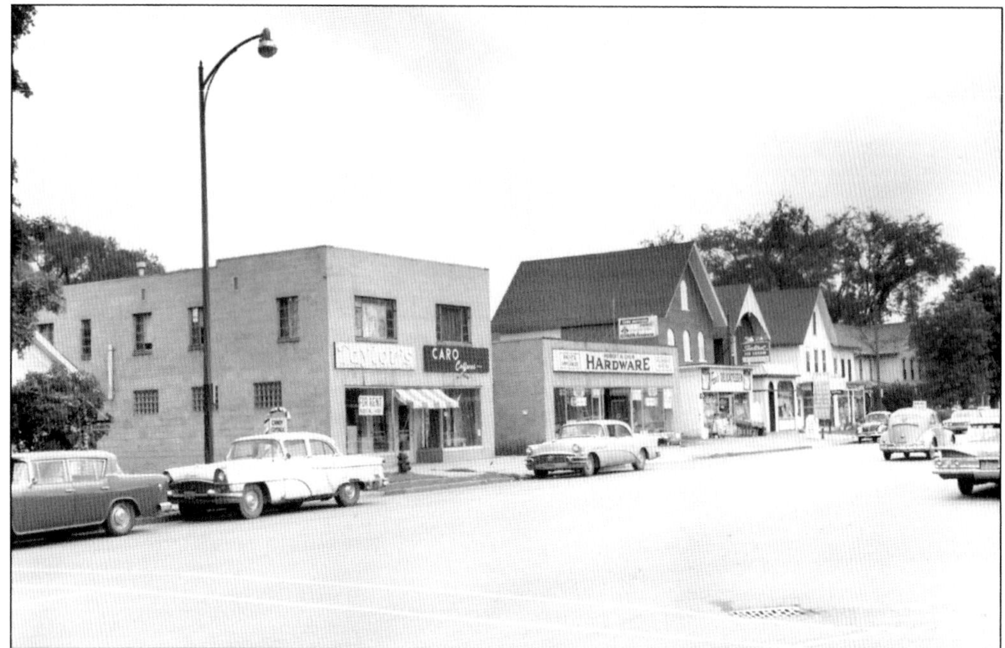

The south side of Main Street at Hamlin Avenue is shown in this photograph taken August 1, 1962. Taylor's, a dry goods and notions store, had just gone out of business. The buildings at the far right were later taken down to make room for a gas station. The Sealtest ice cream parlor is now Bar-Bill Tavern.

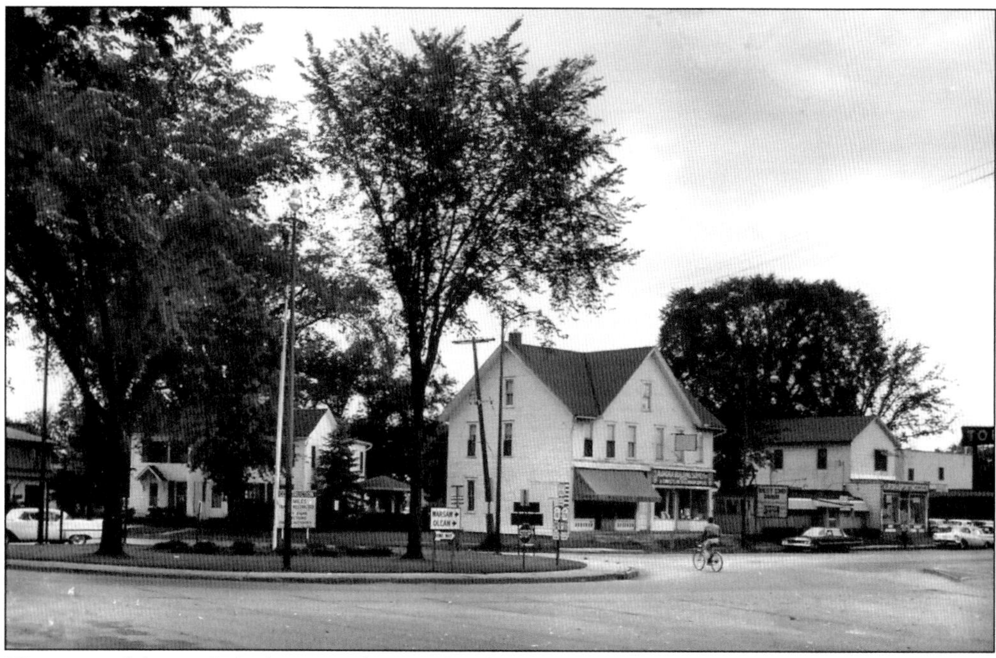

This view of the circle looking north was taken by photographer Rile Prosser August 1, 1962. The sign for the original Tops Friendly Market store can be seen at the far right. All these buildings were removed a few years later to make way for a parking lot. Newer commercial buildings were constructed four decades later. (Courtesy of the *East Aurora Advertiser*.)

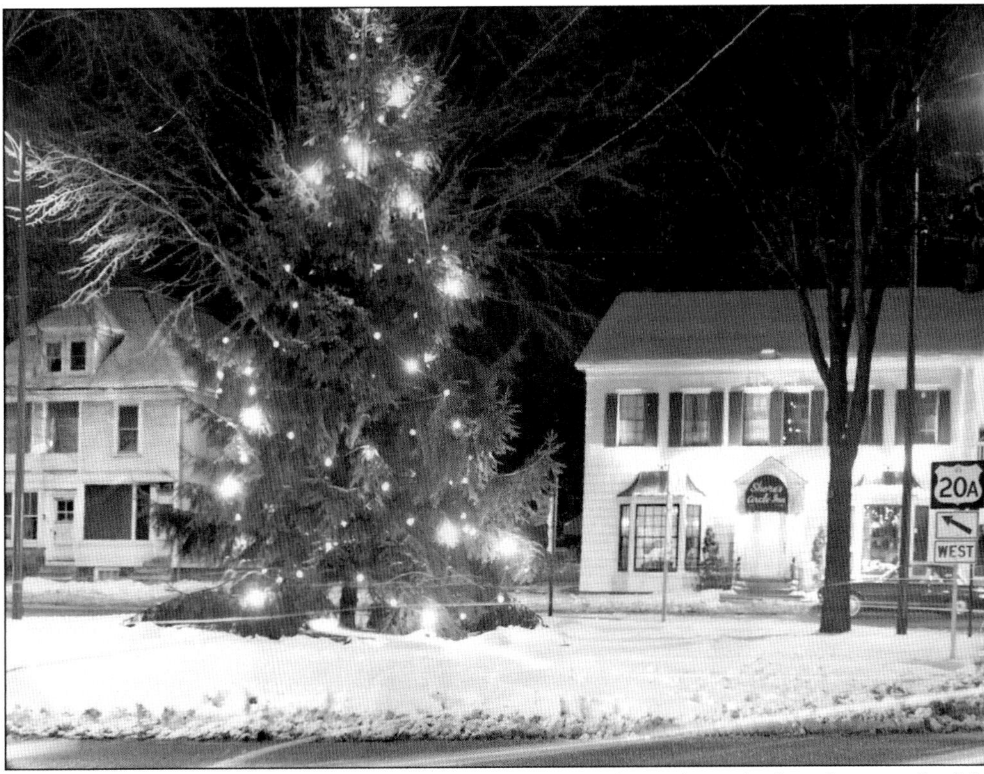

The circle is shown during the holiday season in 1962. It is also perhaps the last photograph of the Shore's Circle Inn before it burned to the ground about a month later. Firefighters were called to the 93-year-old hotel January 28, 1963. They battled the blaze in near-zero temperatures, but they were unable to save the structure. Plans to rebuild a hotel at the site never materialized. Instead, the site became the home of Jester's, a hamburger restaurant. Since the early 1980s, it has been the site of McDonald's. (Courtesy of the *East Aurora Advertiser.*)

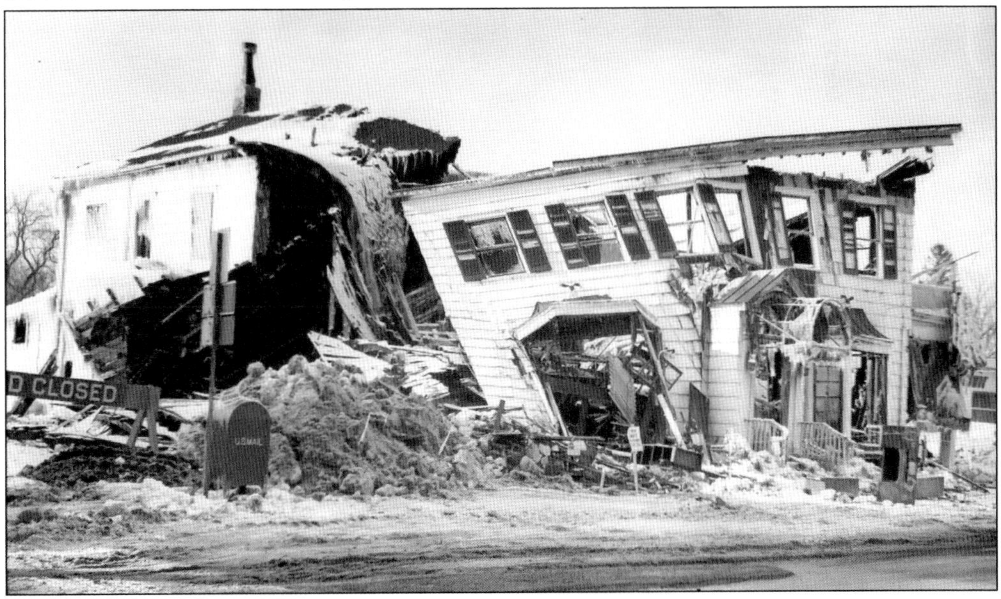

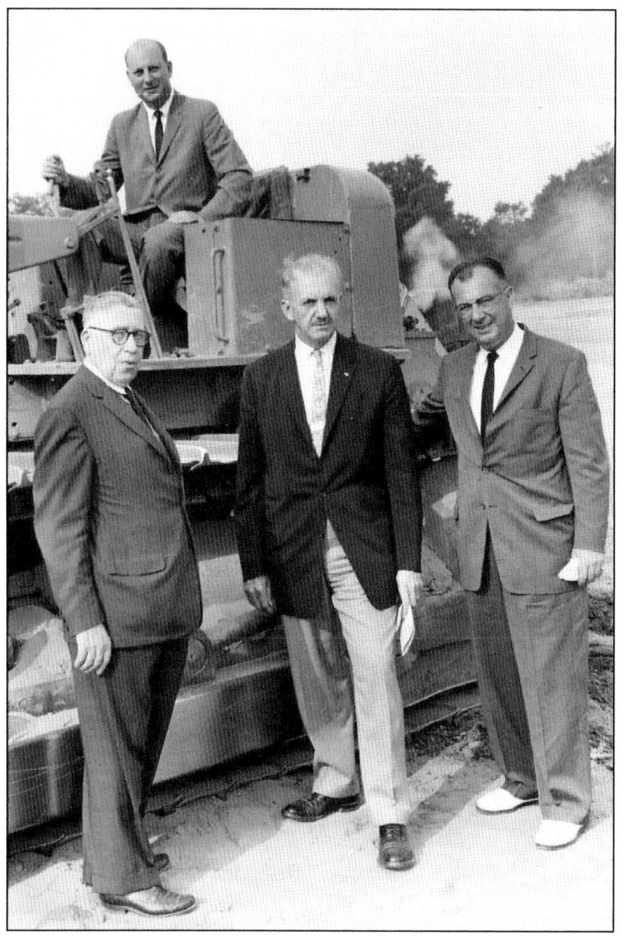

Aurora entered a more modern retail era in 1959, which was when ground was broken on the new $1-million Aurora Village Shopping Center on Grey Street. More than 100 people joined local officials at the site of the future 25-acre plaza for the groundbreaking ceremony in August of that year. The original stores included A&P, W.T. Grant Company, Super Duper, Your Host restaurant, Burn's Barbershop, Lipps Bakery, and Crest Cleaners. Shown at the groundbreaking are, from left to right, town supervisor Dr. Lyle Tillou, Mayor J. Forrest Cain, and developers Raymond and Melvin B. Hoffman. "The mellow traditions and beauty of East Aurora fixed the tone of the Williamsburg, Virginia, restoration-type architecture of the plaza," a local newspaper noted at the time of the opening. During a later restoration, a Roycroft Arts and Crafts style was chosen for the shopping center.

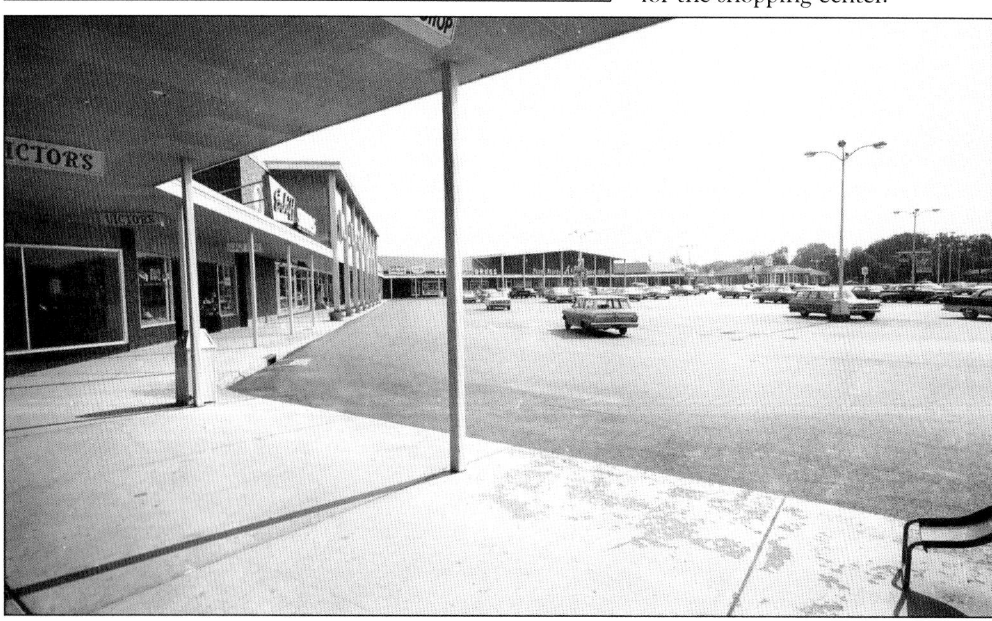

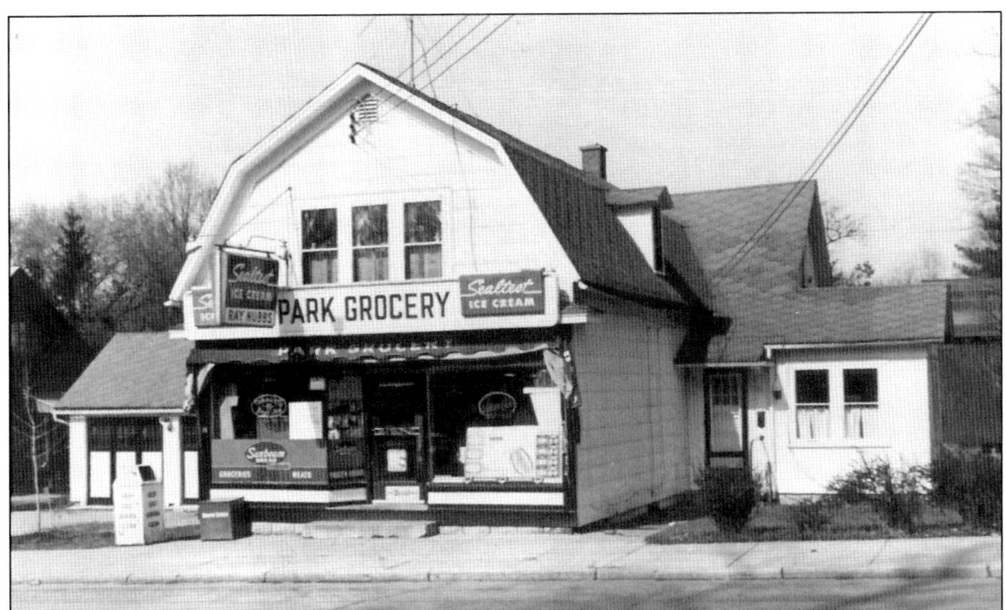

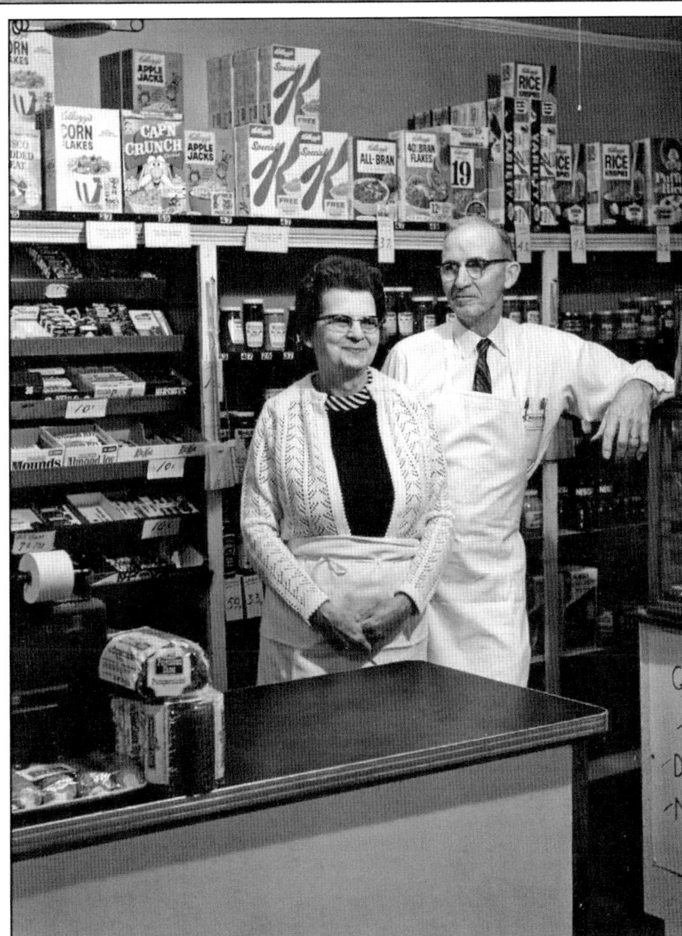

Irene and Raymond Hubbs stand behind the counter at their small Park Grocery, which was located across from Hamlin Park on South Grove Street for 51 years. Roycrofter George Hubbs operated the store before turning operations over to his son. It was said that the Hubbs knew every customer who came into their business and were the unofficial answering service for Hamlin Park across the street, letting callers know if the ice rink was ready or if the baseball game was still on. The store became locally famous for its penny candy and ice cream. Competition from larger chain grocery stores and a transition in family dynamics sounded the death knell for the store. It closed in May 1972. "It has simply gone out of style in our modern transitory life," Hubbs told a newspaper reporter of small groceries.

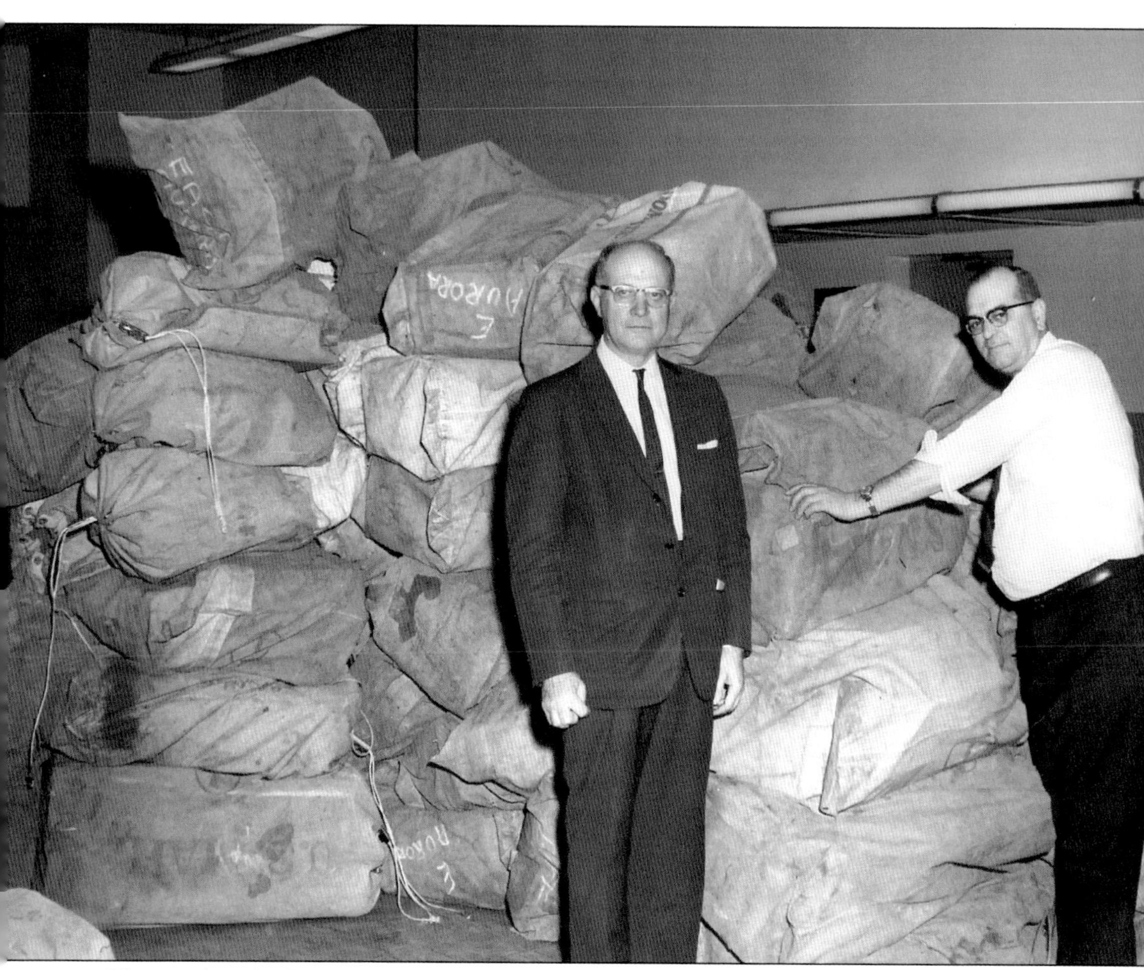

This is what the East Aurora Post Office looked like in December 1962 after nearly 90 sacks of Christmas mail delivered by train and truck. That same year, the post office had moved into a new, brick building on the north side of Main Street, just west of the railroad tracks. It looks like they needed the extra room! Additional help was hired just to handle all this holiday mail. Standing next to the 90 sacks are postmaster Wayne H. Wright, right, and superintendent of mails Charles E. Paul. (Courtesy of the *East Aurora Advertiser*.)

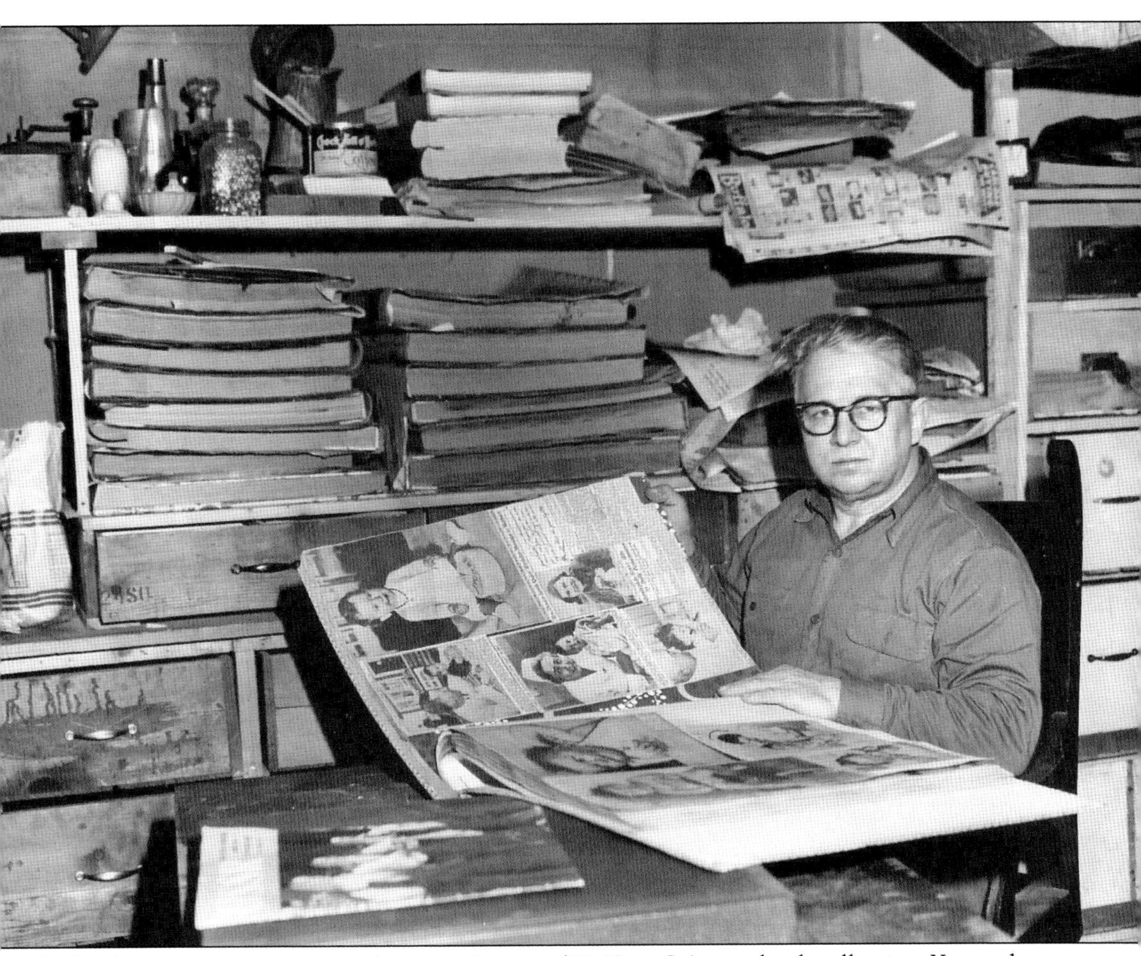

Before Internet search engines, there was Raymond N. Kron Sr.'s scrapbook collection. Kron, who lived on North Willow Street, is shown in January 1963 with his extensive collection. His basement contained shelves and drawers by the dozens. He began the collection as a boy in 1914. There was little to do after a long day's work on the farm. He had no bicycle, so he stayed home and worked on his collection. According to a newspaper profile of Kron, "He often secured newspapers from distant cities, and if an item was interesting, it was placed in a volume and indexed." His collection included clippings about presidential candidate William Jennings Bryan and Pres. Theodore Roosevelt. After moving to East Aurora in 1925, he began clipping and indexing photographs and articles from the *East Aurora Advertiser.* To save resources, scrapbook enthusiasts of yesteryear often reused old budget ledgers. (Courtesy of the *East Aurora Advertiser.*)

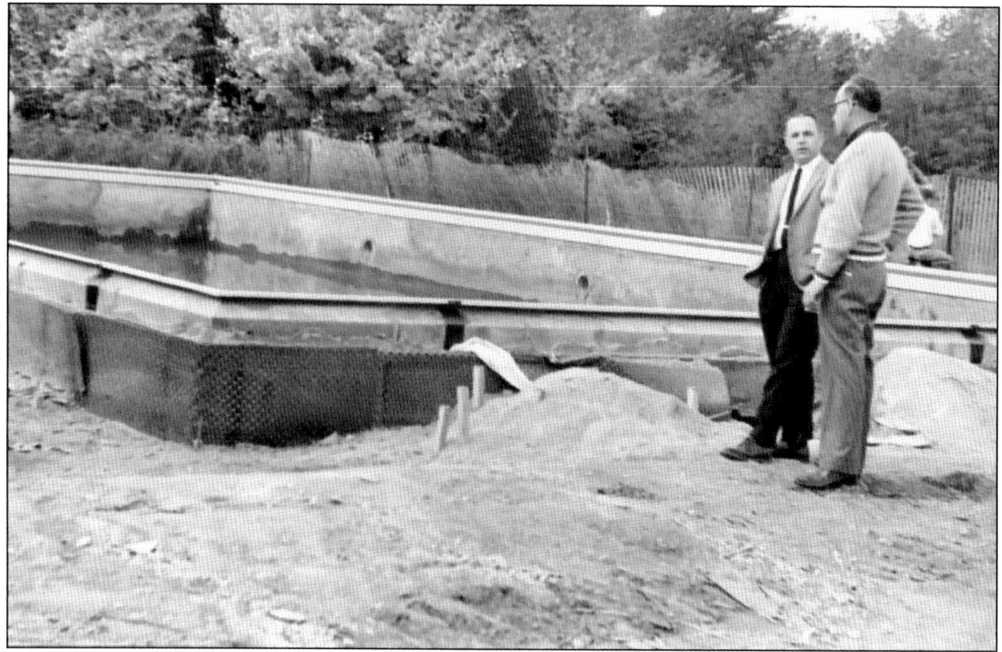

Calvin Potwin, left, the director of the Recreation Commission, and George A. Dye Jr., the president-elect of the Kiwanis Club, look over the progress of construction of the community pool on South Street in October 1965. The pool, which cost $85,000 to build, opened the next July after a three-and-a-half-year community fund drive. Nearly 45 years later, it is still one of Aurora's most popular recreation facilities during the summer months.

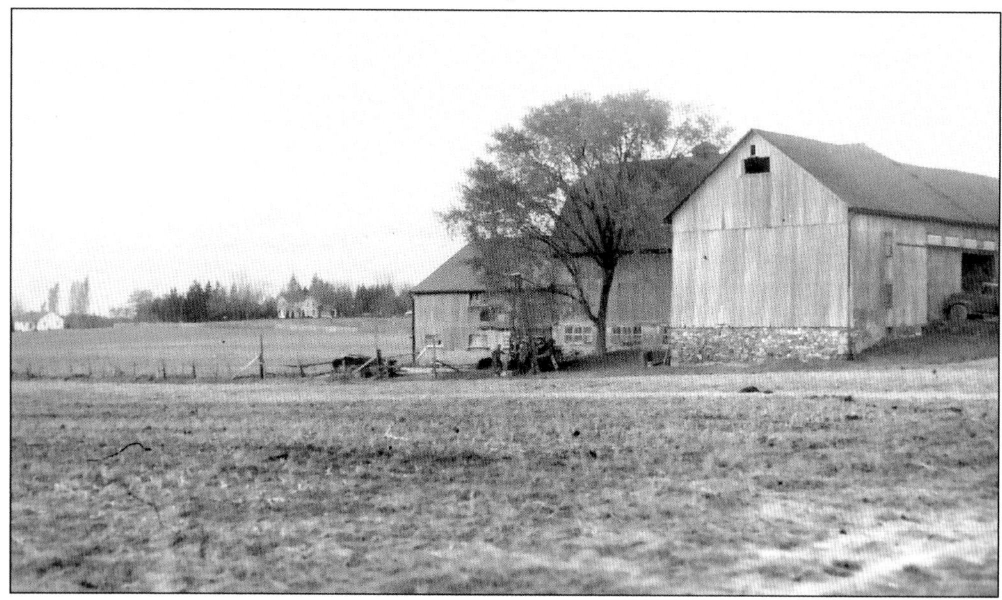

This is what the Becker farm looked like at the southwestern corner of Center Street and Sweet Road shortly before the East Aurora Union Free School District broke ground on the site for the new, more modern high school building and athletic fields in 1969. This view is looking northwest toward Sweet Road. The school district chose the site after considering a handful of other locations throughout the community.

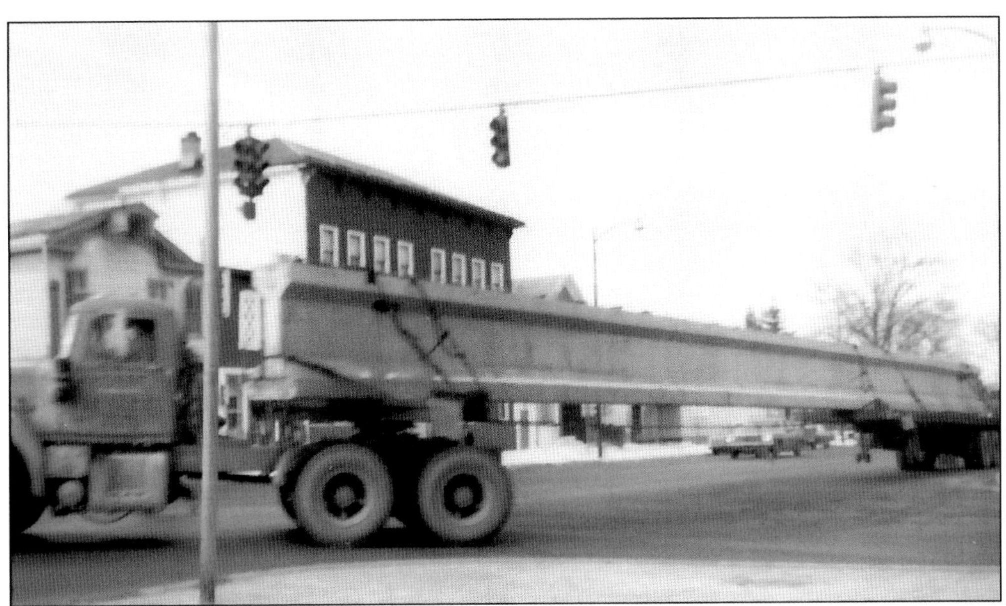

After several years of planning and a great deal of political debate about which path the new highway would take, construction of the Aurora Expressway (Route 400) from the New York State Thruway near Buffalo to South Wales began in 1966. Original plans called for the highway to pass around the west side of the village of East Aurora, but it ultimately ended up on the east side. Above, a support beam is maneuvered around a tight corner at Main and Olean Streets during construction. The Globe Hotel can be seen in the background. Below, cranes are used to lift the beams into place on top of the bridge piers in 1969. The ribbon was cut in September 1971. The expressway drastically cut the amount of time it took motorists to get to Buffalo, and it quickly became a busy commuter route.

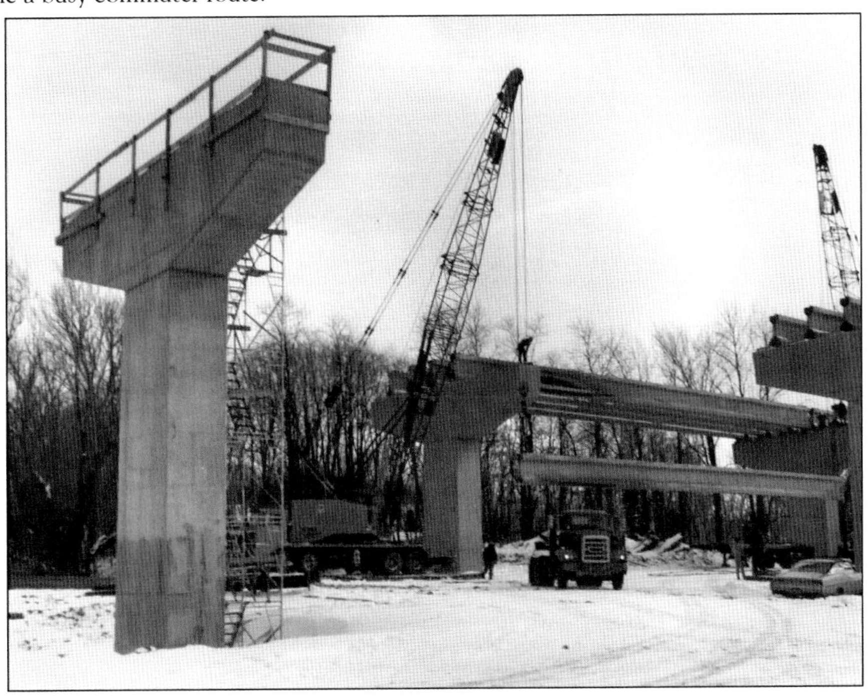

Consistent with our mission to preserve history on a local level, this book was printed in South Carolina on American-made paper and manufactured entirely in the United States. Products carrying the accredited Forest Stewardship Council (FSC) label are printed on 100 percent FSC-certified paper.

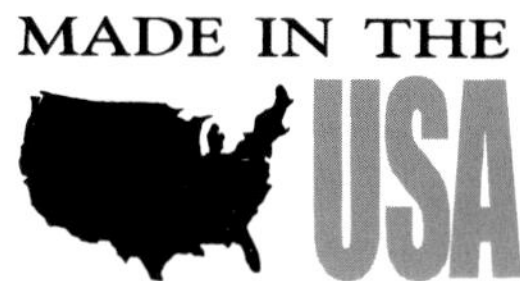